The Call

The Call

Eloquence in the Service of Truth

Craig R. Smith and Michael J. Hyde

Michigan State University Press | *East Lansing*

Michigan State University Press
East Lansing, Michigan 48823-5245

Library of Congress Cataloging-in-Publication Data
Names: Smith, Craig R., author. | Hyde, Michael J., 1950– author.
Title: The call : eloquence in the service of truth / Craig R. Smith, Michael J. Hyde.
Description: East Lansing : Michigan State University Press, [2021] |
Includes bibliographical references and index.
Identifiers: LCCN 2021016780 | ISBN 9781611864090 (paperback) | ISBN 9781609176846
| ISBN 9781628954517 | ISBN 9781628964455
Subjects: LCSH: Eloquence. | Persuasion (Rhetoric)
Classification: LCC PN4129.C6 S66 2021 | DDC 808.5/1–dc23
LC record available at https://lccn.loc.gov/2021016780

Cover design by Shaun Allshouse, www.shaunallshouse.com
Cover art: Architectural Columns, photographed by renaschild, Adobe stock

Visit Michigan State University Press at *www.msupress.org*

Contents

Contents

Preface

The trajectory of our project follows a number of instructive insights: "We speak," writes Jean-Louis Chrétien, "only for having been called, called by what there is to say, and yet we learn and hear what there is to say only in speech itself."[1] Harry G. Frankfurt maintains that "No one in his right mind would rely on a builder, or submit to the care of a physician, who does not care about the truth. Even writers, artists and musicians must—in their own ways—know how to get things right. They must at least be able to avoid getting them too far wrong. In the course of their creative work, they invariably encounter significant problems—for instance, problems of technique and of style. Certain ways of dealing with these problems are clearly far superior to others."[2] To deal with this truth, Ralph Waldo Emerson makes much of the fact that "Eloquence is the power to translate truth into language perfectly intelligible to the person to whom you speak."[3] A hero of the Watergate hearings and later majority leader of the Senate, Howard Baker instructs about the other side of Emerson's coin: "One of the keys to life is to listen eloquently, because it is just possible that the other guy might have something to offer."[4] Moving from public address to fiction, Robert Coles speaks to the wonder of stories when he tells us that "every reader's response to a writer's call can have its own startling, suggestive power."[5] Rabbi Harold Kushner has this power in mind when he notes, "We teach children how to measure and how to weigh. We fail to teach them how to revere, how to sense wonder and awe."[6]

We refocus on negative awe in the third chapter of this book and on positive awe in the concluding chapter. However, at this juncture it is important to note that these insights inspired our study of a communication event that happens every day in the lives of human beings: the call. The most common-sense understanding of this event is displayed, for example, when one person tells another that "I will call you tonight so we can talk about our business meeting." The call enables people to get and stay in touch with others. And with the help of such technological devices as email and cell phones, people can "reach out and touch somebody" and be "on call" for others twenty-four hours a day. Thinking about the call in this way has a role to play in our study, as do the many aspects of the call that remain unacknowledged by this common-sense understanding of an essential feature of human existence.

Our particular way of thinking about the call is based, in part, on our ongoing studies and critical assessments of Martin Heidegger's phenomenological investigations of how the temporal structure of human existence functions to activate a self's moral consciousness. Heidegger describes this event as the "call of conscience," later named the "call of Being" as Heidegger develops his investigations of the ontological nature of language. Heidegger offers an observation that relates these matters and is instructive for our study: "Language has the task of making manifest in its works the existent, and of preserving it as such. In it, what is purest and what is most concealed, and likewise what is complex and ordinary, can be expressed in words. Even the essential word, if it is to be understood and so become a possession in common, must make itself ordinary."[7] Language makes manifest the existent when it works to disclose the presence of what something is—its truth, which is needed to inform the righteous ways of a given public's moral consciousness. The truth must be made understandable, meaningful, and persuasive if it is to become a possession in common in the public realm. The task here necessitates the practice of rhetoric and its art of eloquence: discovering and using the right words, at the right time, and in the right way to move the public to accept the truth in question. Heidegger's 1924 seminar on Aristotle's Rhetoric ("Grundbegriffe der aristotelischen Philosophie: Marburger Vorlesung Summersementer") attests to his interest in this practical art and its employment for educating others. What is lacking in this interest is any appreciation of the intricate nature and actual workings of eloquence. This deficiency is, in part, the result of Heidegger's decision not to examine the ethics involved when communicating with and respecting the value of others in a given audience.

Emmanuel Levinas's phenomenological analysis of the "call of conscience," which also plays a significant role in our writings, is quite critical of Heidegger's decision to avoid what Levinas terms an "ethics of the other." Levinas emphasizes that we exist in a world of otherness (alterity), of all that is but that is not ourselves. Otherness is a fact of life. "To be for the Other is to be good.... The fact that in existing for another, I exist otherwise than in existing for me is morality itself."[8] Like Heidegger, however, Levinas lacks an appreciation of the fundamental purpose of the rhetorical art of eloquence. He associates this art with "ruse, emprise, and exploitation." Levinas's one all-too-brief example is the media: "The media of information in all forms—written, spoken, visual—invade the home, keep people listening to an endless discourse, submit them to the seduction of a rhetoric that is only possible if it is eloquent and persuasive in portraying ideas and things too beautiful to be true."[9] With this example we believe Levinas is justified to associate eloquence with the use of beautiful language to seduce its listeners. The majority of corporate-run media organizations are in the business of producing advertisement-soaked entertainment. Nevertheless, Levinas has an obsession with the negative that distorts his vision of the matter. As we intend to show, his is a far too limited understanding of eloquence, especially when considering how this art facilitates communicating the truth to others in an ethical, meaningful, and persuasive manner.

We have acknowledged these and related deficiencies in Heidegger's and Levinas's philosophies in a number of our writings focusing on the practices of rhetoric and communication ethics in social, political, artistic, and health care settings.[10] We, however, have yet to develop a detailed examination of how the rhetorical art of eloquence advances in significant ways an understanding of the scope and function of the call. Thus, the goal of this project. Briefly stated, here are some of the key features of the call that will be discussed in our study and that speak to the importance of the art of eloquence.

The act of calling is an act of "saying." To say something involves showing and letting something be seen. The call thus functions discursively: It has the formal structure of "discourse," which is a mode of disclosure in which something is said, pointed out, revealed, and shared. The mere presence of a thing's existence sounds a call, for this presence is a showing, a disclosing and revealing of the givenness, the bare "that it is" of the thing's really being present here and now. The philosopher Jean-Louis Chrétien's way of making the point is captivating: "Our eyes are able to watch over the call that rises from things and truly see things only because they have heard it."[11] A tall wooden structure bearing limbs and leaves stands before us. Its presence calls. Hearing this call, the poet Joyce Kilmer famously replied: "I think that I shall never see a poem as lovely as a tree."[12] Theodore Rousseau saw leaves shimmering on a tree and called out "Isn't that romantic."[13] He reinforced the cry of the Romantics to "go back to nature" for it was the repository of truth and beauty. Nature called them over the bustle of the city and the roar of the machine.

Calls invite responses, which emerge as people engage in the activity of witnessing, interpreting, and expressing in meaningful ways whatever calls for their attention and thereby beckons us to be in touch and stay in touch with the presence of a thing's existence. As demonstrated in the words of Kilmer and Rousseau, the call addresses our emotional capacity to be moved, to feel and have a heart for, and thus be touched by what is other than ourselves and in need of acknowledgment. The call is a touching phenomenon. Here is another example: the presence of Van Gogh's painting *Starry Night* and what it says and shows, discloses and reveals, about its subject matter. Readers who search for the painting online will find that as did the various things that called for attention, moved, and touched Van Gogh, the painting calls for attention and awaits an appropriate response.[14] Such a response is heard as a person is taken with the painting and admits that "this painting speaks to me." The admission is evidence that what the painting has to say touches her. What helps to facilitate the admission is the call's rhetorical function: its eloquence, its employment of the "right" symbolism, in the "right" way, and at the "right" time so as to be worthy of a person's attention. Eloquence enhances the ability of a witness to identify to some degree with what something has to say about its being. Following Van Gogh's lead, the person sustains the value of the call with what she has to say about its effects on her life. The success of this saying, a call in its own right, is likewise dependent on its rhetorical competence and whatever degree of eloquence can be put into practice. Call, response, call, response, call, response. . . . The value of a thing's presence, its meaning and truth, is determined and sustained throughout time with the happening of this communication event, an ongoing experience of people being touched by and identifying with the meaning and significance of the presence of things. In this way, the power and influence of calls take form. For example, expanding on our brief references to Rousseau noted above, his revelation led to a new back-to-nature movement that changed landscaping from classic French sculpting to wild, more natural gardens. More importantly, he argued that humans, when taken back to their natural state, were kinder, caring, and interested in reciprocity. That reformation went hand in hand with his ideology that placed government in the service of its constituents instead of the other way around, which in turn inspired America's founders to incorporate inalienable rights into their Declaration of Independence. They eventually became the Bill of Rights of the U.S. Constitution, which was further perfected with other amendments that guaranteed equal protection under the law, abolished slavery, and gave women the right to vote. The process continues to this day.

Importantly, our ability to perceive and create these calls is made possible by a more fundamental presence of the call that lies at the heart of the spatial and temporal fabric of human existence and that we are thus in touch with every second of our lives. This most essential call is heard as the objective uncertainty of the future calls human beings to demonstrate responsibility in being open to, acknowledging, and communicating to others as perfectly as possible the truth of the presence of things that call for attention and acknowledgment. If people are to remain ethically and morally responsible while living the decisions they made in responding to this challenging call, they must be prepared and willing at any moment to question the supposed correctness of what they are thinking and doing as a result of having made these decisions. The constancy of the call demands as much with its objective uncertainty, for it speaks to how human beings are forever open to the possibility of change, of things being otherwise than usual, of how what is yet to come in our lives may require people, for truth's sake, to rethink and revise what they currently hold to be correct about their circumstances, involvements, and interpretive practices. Since we are constantly hearing, we are constantly open to calls, and hence constantly make decisions about how to respond. That is a primordial condition of human being. The constancy of the call is forever calling into question and thus interrupting our decisive ways of being in the world.

Responding to this call is the original calling (vocation) of human beings—a calling that is motivated by a passionate longing for some degree of meaning, order, and completeness or perfection in our lives. This longing is the result of having to deal with the call's objective uncertainty, its constant questioning and interruption, and the unease that manifests itself when, not knowing what is to come in our lives, we experience the discomforting and potentially dreadful emotion of anxiety. The effort needed to deal with this ever-present state of being involves people in the construction of dwelling places or worlds of meaning where a more stable and comfortable way of existence is created and maintained, at least for the time being, and where they can feel at home in their environmental surroundings and engagements. Van Gogh's *Starry Night*, for example, provides such a dwelling place where witnesses can be touched and moved by its presence, sound a call to others about its significance, and thereby assist in maintaining the value of Van Gogh's awe-inspiring response to a call that lies at the heart of human existence and that calls human beings, as noted above, to demonstrate responsibility in being open to, acknowledging, and communicating to others as perfectly as possible the truth of the presence of things that call for attention. How the communication is structured to achieve this goal testifies to the workings of rhetorical eloquence in presenting matters of concern in an enlightening and persuasive manner. The call that lies at the heart of human existence calls for the practice of this art. All of the case studies presented in each of the chapters of this book offer detailed examinations of this practice.

These examinations are our response to the call's calling, and a call that speaks to the call's importance for human beings. This status of the call is brought to mind with a question: What would life be like if people cared not to attend and respond to the calls going on in their lives? "Chaotic and crushing" is a generous answer. All meaning, knowledge, and truth begin with the call. Vocations, callings—exemplars being those worlds of expertise called "professions," or that we call our professional "callings"—are dependent on these three creations of the call. Callings harken back to the original call for attention that lies at the heart of human existence. No call, no callings. And more than that: No call, no human beings.[15]

Two final prefatory notes: Our devotion to the call results in our mentioning this name many times in all of the chapters. One's tolerance for repetition is thus tested and perhaps may lead to the accusation that we are stacking the deck in our favor. The use of any number of official synonyms might help remedy the problem. Indeed, paraphrasing Shakespeare a bit, one might ask and suggest: "What's in a name? That which we call a 'call' by any other name would still tell your story." Not really. The substitution would be less evocative and provocative than we need it to be. It is a call that calls for our attention, not what a thesaurus names a cry, shout, yell, whoop, bellow, roar, scream, holler, exclamation, or other listed terms. None of these terms are eloquent enough to maintain focus on our topic. Eloquence lends itself to disclosing the truth. The literary and rhetorical critic Kenneth Burke puts it this way: "The primary purpose of eloquence is to 'convert life' to its most thorough verbal equivalent."[16] For us, the name "call" is such an equivalent, so we are willing to risk the charge of being too repetitious. We tell a story encouraged by the fact that the call is an essential feature of human existence. Remember: No call, no callings. No call, no human beings.

For our purposes there were two options for organizing our project: offering one case study that provides a single perspective for understanding the relationship between the call and eloquence, or offering a variety of perspectives that if organized well enough into a narrative that displays coherency and fidelity—that is, its material fits together in a way that makes sense, is interesting, rings true with reality, and is educational—would add credence to the ranging applicability of our story. This second option enhances the risk of this project, but it also adds to the challenging and exciting nature of what we seek to accomplish. Our theory and case studies run from 600 BC to the present. We hope the diversity of our case studies provides a broad sweep of times, venues, speakers, and audiences that experienced the call and thus provides a more complete study than would otherwise be possible. One theme that pervades this study is how we are called to a home, a better dwelling place. As we shall see, that home is often the "more perfect union" mentioned in the preface to the United States Constitution.

Chapter 1 continues our definitional work by examining the tension between religion and science in their respective understandings of the scope and function of the call. This tension is eased somewhat when realizing that these callings are responses to the call that lies at the heart of human existence. With these responses there is eloquence at work. That leads to our analysis of the elements of eloquence in chapter 2. Here we provide a toolbox of rhetorical strategies that can be used by orators issuing a call to action or to the transcendent. These tools are then employed in the remainder of the book to determine how and when eloquence is used in the service of the truth. However, it is important to make clear that eloquence can be used for wrong-headed or even evil purposes. Chapter 3 explores cheating eloquence in the public address of presidents George W. Bush and Donald J. Trump to put us on guard against the misguided or the charlatan. Trump in particular provides a case study in negative awe and the shock of the sublime.

With these preliminaries out of the way, we turn to examples of eloquence in the service of truth starting with chapter 4 on epideictic eloquence. We examine two addresses delivered by Barack Obama, one assessing America's values in the wake of racism and the other a eulogy in the wake of a tragic shooting in Tucson, Arizona. Each speech in its own way calls Americans to a higher standard of action and ultimately to transcendent values of a more perfect union. Chapter 5 turns to deliberative eloquence, focusing on two case studies. The first is the eloquence of Senator Daniel Webster in his defense and preservation of Union. The second is the last State of the Union Address delivered by Ronald Reagan. Here we show that eloquence can serve the truth even in the rough-and-tumble world of politics. Chapter 6 also has a pragmatic lens as it examines forensic eloquence. Three senators speak to their colleagues at a crucial moment in American history. Margaret Chase Smith, Susan Collins, and Mitt Romney rise on the floor of the Senate to issue the call of conscience over questions of guilt or innocence. Bucking her own party, Smith declares that her conscience will not let her tolerate a demagogue in our midst. In the course of defending fundamental justice, Collins speaks to the nomination of Brett Kavanaugh to the Supreme Court. Attempting to overcome partisanship in the trial of the president, Romney justifies his vote for removal from office. Each of these advances a call to a more perfect union.

Chapter 7 turns from the pragmatic to the transcendent where we look at higher forms of public address. The chapter examines the religious eloquence in the epistles of St. Paul, the writings of St. Augustine, and the preaching of

Jonathan Edwards. Chapter 8 turns to the existential call eloquently represented in creative activity. It begins by exploring how films can function as narrative arguments while also causing audiences to identify with characters. After exploring several cases of one artist influencing another, whether in prose, poetry, or music, we provide a close examination of the relationship of Vincent Van Gogh and Paul Gauguin from the perspective of their letters and artwork. In each case we show how the artists called one another to a transcendent state and then shared it with the world through their art to bring others to transcendence.

Chapter 9 offers a discussion that elaborates on the relationship between the call and the emotion of awe, the sublime, the ultimate eloquence. Our discussion is structured to associate awe with the other happenings that are called for by the call. Awe lends itself to this arrangement and thereby enables us to provide what we hope is a fitting conclusion to and summary of our response to the call that we ourselves are. Selected writings of the Pulitzer Prize–winning author, nature writer, and narrative essayist Annie Dillard provide material for assessing the experience of being awed by the presence of whatever calls for attention.

Acknowledgments

Craig Smith wishes to acknowledge the home that was created for him by the Department of Communication Studies at California State University, Long Beach starting in 1988. He is also indebted to too many colleagues to name who have inspired him with their scholarship in public address, freedom of expression, and rhetorical theory and criticism. He is very grateful to Catherine Cocks for providing another publishing opportunity for him at Michigan State University Press. Along with the anonymous reviewers, her perseverance and attention to detail sustained this project. Finally, he thanks the raft of students who sustained him over the course of his career by teaching him more than he knew. Many of them became his "sons" and "daughters," and for that he will be eternally grateful.

I, Michael Hyde, am indebted to the faculty, staff, and students of the Department of Communication and the Program for Bioethics, Health, and Society, School of Medicine, Wake Forest University, for providing me with communities that make teaching and research an immense joy. I am also indebted to members of the Divisions of Communication Ethics and

Philosophy of Communication, National Communication Association, for their generous assessments of my research in university and conference settings. For their willingness to answer my call for conversation, education, and inspiration, special thanks are due to Chris Aiken, Arthur Bochner, John Bost, Candice Burris, Barbara Ewbank, Ana Iltis, Nancy King, Itoo Lewin-Arundale, Andrew Lopez, Jo Lowe, Ananda Mitra, Lee Reichbaum, Randall Rogan, Richard Robeson, Calvin Schrag, and Susan Stevens. For her expertise and caring kindness, I wish to thank Catherine Cocks, assistant director and editor in chief, Michigan State University Press. And most of all I thank my wife, Bobette, who is my guiding source for appreciating the all-important spiritual exchange: "Where art thou?" "Here I am!".

CHAPTER 1

In the Beginning, and Before That, Too

n his book *Before the Beginning: Our Universe and Others*, the highly acclaimed cosmologist and astrophysicist Martin Rees tells us that "Our universe sprouted from an initial event, the 'big bang' or 'fireball.' It expanded and cooked; the intricate pattern of stars and galaxies we see around us emerged thousands of millions of years later; on at least one planet around at least one star, atoms have assembled into creatures complex enough to ponder how they evolved."[1] To ponder is to be in touch, stay in touch, and think about something that calls our attention to its presence. Pondering is an activity that initiates a quest to know the truth of whatever some presence is. Rees is interested in pondering what perhaps was happening "before the beginning." Human beings began pondering this specific presence of this call long before Rees's scientific ancestors took on the task. The Judeo-Christian tradition names this presence "God"—a presence that, as far as the authors of the Bible conceive It, has no history. God comes from "nowhere." Nothing that exists comes from nowhere. It follows, then, that God's existence is Other than what human beings are able to conceive. Still, this unconceivable

Otherness calls for attention from those creatures who have the symbolic capacity to name it.

Religion

We are told that "In the beginning was the Word. And the Word was with God. And the Word is God." Apparently, then, before the beginning, before there was space and time as human beings know them, and from out of Nothingness and Nowhere, God decided to be the Word. The Word created, called into being, the presence of everything that exists. Now it was possible for words to recall a founding call by calling attention to presences that call for attention, especially since these presences speak of God's presence. This recalling activity is most pronounced when words enhance the identity of things by naming them, thereby aiding them in their call for attention. The activity of naming is a calling on behalf of the presence of things and what, in truth, they are. Naming thus puts to use what Kenneth Burke identifies as the "perfectionist" function of language: "The mere desire to name something by its 'proper' name, or to speak a language in its distinctive ways is intrinsically 'perfectionist.' What is more 'perfectionist' in essence than the impulse, when one is in dire need of something, to so state this need that one in effect 'defines' the situation?"[2] We are creatures who would enhance and better (perfect) our understanding of the world in order to live wise and fulfilling lives. To define what something is, is to engage in an act of truth-telling, of telling it like it is. Truth happens first and foremost as a disclosing of the world, a revealing of something that calls for attention (for example, a flower blooming). Any truth claim (such as "That rose is in bloom") presupposes this act of disclosure. Truth shows itself in discourse that warrants praise for being revelatory and perhaps even awe-inspiring because of the way it calls forth and discloses its subject matter, thereby enabling us to perfect our understanding and appreciation of what is being talked about. The philosopher Georges Gusdorf has this specific goal in mind when he writes:

Each [human being] can contribute to creating a better world, a world prepared, announced, and even brought into being by every world that is a harbinger of good faith and authenticity. Each [human being] may see to it that words take on value wherever [he or she] is, that is that confidence and peace reign in the commonwealth. The meaning of every fate may be written along the sad and yet triumphant road from Babel to Pentecost. But the moral person can still undertake the task of accomplishing in the world his supreme function [of discovering names that speak to the truth of the presence of things].3

The Word is God. "God" is a name. Throughout the Bible this name also goes by other names—for example, "Father," "Teacher," "Physician"—intended to tell something of the truth of whatever the Word is. God is also called many other names, like the one announced in the Kabbalistic tradition of Judaism, which speaks of God as "Limitless Light" (*Ein Sof*), so to acknowledge the ultimate event of transcendence or "infinity" of God's presence.4 And then there was that one and only moment, recorded in Scripture, when God proclaimed Its own name—who and how God truly is. This most holy act of naming came shortly after God called out to a man tending his flock: "Moses." The call was reminiscent of a much earlier call directed at a sinful Adam: "Where art thou?" The call demanded a response, and Adam was wise to answer: "Here I am." Moses did the same, ascending Mount Sinai to hear what God had to say. Before that event, Moses stood in God's light, the burning bush, and was told that the Jewish people have a future. When Moses asks for God's "Name," he is told, *"Ehyeh-asher-ehyeh."* English renders this reply in a static way: "I am who I am." In Hebrew, however, the dynamic of being open to the future is unequivocal: "I shall be who I shall be." So what is the case? Is the Word a static, all-in-one, never-changing, complete and thus perfect presence, or is this presence rightly understood as a dynamic happening whereby "the whole truth and nothing but the truth" is yet to come? The static and the dynamic depictions of the Word need not oppose each other, for it is possible to hear the name calling for attention by saying "I am what I shall be." In this case, the dynamic takes priority. According to Rabbi Lawrence Kushner, "Here is a Name (and a God), who is neither completed nor finished. This God is literally not yet."[5] God needs acknowledgment and help in materializing the future; hence, God's reply to Moses, which admits as much. The perfection of God's being ("I am") is still in the process of becoming ("I shall be") whatever it is. We have a responsibility to answer the call for both God's sake and our own. The lived body is a moral being.

It is important to realize that this understanding of God's name is the result of trying to resolve the issue of its ambiguous nature. If intended by a speaker or writer, ambiguity functions as an interruption of established common-sense ways of interpreting and understanding some matter of concern. Ambiguity is a rhetorical device that encourages "pause for thought" on the part of people who think they know, because their common sense says so, that they definitely have it right in determining what some presence is telling them about its truth. Ambiguity calls a question with its interruption. Phrased in the Judeo-Christian tradition, the question asks: "Where art thou?" in coming to terms with the truth of God's Word, and are you sure that you're right? The question calls for a response. Be it definite or not, the response calls out: "Here I am" with my stand on the matter at hand. Perhaps it is fair to say that "in the beginning" and thereafter, God's calling is that of an eloquent rhetorician. God employs the right word (name), in the right way (ambiguity), and at the right time (given the trials and tribulations of Moses and his people) to call attention to what God's name names: the truth of Its Presence and the concerned thought and behavior that It calls for in order to respect the most holy instance of otherness to be found in the cosmos.

The radical Christian philosopher Soren Kierkegaard provides a similar case of an ambiguity calling us to an edifying discourse. Kierkegaard uses the ambiguity of Jesus as a rhetoric of enlightenment. For example, Jesus tells us to turn the other cheek—in other words, to be pacifists. However, Jesus chases the money changers from the temple with a whip made of rope. He withers a fig tree for not rendering its fruit to him. This ambiguity invites investigation; it makes one ponder.

Returning to the rhetoric of God, we see Its diverse ways of calling in the story of Elijah after he placed himself into a state of harkening attunement, a state we will return to later in this book. After much isolation, prayer, and fasting in a desert cave, Elijah, prophet in the 1st Book of Kings, gets the call in a subtle way. "And, behold, the Lord passed by, and a great and strong wind rent the mountains and broke in pieces the rocks before the Lord; but the Lord was not in the wind: And after the wind an earthquake; but the Lord was not in the earthquake: And after the earthquake a fire; but the Lord was not in the fire: And after the fire a small voice. And it was so, when Elijah heard it, that he wrapped his face in his mantle, and went out, and stood in the entrance of the cave." We should note that Elijah does not move through the threshold separating humans from the Transcendent using a big voice. Only when he hears the small one is he moved to act. Clearly, we need to be careful not to ignore the small, even silent callings that cross our path. And, of course, we need to be ready to hear them, which takes some work.

An influential response to God's call is offered by the sixteenth-century rabbi Isaac Luria. His interpretations of the five books of Moses and the Zohar (a mystical commentary on these books) give rise to a cosmological myth intended to clarify the workings of the self-manifestation of divinity and how human beings come to play a fundamental role in sustaining this holy happening. The myth calls into question the fundamental belief of older rabbinic theology that God's own well-being is not contingent on human action. Luria insists, on the contrary, that the Creator does need our help. Luria thus creates a new narrative that redefines the traditional understanding of the static conception of God's perfection. A brief summary of Luria's teachings is sufficient for our purposes.[6] According to Luria, the Creator's first act was not the interruptive event of "revelation" but rather withdrawal, the creation of an opening, a "void" or empty place within the Creator's infinite presence and perfection. *Ein Sof,* the "endless light" of the Creator, withdrew "from Itself into Itself" in order to make room in the midst of Itself for the entire cosmos to come into being. This act of withdrawal is the Creator interrupting Itself. The action is the ultimate act of self-effacement.

Otherness is granted priority in God's workings, a giving way to a place, an infinite dimension of space-time, which allows for life and its development. The essential nature of the Creator is that of sharing and compassion, a desire to give of Itself. This entire process occurs before God's interrupting avowal "Let there be light!" The creation of the cosmos presupposes a more primordial creation: with the Creator's withdrawal there arises an absence, which calls attention to Itself every time people prove unable to know God in Its entirety.

Luria teaches that with the creation of the cosmos a crisis occurred. The crisis was that the dynamic operations intrinsic to God's perfection were flawed. God's perfection entails imperfection, acknowledged by God when God names Itself: "I am what I shall be." Indeed, God needs a future to achieve completeness. Moreover, as Luria insists, God needs our assistance to achieve this goal. According to Rabbi Marc-Alain Quaknin, as human beings accept the responsibility of offering this assistance, their "ethic is no longer that of perfection but of perfectibility."[7] Not being God, that is the best we can do for the One who, with an awesome interruption, acknowledged our existence in the beginning. We return the favor by heeding God's call for help. Rabbi Abraham Heschel's way of phrasing the last point is noteworthy: "All of human history as described in the Bible may be summarized in one phrase: God is in search of man."[8] Indeed, "Where art thou?" The reciprocity of acknowledgment is called for: "Here I am."

God is an interruption. Owing to this feature of Its existence, God admits that Its perfection is a question yet to be answered. God is completely incomplete, perfectly imperfect. God is in the process of becoming what God is. "And the Lord said, walk before me and be thou perfect [Hebrew, *tamin* or 'wholehearted']."[9] To involve ourselves in this process is to accept the responsibility of helping God achieve perfection. Whether you are or are not a believer, the dynamics at work here are intriguing, especially if you accept the claim announced in the Bible that human beings were "created in the image of God." Indeed, for God's way of being a process of becoming and what this process calls for finds expression in a presence that is no further away from us than the structure and function of our own existence. It's a fact of life: Human being is fundamentally a process of becoming, which is grounded in the spatial and temporal fabric of our existence and whose trajectory opens us to the objective uncertainty of the future. This trajectory is forever presenting us with the possibility of change, of things being otherwise than usual, of how what is yet to come in our lives may require us, for truth's sake, to rethink and revise what we currently hold to be correct about our ongoing commitments, involvements, and interpretive practices. Owing to the objective uncertainty of the future, our self-assured beliefs regarding what we claim to know about ourselves, others, and the world in general are always being called into question, whereby the security, stability, and comfort of our feeling at home with ourselves and others is disrupted. What can happen tomorrow? Who can say for sure? A call that lies at the heart of our existence necessarily raises these questions.

A question is an interruption. It follows, then, that human existence is fundamentally an interruption. It never stops putting us and our beliefs to the test; it never ceases bringing to mind the issue of contingency. The interruption that we are speaks to us of how our existence is always "on the way," always in a state of becoming, and thus always being completely incomplete, perfectly imperfect. (You can't get more god-like than that.) The interruption that we are is a question always being asked: Are you sure? The questioning function of our existence is a reality check: it calls us to perfect our capacity to be as open-minded and receptive as possible to the ways the world speaks and shows its truths and to think and act in accordance with these truths, at least for the time being. The call thus speaks to us of an ethical responsibility that becomes all the more apparent as we attempt to be true to our openness. (And thereby do all that God calls us to do.) Hence, in so doing, the call shows itself to be a perfective impulse at work in the presence of human existence. We are called to improve, better, and perfect ourselves (from the Latin *perficere—facere*, "to make"; *per*, "thoroughly"). God is well known for being the highest reference point for coming to terms with perfection. Something that is perfect, by definition, cannot get better than it already is.

The *Oxford English Dictionary* thus instructs us that describing something as "most perfect" is redundant, not "proper" English, not a "perfect" way of expressing "perfection." The human tendency to emphasize, and beyond that, to exaggerate and become hyperbolic, is certainly related to who we are as beings bound for perfection and the progress it affords. "If the idea of progress" ever dies in the West, writes historian Robert Nisbet, "so will a great deal else that we have long cherished in this civilization."[10] The same can be said about what progress presupposes. A sense of perfection, as it is sometimes phrased, is "absolutely essential" to the well-being of humankind. Our mindless acceptance of the unneeded adverb found in this common expression is evidence of how perfect we want perfection to be. Endowed with this passion we are fated to struggle with the ever-present challenge of "getting things right," "making things better," "improving ourselves," and being as "complete" as we can be as we grow, mature, and become wise with experience. We are beings who must continually engage in the process of acting and planning, planning and acting, in order to sustain the best of times and to overcome the worst of times. A person who admits that he or she has no purpose in life is likely to be considered irresponsible, if not worthless. Even a person who, owing to some accident, is in a persistent vegetative state but who is still being kept alive artificially by the technologies of medical science is recognized by right-to-life advocates as serving a crucial purpose: encouraging a heartfelt respect for God's gift of life and the struggle that is needed to put this gift to its proper and perfect use.

The call's perfective impulse speaks to us of the importance of progress, which in its most basic form is what evolutionary biologists term "survival of the fittest." We desire to exist, to stay alive, and to create and maintain habitats where we feel at home in our surroundings. Gaston Bachelard emphasizes the life-giving quality of this feeling when he notes: Home "is one of the greatest powers of integration for the thoughts, memories and dreams of mankind. . . . Without it, man would be a dispersed being. It maintains him through the storms of the heavens and through those of life."[11] Indeed, feeling at home is a "beautiful" experience to the extent that this specific habitat, as it is commonly defined, is a dwelling place of welcome, security, convenience, cordiality, relaxation, happiness, and love; a place that encourages the development of personal relationships and strong family ties; a place where one need not worry about "being oneself"; in short, a place of genuine care and comfort. The longing to inhabit such a place is demonstrated, for example, as religious souls pray to God, hoping that when their time on earth has ended, they will experience the joy of "going home to their Maker." Answering the call that lies at the heart of existence and doing all that it calls us to do, a person engages in the process of becoming, as they say, "one with God."

Such behavior displays what the philosopher William Earle describes as a human being's passionate longing or "metaphysical impulse" for some degree of meaning, order, and completeness or perfection in her or his life: "a nostalgia for something final and absolute."[12] This description is especially appropriate in that the feeling identified here—"nostalgia," from the Greek *nostos*: to return home—speaks of that state of being wherein one is "homesick." Such sickness threatens the health and well-being of human beings. The beauty of feeling at home is lost. The loss of this feeling can bring about the disruptive emotions of anger, depression, anxiety, and hopelessness—emotions that fuel the intensity of the call's challenge to deal with the ever present uncertainty of existence and to be as complete (perfect) as we can be in constructing worlds of meaning and understanding that serve the purpose of remedying to some extent the discomforting situations at hand. The call's perfective impulse thus gives rise to our being the purposive creatures that we are. (Supposedly, God did this on purpose.) When we lose our sense of purpose in life, we find ourselves in a state where the perfective impulse of existence has all but vanished. Without the experience of the call, its perfective impulse, and its purposive function, the callings of religion would never exist, nor would any other callings whose professional dwelling places arise from its inhabitants have succeeded in creating and using specialized languages to name and understand in a meaningful way whatever directs their expert attention and commitments. So using the example of religion again: Without our ability to hear and respond to the call, the name of God and all the language that is invented to explain what, how, and why this named presence is "real" would never come to mind and be put into practice. Arguments about whether or not the call that lies at the heart of human existence is a God-given gift are themselves continued responses to this call and the question that it poses: "Are you sure?" Did God create the call that lies at the heart of our existence and its process of becoming, or did we create God as a response to this call whereby we could feel at home with ourselves and others? Let the reader decide. We are content to maintain our empirically oriented existential understanding of the call that lies at the heart of our existence. It is a communication event whose presence is undeniable—a fact of life, without a doubt. With our empirical orientation we value the importance of a scientific outlook and its commitment to disclosing the truth of "the things themselves." This is not to say, of course, that science knows without a doubt what the call is all about.

Science

The physicist Leonard Susskind tells us that scientists "resist, to the death, all explanations of the world based on anything but the Laws of Physics, mathematics, and probability."[13] The physicist and Nobel laureate Steven Weinberg makes the point this way: "One of the great achievements of science has been, if not to make it impossible for intelligent people to be religious, then at least to make it possible for them not to be religious. We should not retreat from this accomplishment."[14] As noted by the physicist Paul Davies, however, such reductionism and skepticism emphasized by these physicists does not necessarily lead to a complete and final dismissal of God: "Our ignorance of the origin of life [and the universe] leaves plenty of scope for divine explanations, but that is a purely negative attitude, invoking 'the God-of-the-gaps' only to risk retreat at a later date in the face of scientific advance." Hence, "to invoke God as a blanket explanation of the unexplained is to invite eventual falsification and make God the friend of ignorance. If God is to be found, it must surely be through what we discover about the world, not what we fail to discover."[15] Notice that with this way of thinking, scientists do God a favor by acknowledging the possibility of the Creator while, at the same time, saying that the best way to do this is not to acknowledge this possibility because it gets in the way of and undercuts the scientific endeavor. A historical fact omitted in Davies's prescription for dealing with the question of God is important for our story: the prescription dates back to ancient Greece, when the callings of science and philosophy began to take form in the sixth century BCE with the teachings and findings of Milesian philosophers and scientists and those of the philosopher Heraclitus. Then as now, these callings, as well as the calling of religion, are primarily different ways of responding to two separate and related calls. The first is that original call that comes from the presence of the temporal structure of human existence and incites a metaphysical impulse of human beings to long for some degree of meaning, order, and completeness or perfection in their lives. The second call emanates from the presences of objects of consciousness that are ready to be named—for example, "God," the "big bang"—by witnesses so to make known what is maintained to be the truth and significance of these objects.

In the case of Milesian philosophers and scientists, such as Thales and Anaximander, this second call came from the presence of the cosmos (Greek: *kosmos*—the "fitting order" or "beautiful arrangement" of the universe). Pondering this call led the Milesians to break away from Homeric notions of the gods that prevailed at the time and that offered a version of what was referred to earlier as the short-sighted investigative mentality of "God-of-the-gaps" thinking. Homer's gods are not spiritual, but are physical beings that personify what called for Homer's attention: the presence of the attributes and forces of nature that now could be named in a way that made them easy to understand. Homer thus emphasized an anthropomorphic understanding of the gods, whereby, for example, the gods are similar to but more powerful than human beings and they never die; they engage in sexual love; they are quite competitive; they get jealous and envious of one another and wish to hurt those gods that challenge their authority; and they deceive one another and mortals and are willing to let human beings massacre one another in wars in order to injure those aligned with rival gods. The Milesians countered this blinding mythology and its use for explaining how nature is structured by offering an empirically based naturalistic approach to the study of nature, providing numerical measurements of astral cycles and creating a geometric model of the cosmos. According to the classical scholar Charles Kahn, this specific appreciation of the cosmos "was something new, and its novelty is identical with the emergence of Western science and philosophy as such." Hence, Kahn emphasizes that Milesian cosmology was "not so much a revolution within science as a revolution into science for the first time."[16]

With this revolution, the Milesians tended to the agricultural and seafaring needs of their culture by taking special notice of such phenomena as the daily, monthly, and annual cycles of weather, the atmospheric phenomena of evaporation and precipitation, and how these phenomena were directly associated with the ebb and flow of life. The change involved in this dynamic process was characterized by the Milesians as a cosmological conflict between opposing powers (e.g., the heat and dryness of the summer compared to the cold and wetness of winter; the light of day compared to the dark of night) forming a cycle of elemental and dialectical interchange. In the one surviving fragment that we have from Anaximander, the philosopher/scientist describes the cycle this way: "Out of those things [namely, the opposing powers] from which their generation comes, into these again does the destruction of things take place, in accordance with what is right and necessary; for they make amends and pay the penalty to one another for their aggression (*adikia*, injustice) according to the ordinance of Time."[17] In short, for the Milesians change is a constant, which operates dialectically as a conflict of opposing powers; it requires a reciprocity of these powers (i.e., a unity of opposites), regulates the potential of excess and aggression of the opposing powers to maintain the unity of opposites over time, and defines an inevitable rule of justice that emanates from the orderly and beautiful arrangement of the cosmos. The beautiful order of nature entails a moral imperative. Moreover, as Kahn suggests, we can understand the Milesians as granting the world order a starting point (*arche*) that, naturally, came before everything else. This origin lends credence to the existence of an ever-present and monolithic "cosmic god" who initiated the whole process.[18]

The philosopher Xenophanes of Colophon, who was much influenced by the Milesian's scientific investigations, acknowledges this divine entity when he criticizes mortals for their anthropocentric way of understanding "the gods to be created by birth, and to have their own raiment, voice and body." No, says Xenophanes, "There is one god, among gods and men the greatest, not at all like mortals in body or in mind. He sees as a whole, thinks as a whole, and hears as a whole. But without toil he sets everything in motion, by the thought of his mind."[19] The ancient Greek term for "to set in motion" (*hormáein*) is also properly translated as "to agitate," "to shake up," or "to jolt." These alternative translations suggest that we are talking about a primal interruption or call that changes a state of being that was not in motion (before the beginning) into one that now is (in the beginning and after). Unlike Homer and his followers, the Milesians listened attentively to the saying and showing of a specific presence that called for acknowledgment of what, in truth, it is. Hippocratic physicians, the first men of scientific medicine, emphasized a teaching that is relevant here: "There are in fact two things, science and opinion. The first begets knowledge, the later ignorance."[20] Another instructive saying is offered by the literary writer Vladimir Nabokov: "Common sense at its worst is sense made common, so everything is comfortably cheapened by its touch."[21] Trying to be as attentive as possible when witnessing what is called for by the presence of some object of consciousness is much influenced by the mindset that up to this point has been accepted by the witness as common sense and that conditions one's ability to ponder the truth of this particular presence. The Milesians' science, mathematics, and geometric skill called into question Homer's common-sense understanding and portrayal of the attributes and forces of nature. For the Milesians, Homer's common sense was common sense at its worst and thus a source of ignorance.

The teachings of the Milesians and philosophers like Xenophanes suggest that science and God can go together. Something of God's presence can be verified by a scientific assessment and understanding of the ways and means of nature. The philosopher Heraclitus agrees; hence he tells us in two related fragments: "The lord whose oracle is in Delphi neither declares nor conceals, but gives a sign"; "The wise is one alone, unwilling and willing to be spoken of by the name of Zeus."²² At least something of the "sign" mentioned here is evident in the findings of the Milesian cosmologists. A trace of the "lord" is found in the workings of the cosmos and nature. The "wise" is willing to grant a degree of disclosure, presumably so that at the appropriate time the truth may be known to the fullest extent. Yes, there is something happening that may be god-like (e.g., Zeus), but the truth transcends our common-sense way of naming and understanding the world. The force of this truth registers itself as a contradictory (interruptive) logic: To know this truth is to understand that one does not know it. Still, there is room for improvement. Xenophanes puts it this way: "Truly the gods have not revealed to mortals all things from the beginning, but mortals by long seeking discover what is better."²³ With this statement Xenophanes is credited with offering the first statement in Western history of the idea of "progress," of advancing and perfecting an understanding of the truth of the presence of things. Influenced by the call of Milesian cosmology, the philosopher Heraclitus assumed the task in a bold and influential way—what we take to be an original effort in the philosophy of science.

Heraclitus is famous for his cosmological "doctrine of conflict or opposition," which he associates with the presence of what he terms "the Logos" (commonly translated as "the Word"): the way reality presents and discloses itself and thereby "speaks" of what and how it is. To grasp the fundamental truth of all that exists, we must hear the call that is spoken here. "It is wise, listening not to me but to the report [Logos]," writes Heraclitus, "to agree that all things are one."[24] The Logos is the monolithic ruling principle of an orderly universe. Heraclitus sometimes refers to the dynamism of this ruling principle as "the Divine," but this naming of the Logos is not meant to suggest that it is God. On the contrary; Heraclitus maintains that the monolithic ruling principle is "not [something that] god nor man has made, but it ever was and is and will be."[25] The Logos was there in the beginning and before the beginning; its presence is ever present. The primary substance Heraclitus uses to demonstrate the dynamism of the Logos is "fire." The "flame" of the fire burning steadily remains what it is only as the flame's nature is continually changing, maintaining a state of flux and organizing the "polar oppositions" characterizing everyday existence into a unity. For example, death negates life, but without the former the latter would not make sense. Life needs death to be the life that it is. Life and death go together in a dialectical manner. With Heraclitus's theory of the Logos and its doctrine of opposition, dialectics assumes a life-affirming character made possible by that which speaks the truth of all that is. This most original speech act and the call that we are instructed to listen to announces an ethical precept, which Heraclitus states as follows: "Speaking with understanding . . . [people] must hold fast to what is shared by all, as a city holds to its law, and even more firmly. For all human laws are nourished by a divine one. It prevails as it will and suffices for all and is more than enough."[26] The declaration is meant to have people engage in the practice of acting and speaking with praiseworthy competence, which Heraclitus insists "is the greatest excellence and wisdom: to act and speak what is true, perceiving things according to their nature"[27] Although he does not credit Heraclitus for this teaching, Socrates famously employed this practice in his dialectical and dialogical exchanges and pondering with his students. The practice allows for an experience of beauty (*kalon*), which takes place as pondering "calls forth" (*to kaloun*) and "names" (*kalon*) the truth of matters of concern. Heraclitus certainly would welcome such Socratic wisdom. Recall that Heraclitus, following the Milesian cosmologists, understood the Logos to speak the "fitting order," the "beautiful arrangement," the truth of the cosmos.

The truth be told! Heraclitus wants exactly that—the truth as it shows itself empirically in nature. "Whatever comes from sight, hearing, learning from experience: this I prefer."[28] Like the Milesians, Heraclitus is critical of a tradition of mythic belief about supposed divine referents by speaking of a truly fundamental referent that is more than the fabled gods: the Logos. Heraclitus berates the common sense of his time—the way its traditions, routines, and habits too readily dull humankind's perceptional and cognitive capacities for comprehending the ultimate truth. "Most men do not think things in the way they encounter them, nor do they recognize what they experience, but believe their own [conditioned] opinions."[29] The error borders on blasphemy: "Eyes and ears are poor witnesses for men if their souls [*psychai*] do not understand the language," the Logos, the disclosing of nature as being a cosmic order, the one and the many, the basis of rational thought.[30] Not comprehending the language and truth of the Logos, the masses, declares Heraclitus, "hear like the deaf. The saying is their witness: absent while present."[31]

Heraclitus is determined to "go beyond" (*para*) the "received opinion" (*doxa*) of the masses' common sense; hence, he is compelled to offer discourse that interrupts and thus conflicts with this domain of normalcy. Heraclitus is a "paradoxicalist." It is thus especially appropriate and fitting for Heraclitus to say, for example, that "One must realize that war is shared, and conflict is justice, and that all things come to pass . . . in accordance with conflict."[32] Heraclitus's use of the metaphors war and conflict are not meant to encourage carnage and bloodshed; rather, they are intended to echo the force of interruption that comes with the Logos and its continua of opposites, and that calls on us to learn the importance of being just by finding a balance between opposing forces. Heraclitus writes this declaration in an oracular style; his discourse thereby gives the impression that he is a person through whom a deity is believed to speak. Heraclitus reads and reports on "signs" that are found in nature and in the workings of language and are informed by the interruptive force of the Logos. The rhetorical figures of antithesis, contradiction, and paradox (e.g., "absent while present") thus become linguistic devices for communicating a wisdom that is obscure. "Nature loves to hide."[33] Hence, the famous saying by Heraclitus that contrary to common sense, "you cannot step twice into the same rivers; for fresh waters are ever flowing in upon you."

Here, again, Heraclitus uses a familiar object to demonstrate the essential interruptive function of the Logos. His paradoxical formulations are not intended to be mere rhetorical ploys against traditional standards of common sense. On the contrary, his statements represent a serious reflection of reality, one that sees and hears the Logos as a force that "rests [maintains its identity] by changing."[34] The reality of a river can be named whereby we preserve its identity in linguistic form despite the constant change of its parts. We can do this because of the regularity and continuity of that change. Constant change lends itself to being perceived as some static state of existence. Heraclitus writes so to interrupt this commonsensical and misleading way of perceiving the interruption that is the Logos and whose presence is "unexpected" due to the limiting habits and routines of everyday common sense and language use.[35] Heraclitus not only expects the unexpected to show itself, he welcomes and praises its presence with discourse meant to puzzle and provoke his readers to ponder the truth of what is always present, calling for attention and acknowledgment. Heraclitus wants good listeners and speakers so that they can understand and share with others the wisdom of the Logos, the Word, which operates dialectically, enacting interruption. Kahn emphasizes the point this way: "The world order speaks to [human beings] as a kind of language they must learn to comprehend. Just as the meaning of what is said is actually 'given' in the sounds which the foreigner hears, but cannot understand, so the direct experience of the nature of things will be like the babbling of an unknown tongue for a soul that does not know how to listen."[36] The role that language plays in Heraclitus's philosophy cannot be overestimated.

The Logos disclosing itself marks the initial manifestation of the power of language and articulate speech, a power that, as it demonstrates itself in everyday discourse, displays how well a given discourse is able to uncover and reveal what something is, its truth. This revelation functions as a call to attend to the presence of a thing's existence that calls for acknowledgment. As noted in our introduction and detailed in our discussion up to this point of our story, the act of calling is an act of "saying." To say something involves showing and letting something be seen. The Logos is translated as the Word. It is also translated as a "Saying" (Greek: λόγος [Logos] from λέγω "I say"). The presence of the Logos is a Saying that shows itself and thereby calls for the acknowledgment of its truth. This is the call that Heraclitus wants people to listen to such that they can develop their ability of "thinking well" in order to "speak what is true." Without admitting it explicitly, Heraclitus thus associates Logos with what ancient Greek rhetorical theory terms "epideictic discourse." Such discourse is commonly associated with the employment of language to bestow praise and blame on others. The primary function of epideictic discourse, however, is a "showing-forth" (*epi-deixis*), a disclosing, displaying, saying of the truth of some matter warranting concern.

A classic example that illustrates what we are saying here about epideictic discourse is Pericles's funeral oration on the Athenian dead in the first year of the Peloponnesian War. The Greek general insists that his fellow soldiers, in sacrificing their lives to defend their homeland, have "won praises that never grow old, the most splendid of sepulchers—not the sepulcher in which their bodies are laid, but where their glory remains eternal in men's minds, always there on the right occasion to stir others to speech or to action. For famous men have the whole earth as their memorial: it is not only the inscriptions on their graves in their own country that mark them out; no, in foreign lands also, not in any visible form but in the people's hearts, their memory abides and grows."[37] The praise offered here is obvious, but how Pericles structures this praise to emphasize the lasting character of his comrades, their true "glory," is what makes the oration memorable: By way of our minds and hearts we provide accommodations that enable the dearly departed to come back to life, to be there with us and to guide us as we carry on their teachings. The polar opposites of life and death form a unity in Pericles's oration. Here on earth, our lived bodies offer a "home" (sepulcher) for the dead. Pericles's speech is designed to register this point in the hearts and minds of an audience whose members, he believes, need not only "commiseration" but also "comfort." Home is a "dwelling place" (Greek: *ethos*) that caters to this longed-for state of being, and Pericles's epideictic rhetoric creates a narrative structure whose workings acknowledge this human desire. As he offers unqualified praise for his troops, Pericles constructs a home where personal relationships and strong family ties can flourish, and where people can know together the truth of whatever calls for concerned thought and thoughtful behavior. Feeling at home with the truth and others is an honorable way to live.

Pericles's epideictic rhetoric is enhanced by its eloquence, its evocative use of discourse that facilitates the vividness of Pericles's subject matter and the attendant emotions and moods that are invoked by the power of this rhetorical activity. The philosopher Raphael Demos offers a perceptive description of the evocative workings of this activity. "Evocation," he writes,

> is the process by which vividness is conveyed; it is the presentation of a viewpoint in such a manner that it becomes real for the public. It is said that argument is a way by which an individual experience is made common property; in fact, an argument has much less persuasive force than the [eloquent and] vivid evocation of an experience. The enumeration of all the relevant points in favor of a theory and against its opposite can never be completed; far more effective is it to state a viewpoint in all its concreteness and in all its significant implication, and then stop; the arguments become relevant only after this stage has been concluded.[38]

Stating a viewpoint in all its concreteness and all its significant implication helps to stimulate the emotional dispositions of an audience that must be called into play if the members of the audience are to take an interest in the matter at hand. Eloquence is the perfective impulse of language at work helping to disclose something of a given presence's truth.

What we are saying about Pericles's discourse is applicable to Heraclitus: He hears and responds to the epideictic discourse of the Logos, its call, its saying and showing of its truth and what this truth calls for—"the greatest excellence and wisdom: to act and speak what is true, perceiving things according to their nature." Heraclitus's response is itself a call that calls attention to an all-encompassing call. He sounds his call with an interruptive and evocative rhetoric that displays eloquence in its paradoxical and metaphorical formulations that call into question the limiting habits and routines of everyday common sense and language use. Although his words are intended to be disruptive, they nevertheless warrant credit for their eloquence. Even the ancient literary theorist Longinus and the eighteenth-century philosopher and statesman Edmund Burke, authorities on the matter, confirm this point with their related theories of eloquence. For they associate eloquence with a speaker's and writer's ability to "torture his language" in order to "enthrall" (awe) an audience and enhance its understanding and appreciation of some "awe-inspiring" experience—such as the presence of the Logos.[39] Pericles's epideictic and eloquent discourse was offered to help others feel at home with the sacrifice of his fellow soldiers. Heraclitus's epideictic and eloquent discourse, on the other hand, was structured to dismantle what he maintained was a misguided way of feeling at home with a prevailing common-sense understanding of everyday existence. But this was not an abandonment of this much needed feeling. On the contrary: for Heraclitus, nothing less than this feeling is called for by the Logos and what it has to say and show with its epideictic discourse. One way that Heraclitus recalls this call was noted above and may be supplemented with words that enhance its meaning: "Speaking [the truth] with understanding . . . [people] must hold fast to what is shared by all [the Logos], as a city [a dwelling place where people can feel at home with the truth and others] holds to its law, and even more firmly. For all human laws are nourished by a divine one. It prevails as it will and suffices for all and is more than enough." Educated by the call, Heraclitus calls to others to acknowledge the relationship that exists between truth and the feeling at home and that plays an essential role in maintaining the well-being of a citizenry. The philosopher Harry Frankfort offers a lucid assessment of the relationship:

> To the extent that we grasp the truths that we need to know, we can develop sensible judgments concerning what we would like to happen and concerning the outcomes to which various possible courses of action will probably lead. This is because we are then more or less fully aware of what we are dealing with, and because we know how the objects and events that would be implicated in our following one course of action or another will respond to what we do. In a certain part of the world, we are therefore somewhat more relaxed and secure. We know what the important constituents of our environment are, we know where to find them, and we can maneuver freely without bumping into things. In that region of the world, we can begin—so to speak—to feel ourselves at home.[40]

The experience of feeling at home has a very far reach. To speak of going home to one's Maker, although soothing, is God-of-the-gaps thinking. Such thinking is uncalled for by science, which is content to speak of Planet Earth as being our "home in the universe," which is empirically verifiable. Here we live, die, and nothing more. But the universe may also have a home that was there before the big bang. Speculation regarding "the before" of the big bang is based on science's mathematical ability to extrapolate from what is known about the observable universe and predict what was going on in a state of nothingness and nowhere. So, for example, there is Alan Guth's theory of cosmic inflation, from the early 1980s, which explains how our universe has been expanding since the big bang.[41] This theory, which is built into the standard quantum theory of elementary particles, grants the possibility that the phenomenon of inflation was happening prior to the big bang. The inflation may be due to the presence of "dark energy." Dark energy is neither atomic nor visible, which is to say that it is not composed of quarks and electrons. This energy, which defines approximately 70 percent of the density of our present-day cosmos, is in conflict with gravity: The presence of regular matter causes the expansion ratio of the universe to slow down, while dark energy speeds it up. In a heuristic sense, then, dark energy acts as if it is a repulsive force, and just before the big bang occurred the repulsion inflated exponentially, instigating an interruption of momentous proportion. Out of a location of nothingness and nowhere (a "space" that is dramatically otherwise than everyday space) came the existence of the universe. The more space grew, the more repulsion and inflation transpired. The universe is expanding. There are currently more than 100 billion galaxies in the observable universe. Our universe is at home in the multiverse, which for the religious soul is a further testament of the power and glory of God and the home of heaven that awaits us.

Like it or not, God-of-the-gaps thinking is here to stay, and for the same reason that motivates science to question its legitimacy. It is a matter of finding a way to feel at home with one's environment. Consider, for example, this life-changing moment of scientific discovery: the thirteen-year scientific and technological research endeavor known as the Human Genome Project. The human genome consists of all the DNA of our species, the hereditary code of life. The goal of the project was to decipher this code. The leader of the project, geneticist Francis S. Collins, tells us that the "newly revealed text was 3 billion letters long and written in a strange and cryptographic four-letter code. Such is the amazing complexity of the information carried within each cell of the human body, that a live reading of that code at a rate of three letters per second would take thirty-one years, even if reading continued day and night." Collins and his associates thus produced what he terms an "amazing script" that carries "within it all of the instructions for building a human being."[42] With this script, science takes a giant step in getting rid of God-of-the-gaps thinking and its attending rhetoric regarding the evolution of our species. The Bible's language and call is far from being fine-tuned enough in its account of the creation story and human development. Religious fundamentalists, however, would have us believe that "evolution's lie permeates and dominates modern thought in every field. . . . When science and the Bible differ, science has obviously misinterpreted the data."[43] Collins takes offense at such closed-minded thinking. Still, his book about his experience with the Human Genome Project is entitled *The Language of God*. Collins was an agnostic before he began work on the project. The script that he and his colleagues deciphered, however, was wondrous enough for him to dismantle his taken-for-granted hesitancy to believe in God and to reconstruct his thinking about the matter. For Collins, "the experience of sequencing the human genome, and uncovering this most remarkable of all texts, was both a stunning scientific achievement and an occasion of worship."[44] Faith in science and faith in God are not incompatible. The call that lies at the heart of human existence calls to scientists and religious souls alike. "Evolution, as a mechanism, can be and must be true. But that says nothing about the nature of its author. For those who believe in God, there are reasons now to be more in awe, not less."[45] The human genome sequence "was written in the DNA language by which God spoke life into being."[46] Making perfect use of the perfectionist impulse of language was at work in the beginning. The DNA language is as eloquent as one can get.

Collins writes as both a scientist and a religious soul. He associates genetic mutations that cause serious illnesses with our evolutionary history. He also maintains that these mutations and the suffering they produce serve God's purposes. Suffering educates people about the importance of being strong, supportive, and faithful even in dire situations. Awed by his interpretation of the human genome, Collins speaks with assurance: "Science is not threatened by God; it is enhanced. God is most certainly not threatened by science; He made it all possible."[47] Critics of Collins's statement were awed by his "ridiculous" interpretation. In the most brutal review of Collins's book by the neuroscientist, philosopher, and atheist Sam Harris, we are told that what Collins has written is "a genuinely astonishing book. To read it is to witness nothing less than an intellectual suicide. It is, however, a suicide that has gone almost entirely unacknowledged: The body yielded to the rope; the neck snapped; the breath subsided; and the corpse dangles in ghastly discomposure even now—and yet polite people everywhere continue to celebrate the great man's health."[48] Harris does not feel at home with Collins's worldview. Indeed, the harshness of his rhetoric suggests that Harris found this worldview to be an insulting interruption of science's commitment to telling "the truth and nothing but the truth." Collins must be charged with committing an act of home invasion. The "godly" rhetoric of religion is well-known for its evocative and eloquent phrasings and declarations: for example, "I will give them a heart to know Me that I am the Lord." But such rhetoric warrants condemnation. The philosopher and political theorist John Locke makes the point this way in his argument for the truthful ways of scientific discourse:

> If we would speak of things as they are, we must allow that all the art of rhetoric, beside order and clearness; all the artificial and figurative application of words eloquence hath invented, are for nothing else but to insinuate wrong ideas, move the passions, and thereby mislead the judgment; and so indeed are perfect cheats: and therefore, however laudable or allowable oratory may render them in harangues and popular addresses, they are certainly, in all discourses that pretend to inform or instruct, wholly to be avoided; and where truth and knowledge are concerned, cannot but be thought a great fault, either of the language or person that makes use of them.[49]

Eloquence is a manipulative tool, a perfect cheat, for making people feel at home with bogus truth-claims. The call that lies at the heart of human existence demands far more than that. In defending its response to this demand against those "who know not what they speak," science does, however, grant exception to its practitioners who would employ the evocative ways of eloquence for "the best of reasons." Harris's critique of Collins is a case in point. Even at the risk of insulting those who are not wise enough to stand the truth, Harris's evocative flourishes are granted permission to be merciless.[50]

The callings of religion and science are the result of people answering a call that lies at the heart of existence, in the fabric of space and time that we did not create, opens and exposes us to the uncertainty of the future, and thereby triggers our evolutionary developed passionate longing for some degree of meaning, order, and completeness or perfection in our lives. This is how we are at home in the multiverse, the universe, and here on earth. It is empirically verifiable. Making the best of this situated way of existing in these dwelling places, we put our longing for completeness and perfection to use by engaging in the rhetorical activity of constructing habitats where, with the help of eloquence, we can as much as possible feel at home with ourselves and others. We term this rhetorical activity "homemaking."

Beginning with Socrates's favorable assessment of the scientific outlook advanced by Hippocratic physicians and his critique of how the Sophists of his day too often employed eloquence to manipulate and deceive audiences, the rhetorical activity of homemaking would become well-known as a "perfect cheat" for commending bogus truth-claims. Yet, Socrates's employment of eloquence in his dialectical and dialogical interactions with students and other members of the public commended the workings of this activity as a way of disclosing as much as possible the truth of matters of concern. In this way his interlocutors could feel at home with the thought and behavior called for by the truth in question. It is this well-deserved favorable understanding of the activity of eloquence that is especially important for our study, although we are also attentive to how eloquence operates as a perfect cheat. The contrast here serves the purpose of heightening an appreciation of the importance of the rhetorical art of eloquence for establishing and maintaining the moral ecology of our home environments. The history of this art is far more robust in detail and complexity than what we have to say about the matter throughout the chapters of this book. Those features of the art that are essential to our project are introduced later. As our study proceeds, we also will be further referencing and developing a host of phenomena that call for attention in examining the scope and function of the call. These phenomena include presencing, touching, naming, language, otherness, perfection, truth, ambiguity, temporality, the process of becoming, interruption, common sense, rhetoric, and responsibility. The call is a robust and essential communication event. Let us not forget: No call, no callings. And more than that: No call, no human beings. We *are* beings on call, beckoned to hear and to communicate to others what the presence of things, including ourselves, have to say about their existence. It's a call for judgment awaiting a judgment call. Hence, the task before us.

CHAPTER 2

The Elements of Eloquence

f you have ever watched a football game, college or professional, on television, you have undoubtedly suffered through the judgment call of an official. A player, football tucked under his arm, runs for the end zone hoping to score a touchdown. There is only one defensive player left in his way. The defensive player tackles the offensive player with the ball just before he reaches the end zone. The offensive player switches the ball into his hand and stretches it out just as his knee hits the turf. Did the ball break the plane of the goal? The question is an interruption: Are you sure? In the wink of an eye, the referee must make the judgment call. He raises his hands over his head indicating a touchdown has indeed been scored. However, the call is challenged. Suddenly, the play is "under review." Another interruption in pursuit of the truth—a call for perfection.

Now another official enters the fray. In a booth somewhere in the stadium, that official reviews the "touchdown" with the aid of many camera angles. To overturn the call on the field, she must have incontrovertible evidence that the ball did not break the plane of the goal before the offensive player's knee touched the turf. With more visual evidence than the referee on the field, the official in the review booth overturns the call because she sees the truth of what occurred that could determine the outcome of the game. Because she has witnessed the truth, she makes a more robust and perfect call.

Clearly, there are judgment calls that are much more momentous. Drone operators sit in the Nevada desert and make judgment calls about when to approve and/or order a strike. If the targeted combatants are shooting at allies, the judgment call is pretty easy. However, if those targeted are not clearly enemy forces or if they are armed children, ambiguity and issues of responsibility enter the picture. The judgment call is much more difficult and may require more evidence.

Furthermore, the element of timing is added to the element of visual evidence to make the call. If the timing isn't right, drone operators can miss their shot. This happened with the first sighting of Osama Bin Laden. He was in the sights of a drone operator in Kandahar province, but approval could not be obtained in time, and Bin Laden escaped his fate. Years later, with ample evidence from sources on the ground and the air, it was determined that Bin Laden was holed up in house near the Pakistani border. Based on this evidence, President Obama made the judgment call. He bet that Bin Laden was in the house and that a special forces team could capture or kill him. The truth for Obama was not absolute but based on a high degree of probability. His way of thinking is perfectly compatible with Aristotle's thesis that in a contingent world, our most important decisions are based on probability, not absolute truth. Aristotle contended that all things being equal, including equal eloquence on all sides, the truth will prevail. The truth is not made up and therefore can be reconstructed and recalled more easily and accurately than fiction. This was particularly important to Aristotle in the forensic arena where the judge and jury make the call.

One other observation is important to understanding judgment calls and the call to judgment. Each implies a dialectic. Did the football play result in a touchdown or did it not? Does the evidence support a drone strike or does it not? In the latter case, there is also a dialectic between doing the right thing and doing the wrong thing from a moral standpoint—that is, the issue of responsibility. There is need for eloquence, and the more sublime the better.

Earlier in this book we established the fact that naming calls to us. In this way, eloquence is naming. Recall Kenneth Burke's related directives noted earlier: "The mere desire to name something by its 'proper' name, or to speak a language in its distinctive ways is intrinsically 'perfectionist.' What is more 'perfectionist' in essence than the impulse, when one is in dire need of something, to so state this need that one in effect 'defines' the situation? The primary purpose of eloquence is to 'convert life' to its most thorough verbal equivalent." In what follows, we review the major constituents of eloquence so that in the chapters that follow we can assess the calls that are being made. Eloquence helps us make our calls more appealing, more attuned to our audience, more present in the moment, and better able to describe disclosive moments. Calling needs words to enhance the experience and make it present. Calling requires eloquence; the more eloquent one is, the more robust the call. Thus, this chapter reviews the primary tools available for issuing a call and for building the dwelling place where the call is issued and heard. The tools have been provided over time by important philosophers and rhetorical theorists. They give us a vocabulary for talking about eloquence and hence eloquent calls.

Generally, rhetoricians have defined three types of discourse that to different degrees engage in what we call "homemaking," that is, creating a comfortable dwelling place (ethos) for speaker and audience, whether that be a public forum, a quiet dialogue, or a prayer at the foot of a bed. This rhetorical act of creation defines the "architectural" function of the art: how, for example, its practice grants such living room to our lives that we might feel more at home with others and our surroundings. The ethos of rhetoric would have one appreciate how the premises and other materials of arguments not only are tools of logic but also mark out the boundaries and domains of thought that, depending on how their specific discourses are designed and arranged, may be particularly inviting and moving for some audiences. The ethos of rhetoric makes use of our inventive and symbolic capacity to construct dwelling places that are stimulating and aesthetically, socially, and perhaps theologically instructive. We are creatures who are destined to be caught up in the process of providing openings of these places where good (and bad) things can happen. These venues serve the purposes of those who would perfect the world, heal the nation, or care for others. The call that lies at the heart of human existence demands as much.

The first discourse involved in responding to this call is ordinary rhetoric. It tries to get things done in the here and now. It is quotidian, pragmatic, and often mundane. It can certainly be used for good or evil. The important thing to remember is that if rhetoric is like chemistry, it is important to master all of its strategies if one is to combat its misuse. If you visit the floor of the U.S. House of Representatives, you will often hear rhetoric as members try to pass or stop legislation that concerns ways and means, budgets, foreign policy, and the like. If you go to any courtroom, you can hear it in the appeals to judges and juries. If you attend a wedding reception, you can hear it in the toasts. But it can also be essential to surviving in a contingent world. The shout can save you from being run down by a car.

The second type of discourse is rhetoric taken to a higher level with appropriate language that may achieve literary quality. Here is where eloquence is at work. It can be concerned with the issues mentioned above, but it also seeks to last over time. It often taps the beautiful and sublime to advance its cause. Here again, we must be careful, because this kind of eloquence can become the perfect cheat when disguised as flattery, some ism, or emotional appeal. It can be deceptive and dishonest.

Finally, there is what we shall call "true eloquence." In this case, the discourse is not only appropriate in terms of timing and language, it discloses a truth and/or perfects something, be it the nation or the souls in the audience. The transcendentalist Ralph Waldo Emerson has true eloquence in mind when he writes of the heroic and performative nature of the orator's art: "Certainly there is no true orator who is not a hero. . . . The orator must ever stand with forward foot, in the attitude of advancing. . . . His speech is not to be distinguished from action. It is action, as the general's word of command or shout of battle is action."[1] This claim calls into question and thus interrupts a well-known maxim of our culture—"actions speak louder than words"—a "putdown" of the practice of rhetoric. The metaphor that informs the eloquence of Emerson's claim lends it further force, for indeed, heroes and war are readily related. When Emerson speaks of the true orator's heroism, however, his understanding of "war" emphasizes what he terms "a military attitude of the soul" that is not directed toward the actual killing of others. Instead, this attitude is needed by the orator who would "dare the gibbet and the mob," the rage and retribution of a misinformed and closed-minded public, when attempting to move its members beyond the blinders of their "common-sense" beliefs and toward a genuine understanding of what, for the orator, is arguably the truth of some immediate matter of concern. For Emerson, the heroism and dignity of the true orator are made possible not only by his "power to connect his thought with its proper symbol, and so to utter it" but also, and primarily, by his "love of truth and . . . [the] desire to communicate it without loss." The process presupposes the imaginative capacity of the orator to construct dwelling places for his or her audience, to create openings for others that allow for collaborative deliberation about the truth of the matters at hand.

Eloquence need not be prim and proper to warrant praise. It does require, however, that its practitioner be especially receptive to how the presence of something's truth calls for attention. Only then can one say that she or he is truly ready to discover and use the right words (vocabulary) in the right way (appropriateness) and at the right time (expectation) to construct a discourse that calls for attention because of what it has to say and show about whatever called this discourse into being with its saying and showing of truth.

Speakers or writers who have a truth to tell and who want this truth to be thought-provoking, influential, and memorable would be wise to be concerned with finding the most appropriate, convincing, and effective way of expressing themselves about the matter at hand. This task calls for an appreciation of eloquence, an art long acknowledged as being essential for the well-being of any civil society that values freedom and that is bent on achieving genuine social, political, moral progress. Just as eloquence can help individuals perfect their well-being, it can also perfect society as a whole and/or the nation-state.

The Roman senator, orator, lawyer, and philosopher Marcus Tullius Cicero had eloquence in mind when he offered counsel in the ways of rhetoric. For "what function is so kingly, so worthy of the free, so generous, as to being help to the suppliant, to raise up those who are cast down, to bestow security, to set free from peril, to maintain men in their civil rights? . . . The wise control of the complete orator is that which chiefly upholds not only his own dignity, but the safety of countless individuals and of the entire State." Like the physician, the complete orator has a significant role to play in maintaining the good health of the people that constitute the body politic. However, even before Cicero, there were rhetoricians who believed that oratory was essential to proper maintenance of the nation.

Timing, Expectations and the Call

The ancient Sicilian rhetorician Gorgias eventually became the ambassador from the city-state of Leontini to Athens. There, he gained fame as an orator par excellence, winning the quadrennial Olympic games three times. He also taught students who could afford his enormous fee. Gorgias discovered a number of important tools for rhetoric and eloquence. He knew that speakers needed to make judgment calls and also induce adherence from their audiences. At one point, Gorgias compared rhetoric to pharmaceuticals. It could cure the body politic, it could ease the pain of a people, but it could also cause hallucination, allowing some to deceive their audiences. He borrowed Empedocles's theory of animation in delivery. He adapted Protagoras's theory of *Kosmos* to define a sense of proportion and refine the proper order of arguments in a speech. As far as we can tell, he was the first to borrow tropes and figures from poetry, particularly songs, for use in persuasive endeavors. They fascinate the audience, make concepts present, and hold attention. He developed the apologia, a speech of explanation or defense, and took epideictic rhetoric, the display of virtue and the condemnation of vice in ceremonial speeches, to unprecedented levels. When he taught about eliciting emotion, he not only covered the common emotions such as pity, fear, and anger; he claimed that the successful orator achieved a "shuddering" in his audience, his version of awe.[2]

Putting those tools aside for the moment, we want to concentrate on one other contribution of Gorgias, his notion of *Kairos*, like *Kosmos* named for one of the sons of Zeus. Kairos refers to "fitting timing" of the speech. The timing of the speech is one of its sine qua nons. Even the best idea presented at the wrong time will fail. So if we are to engage in true eloquence and make a judgment call, we need to master timing. Gorgias saw that opportunities open up at various times for the call.

Fitting timing can come when an opportune moment presents itself for a speech of inspiration to induce a judgment. The speech of inspiration can lead an audience to make the judgment call. Shall we declare war? Shall I vote for candidate X? The opportunity may come when orators find themselves caught in the clash of highly charged conflicting opinions. Here dialectic can be crucial in the search for the truth and the making of the call. The orator seizes the moment by heroically stepping into the divisive scene at the height of conflict.

Cicero insisted that "we are not born for ourselves alone," that "our country claims a share of our being," and that if we intend "to contribute to the general good," we must not disparage and retreat from the politics of public life but instead use "our skill, our industry, and our talents to cement human society more closely together, man to man."[3] The obligation stated here speaks to the importance of rhetoric in his civic healing role. Philosophy is essential for the education of the orator, but it is the "art of eloquence" (*oratio*) practiced by this advocate of the *vita activa* that instructs one on how to equip (*ornare*) knowledge of a subject in such a way that it can assume a publicly accessible form and thus function effectively in the social and political arena. For the good of the community, philosophy and rhetoric must work together. Cicero—who admitted "that whatever ability I possess as an orator comes, not from the workshops of the rhetoricians, but from the spacious grounds of the Academy"—would have it no other way.[4] "To be drawn by study away from active life is contrary to moral duty."[5]

The Roman senator and consul profoundly expands the role of style in language when he develops his theory of decorum: the art of meeting and/ or creating expectations of the audience and the occasion. Obviously, an analysis of what the occasion requires and what is expected of the speaker should precede any construction of the speech itself. At a funeral, mourners expect to grieve and hear praise about the deceased. At a wedding, we expect an exchange of vows and blessing of the union. However, there are times when an audience expects one thing, and speakers need to change their expectation.

Cicero saw expectation as a macro theory that informed eloquence. However, expectations could not be met or changed, nor could ideas become present for the audience, unless the proper naming was employed. Cicero set out a continuum that ran from the plain style through a middle style to a grand style in his process of properly naming and disclosing. The plain style is used to teach and inform; it is expository and has the least need of stylistic devices. The middle style is used to persuade and can be seen in deliberative forums and courtrooms. It employs a modicum of stylistic devices to achieve its ends, such as guilt or innocence. The grand style seeks to achieve conviction and can be seen in speeches of display, such as eulogies that seek to honor or dishonor their subjects. The grand style uses more stylistic devices than the other two styles and is the most likely to evoke the sublime.

And that is where Cicero's micro theory of *ornatus* comes in. *Ornatus*, from which ornament is derived, is the fashioning of the speech with appropriate tropes and figures that enhance the presence of ideas, that is, moving them to the fore. It is artful naming that calls for our attention; it fascinates us. Over a century after Cicero, Quintilian wrote about the positive use of *ornatus*: "Here is the dwelling place of prose; here is the point to which the audience looks forward; here is the orator's whole merit."[6] Quintilian redefined *ornatus* as *copia*, ample style. It provides the speaker with symbolic resources that can amplify the subject matter.[7]

Mastering *ornatus* or *copia* is no easy task. Cicero set out 97 tropes and figures useful to speakers. By the Victorian Era, orators were expected to know how to use 288. Obviously, the larger one's vocabulary, the more choices one has to convey a message accurately and make it present for its audience. The more tropes and figures one masters, the more tools one has to make that message fascinating, timely, and in line with audience expectations. *Ornatus* is like salt: it should be used to enhance the flavor of the speech, not to overwhelm it.

In 1757, in his *Philosophical Inquiry into the Origin of our Ideas of the Sublime and Beautiful*, Edmund Burke argued that the more we are exposed to beauty, the more our sense of taste is developed. As opposed to everyday rhetoric, eloquence perfects an audience by developing its sense of taste, which might be seen as eloquent listening. Eloquence should be pure, that is, purged of defects—grammatical and otherwise—and then enhanced with beautiful images drawn mostly from nature. Beauty appeals to the senses and is associated with them in terms of beautiful sights, smells, feelings, hearing, and tasting. These sensations attract us to the house of the speaker just as ugly images when associated with ideas can repel the audience from the house of an opponent.

As a Romantic rhetorical theorist of the late eighteenth century building on Burke's theory, Hugh Blair sought to move rhetoric beyond "mere declamation" to true eloquence. When operational, eloquence causes human emotions to ignite a "contagion" that flows from the speaker to and among audience members.[8] The audience and the speaker are transformed in the present moment. Furthermore, while rhetoric may achieve immediate effects sometimes by relying on "common sense," eloquence leaves a long-lasting impression, sometimes by relying on insightful truth. Eloquence takes more skill at achieving literary quality. Following Burke's lead, Blair wrote,

"Nothing that belongs to human nature is more general than the relish of beauty."9 He claimed that beauty could be achieved not only by creating images from nature, but by constructing speeches that were harmonious and proportional.

And that insight takes us on to Edmund Burke's notion of the sublime, the highest form of eloquence. He acknowledges that Cassius Dionysius Longinus, who lived in the Second Sophistic age of the Roman Empire, developed the most fulsome notion of the sublime. After reviewing *decorum* and *ornatus*, Longinus laid out ways that a speaker could transport the audience out of themselves; they could have a sublime moment. This step to the transcendent requires the creation of great conceptions because "Sublimity is the echo of great soul."10 Great soul may be the key to individuals as sublime. In 1963, Dick Cavett was waiting for Muhammad Ali, then known as Cassius Clay, to arrive at a scheduled interview. Cavett reports on what happened when Ali arrived: "It was like seeing a god. People were just standing there in awe, just stricken by his presence, and it was really a wonderful thing to see and feel. He had what you call 'it.'"11

In eloquence, the sublime is achieved in several ways. One can combine several tropes and/or figures in one sentence. One can sophisticate a simple figure into a more complex one. Military veterans have a saying: "All gave some; some gave all." This simple form is called a chiasm because if you diagram it forms an X, the Greek letter *Chi*. However, you can sophisticate the form to an antithesis by having the second premise deny the first: "We should never negotiate in fear, but we should never fear to negotiate."12 One can bring majesty to the speech. One can use elevation in terms of great thoughts, vibrant emotions, and word order. For Blair, the sublime was vast and boundless and should "fill the mind with" awe.13 The sublime stresses the spiritual over the material and seeks to overwhelm the audience with awe. It moves the audience from their scattered existences to a transcendent dwelling place, a place where they can hear the call that lies at the heart of existence.

Burke picks up on this last note and develops it further. To make awe present for an audience one can rely on descriptions of vastness, infinity, power, suffering, and horror. The fear of horror is the most potent use of the sublime, according to Burke. His notion of sublime horror, which inspired Mary Shelley to write *Frankenstein*, can be drawn as obscure, dark, or unknown. The image should astonish the audience, chasing all other thoughts and images away. However, we would argue that an omniscient and omnipotent God is more awesome.

Eloquence concerns the ability to use timing, expectation, beauty, and the sublime to convey disclosive moments or to make judgment calls that guide an audience aright. The sublime moves an audience to a new dwelling place and there opens them to the disclosure of truth. The authentic call is often embodied in eloquence that seeks perfection. The authentic call can interrupt our prejudice, our anger, and our common sense to have us reassess where we dwell and how we will act.

Aristotle on Rhetoric

Aristotle's lecture notes were reworked into his book *On Rhetoric*.[14] Rhetoric can disrupt common sense for good or ill. However, if one is to build a house from which to make the heroic call, and display or disclose the truth, one must master the strategies that build credibility, gain attention, change hearts and minds, and seal the persuasion against those who would use the same strategies for ignoble purposes. Engaging these strategies to combat the ignoble may be as important as advancing a noble cause or providing a disclosive moment. In either case, the various forms of the call cannot reach an audience unless its members feel comfortable dwelling with others. That sense of home can be created by a trustworthy source. It can come to the audience in an emotional moment. It can come in the dialectical movement of an argument. In his treatise, Aristotle created a civic discourse that can heal the body politic, much in the way that Gorgias saw rhetoric as therapeutic.

Aristotle's *Rhetoric* provides a framework for assessing whether the use of various appeals is judicious. We use the word judicious because Aristotle is very concerned with making the proper judgments. He often exemplifies what he means by issuing assessments of the speakers he examines. It is no accident that he refers to rhetorical strategies as "proofs." Some are "inartistic," such as laws, statistics, observed objects, and the like. They are inartistic because, while the speaker uses them, the speaker does not create them. The others are "artistic" because the speaker creates them in the course of a speech. These proofs are to be used in the service of truth. In his opening chapter, Aristotle tells us that "rhetoric is useful because the true and just are by nature stronger than their opposites," but if the true and the just are not presented properly, they can be "defeated" by their opposites.[15] This is one of the ways in which rhetoric is a counterpart to dialectic; dialectic finds the truth and rhetoric presents it. The other way in which rhetoric is a counterpart of dialectic is when dialectic cannot determine the truth and a decision must be made on the basis of probability. In such situations, rhetoric discovers the most likely truth and hence, is crucial. It takes on a making-known function—what we are calling "homemaking." Either as a presenter of truth or a discoverer of truth, the heroic orator is judicious because he or she is engaging in civic discourse to heal, protect, and/or perfect the body politic. Aristotle believed that rhetoric was like chemistry; it could be used for good or evil. It could be judged to be noble or ignoble. That is why he wrote a separate book on ethics, to which we will also turn in this chapter.

We begin with what the Greeks called "ethos," from the root word for ethics and a derivative of the Greek word for "dwelling place." The concepts are related by the fact that where a person dwells says a good deal about their character. In terms of a dwelling, we mean the ideological place as well as the physical place. Edifices edify; edifices are where edification can take place. Aristotle believed that when ethos was used as a rhetorical proof, it was the most potent of all the rhetorical strategies. He saw it as a way of constituting the credibility of speakers, making them trustworthy and, hence, safe to believe. By displaying ethos, speakers make themselves present for their audience.

Bad people can have good ideas and good people can have bad ideas. However, there is nothing more persuasive than a good person speaking well. Aristotle put it this way: "Persuasion is achieved by the speaker's personal character when the speech is so spoken as to make us think him credible. We believe good men more fully and more readily than others"; we feel more at home with them.[16] Aristotle tells us how to achieve that attitude.

Aristotle begins by claiming that everyone has ethos whether it be noble or ignoble. Before one even speaks, that ethos has an ontological dimension because it emerges from the way one makes decisions, the way one lives on a day-to-day basis, and the way one dwells. Those decisions are informed by one's values, one's practical wisdom, and one's goodwill. Ethos is the public manifestation of a person. Aristotle reached his conclusion by studying the speakers of his day and their audiences. However, it is not enough for a speaker to be good; a speaker must understand virtue. The virtue of the culture is one of the dwelling places of ethos. The dwelling place of virtue in Sparta was strict, authoritarian, and militaristic. The dwelling place of virtue in Athens was artistic, democratic, and at its best, deliberative. Speakers must adjust to those dwelling places by displaying or praising those values if they are to heal and/or perfect the body politic, that is, rebuild the dwelling place of the citizenry. This healing was often necessary in Athens because it often fell under the sway of a demagogue; it took powerful persuasion to call its citizens back to their democratic roots.

Aristotle turns to the constituents of ethos starting with prior reputation. While it is de-emphasized because Aristotle wishes to focus on what can be created in the speech, it is a potent part of ethos.[17] For example, near the end of the *Rhetoric*, Aristotle advises, "With regard to moral character: there are assertions which, if made about yourself, may excite dislike, appear tedious, or expose you to risk of contradiction. . . . Put such remarks, therefore, into the mouth of some third person."[18] Is not this the advice we give to those who are to introduce us so that we do not sound like braggarts about our prior achievements?

Aristotle claims speakers are judged by their past decisions; that is the grounding of their public personae: "We shall," he writes, "be finding out how to make our hearers take the required view of our own character."[19] What the audience believes is honorable is more important than what is actually honorable. One has to either adapt to the audience's beliefs or change them to make them compatible with the speaker's message. Determining the audience's beliefs is the key to successful homemaking, the building of credibility. In this way, ethos dwells not only in the speaker but in the audience. That is, what the audience believes is honorable and just tells us a lot about the audience, the body politic. If it follows a corrupt leader, it too is corrupt. If it follows an honorable leader, it too is honorable.

How does one become an honorable and judicious leader so that one's call is respected? In Book 2 Aristotle describes the components that comprise ethos: "There are three reasons why speakers themselves are persuasive. . . . practical wisdom [*phronesis*] and virtue [*arete'*] and goodwill [*eunoia*]."[20] Aristotle proceeds to deep-structure his theory; as he begins he says some important things about decision making: "But since rhetoric exists to affect the giving of decisions—the hearers decide between one political speaker and another, and a legal verdict is a decision—the orator must not only try to make the argument of his speech demonstrative and worthy of belief; he must also make his own character look right."[21] Aristotle then lays out his understanding of credibility building by analyzing the three components of ethos—virtue, wisdom, and goodwill. These will be possessed, named, and then displayed by the heroic leader.

Aristotle defines virtue as heroic; it is the ability to produce and preserve the good for the body politic.[22] For Aristotle, the ultimate good is happiness, "at which everything aims," he claims in the opening of his *Nicomachean Ethics*.[23] Happiness is the "telos" of his philosophy of moral values, and hence a guiding light for ethos. Aristotle contends that virtue is a "state of character" concerned with "choice" and the proper choice contains moral and/or intellectual virtue that will lead to or reinforce happiness, which he defines as contentment.[24] Reaching that dwelling place is not easy since humans are often distracted by "gratification . . . a life for grazing animals" or political activity.[25] In his elevation of the process of becoming over politics and gratification, Aristotle demonstrates the influence of his mentor Plato, who believed the truth could be recollected by one's soul.[26] In fact, Aristotle wrote that "by human virtue we mean virtue of the soul, not of the body, since we also say that happiness is an activity of the soul."[27] Thus, Aristotle points out that judicious speakers not only lead bodies to contentment, they lead souls. Contentment (*eudaimonia*) is not passive; it is active in the sense of living well, perfecting ourselves. The judicious speaker calls us to this life and tries to create a nation in which that life can be attained.

Virtue is concerned with moral motivations and actions that lie on a continuum running from excess to deficiency, either end being a vice, the intermediate or mean position being a virtue.[28] Virtues are moving targets established by the audience. These include justice, courage, self-control, liberality, magnanimity, magnificence, prudence, wisdom, and gentleness. Aristotle shows how they are useful in homemaking. For example, justice and courage are the most important because the latter benefits people during war and the former in times of peace. They get us to contentment, the comfortable dwelling place of a people.

By referring his readers to his book on ethics, Aristotle develops the rest of the virtues while also linking them to certain states of mind (*pathe'*, see below). For example, courage is concerned with feelings of fear and confidence, and is the mean, the perfected place between the two. Those who exceed in confidence are rash; those who fall short of confidence and have excessive fear are cowardly.[29] Each one is imperfect and represents vice. Thus, the *Ethics* significantly enhances the understanding of virtue by pointing out how to become virtuous and how virtues emerge in the judicious character. For example, the commander who faces battle must decide to act courageously; however, that may mean a prudent withdrawal, a dashing charge, or a defensive stance, each of which may prove uncourageous in a given context. Because the world is contingent, speakers need to understand not only universal and ideal virtues, but how these same virtues function in the everyday world.

Character is based on what deliberate choices have been made; that is, the "end" achieved by the choice illustrates good or bad character, and makes it present for the audience. The connection between choice and character is further developed in Book 2 of the *Ethics* where a virtuous act reflects virtuous character only when at least two conditions are satisfied: there is knowledge of the act to be performed; the person chooses to perform the act.[30] Here in terms of virtue, intent is elevated over effect. When Socrates chose not to go into exile after he was found guilty of corrupting the youth of Athens, he had knowledge of the consequences and chose to drink hemlock and die. He knew that dying for his beliefs would make his call more robust and longer lasting. In that way more people would be called to his philosophy than if he went into exile, that is, left his home. Virtue and vice serve as the foundation for praise and blame because they describe what is honorable and dishonorable, thereby guiding an audience aright, that is, to their dwelling place of contentment.[31]

Wisdom has been subjected to various interpretations over time—good sense, practical wisdom, sagacity, expertise, and intelligence.[32] Regardless, a public speaker must know a great deal to be successful. Imagine all of the knowledge one must possess on taxes, health care, foreign policy, and the like, and one begins to understand why it is a daunting task to achieve ethos in terms of expertise.

Again, Aristotle refers his readers to his *Ethics*, where he lays out the five "chief" intellectual virtues—scientific knowledge, art, practical wisdom, intuitive reason, and philosophic wisdom.[33] They serve as guides for the homemaking of the judicious advocate and his/her audience. *Nous* is the sensed data that the mind perceives from the senses. *Dianoia* is the ability to make connections and associations among various items. While *nous* and *dianoia* serve as foundational wisdom, humans are also capable of learning episteme or scientific knowledge. *Techne'* is knowledge of scientific or artistic principles that allow for such creative activities as composing music or describing the movement of planets. *Sophia* is theoretical knowledge that Aristotle attributed to the study of philosophy.

Finally, and most important for the speaker, is *phronesis* or practical wisdom. Practical wisdom is what makes a speaker judicious. To put it another way, practical wisdom is a capacity for discerning in the sphere of action where right conduct lies in any given situation. It is a capacity for applying a rational principle to practical situations that call for choice about action.[34] Thus, it often serves as a corrective on common sense. As noted above, a virtuous act reflects virtuous character only if the act reflects deliberate choice; practical wisdom is deliberation that results in the right choice.[35] Would-be leaders need to understand that knowledge based on experience guides good practice (*eupraxis*) in a contingent, diverse world. The experience conditions the leaders to repeat good decisions, to be in the habit of good decision making—that is, to be responsible. This created sense of judicious character becomes the most controlling factor in persuasion.[36] Persuasion results because those who are perceived to be judicious are believed more quickly on general subjects and are believed completely on subjects where there is not exact knowledge but room for doubt.

Goodwill

Perhaps no constituent of ethos is more important to gaining an audience's trust than goodwill. Aristotle compares it to "friendliness," which he defines as wanting others to receive things that are good and things that produce good solely for the benefit of the friend.[37] This definition aligns with another passage in which Aristotle defined a friend as one who is active in providing another with the things that are of benefit.[38] Friendliness appears consistent with Aristotle's brief description of goodwill—the speaker should share the best advice out of goodwill as one would share the best advice for the sake of a friend, a healing process.[39] In the mutual dwelling place, goodwill would be represented by hospitality and altruism.

Aristotle concludes his advice to speakers by arguing that the planning (*dianoia*) and content of the speech enhance the components of ethos and make speakers more worthy of trust, thus making their call more robust. For example, practical wisdom demonstrates judiciousness in two ways: it allows people to construct correct opinions based on knowledge, and it deliberates on the means to reach virtue. Thus, the speech itself conveys ethos when it enhances the fair-mindedness of the speaker in thought and content, is properly constructed, and is well delivered.[40]

Pathos

One of the most difficult rhetorical strategies to deal with is pathos, which concerns using emotional appeals to reinforce or change the state of mind of the audience. In the process, pathos can disrupt the rhetorical dwelling place where the audience feels comfortable; but that may be necessary if that dwelling place is a space of racism or ignorance. Sometimes the orator needs to dissipate emotions and at other times elicit them. Aristotle believed that it is essential to put listeners into the right "state of mind" if the speaker is to perfect them, whether they be a jury or a national electorate.[41] Aristotle's first reason for raising appeals to emotions is because evil persons will use emotion to pervert the legal process. These emotions must be allayed before one can prosecute or defend. Thus, judicious advocates will learn how to counter emotional appeals incompatible with their aim.[42] Secondly, Aristotle claims that decision making is often based on probabilities or emotional responses, a process modern psychology acknowledges. Thus, it is often necessary to appeal to emotions to get something done.

Having established the necessity of knowing how to appeal to emotions, Aristotle moves to a phenomenological analysis of them. First, he tells us that emotions do not exist in isolation; they affect one another. Experiencing fear may make one angry. Or someone who is angry may evoke fear in another person. Second, emotions lie at the ends of various continua, the middle position of which is the soul at rest, or content. Fear and confidence, for example, are at opposite ends of one of Aristotle's continuums.43 You can't feel confident when you are fearful, and you can't feel fear when you are confident. The soul at rest in the middle feels neither emotion. Speakers seeking to move the soul to one emotion or another must rouse it from its resting place and move it toward the emotion that is most compatible with proper judgment. This movement is a measure of intensity; the further out on the wings of the continuum, the stronger the emotion is felt, and hence the more robust the call that is being made.

That leads Aristotle to formulate how this intensity is achieved. He argues that intensity is a product of proximity, that is, a condition of time and space. The closer one is to the cause of an emotion, the more intense the feeling of that emotion. If I'm in the city, a bear in the woods doesn't scare me much. But if I'm camping in the woods and a bear comes near my tent, I am terrified. Aristotle linked his analysis to pleasure and pain. Orators should use descriptions of what causes pleasure or pain to achieve the proper state of mind in their audiences. The plight of the homeless is painful to behold; therefore, it can induce the emotion of sympathy. The more vivid and closer the speaker can make that plight in terms of space and time, the more intense the emotion of sympathy, and hence the more robust the call for help.

For each individual emotion, there are three crucial questions to ask. Aristotle uses anger for his example: "Here we must discover 1) what the state of mind of angry people is, 2) who the people are with whom they usually get angry, and 3) on what ground they get angry with them."44 Aristotle then claims that we get angrier at people than we do at objects, and angrier still at people who are close to us if they cause us pain. Thus, an insult from a foreigner will create less anger than an insult from a close relative. The pain causes a privation that we seek to ameliorate. When we imagine relieving the privation—for example, by seeking revenge for a slight—we feel pleasure and the anger dissipates. The key term in this sequence is "imagine" because the orator must induce the audience to imagine the revenge if he or she is going to move the soul of the listener to action in the future.

Logos

In the ancient world, the truth was the counterpart of the myth. *Logos* (naming) and *mythos* (storytelling) were coupled to cope with the vicissitudes of the human condition. Mythos as narrative rationalized an absurd world of hurricanes, volcanoes, and tidal waves by explaining that the gods were mad at humans. Logos as argument was a search for the truth that often led to transcendence.

If Plato refined the search for truth through his dialectical method, his pupil Aristotle gave us the means for determining validity. To reason inductively, one must collect enough specific examples to establish a general rule. For example, by examining many patients, a doctor somewhere concluded that every patient with the flu ran a temperature. The generalization could then be turned into an argument from sign: a fever is a sign of the flu. Aristotle tells us there are infallible signs, ones that are always true: Ice is a sign that water has been frozen and the temperature is below 32 degrees. However, there are also fallible signs, ones that are usually true but have exceptions: Smoke is sign that there is a fire, but not if the smoke is caused by dry ice. Once a sign is accepted, it can morph into a maxim. Maxims often become part of common sense even though they may contradict one another: "A stitch in time saves nine"; "haste makes waste." "Don't judge a book by its cover"; "clothes make the man."

Aristotle established an elaborate system for determining deductive validity and it can be used to strengthen one's call. Basically, if one has true premises, one can build syllogisms that will produce true conclusions. These syllogisms include the categorical: All cats die by the age of twenty-five; the pet you have is a cat; the pet you have will die by the age of twenty-five.

There are also hypothetical syllogisms: If Donald Trump is in Florida, then he can't be in Washington, DC. Trump is in Florida, therefore he is not in Washington, DC. And finally, there are disjunctive syllogisms: Either Trump is in Florida or he is in Washington, DC. Trump is not in Washington, DC, therefore he must be in Florida.

Aristotle's system of logical validity is set out in his *Organon*, a set of books on logos. However, he takes an ingenious step when discussing logos in the *Rhetoric*. After acknowledging that humans live in a contingent world where they cannot always know the truth for sure, Aristotle tells his readers how to build a syllogism based on probable premises that are accepted as true by the audience; he calls it an enthymeme. These premises can be found in and generated by topoi, location places for lines of argument. These include arguments from the parts to the whole, arguments from opposites, arguments from attributed motives, and the like. Aristotle eventually spins out twenty-eight topoi for the building of enthymemes.[45] These make the audience feel comfortable, at home as it were, in familiar territory.

Aside from its basis in probable truths, the enthymeme usually leaves an obvious premise out. This tactic has at least two advantages. First, it avoids pointing out the obvious and thereby boring the audience. Second, it involves the audience because they fill in the missing premise. In the enthymeme "Fido is a dog, so he will die someday," the missing and unnecessary premise is that "all dogs will die."

Enthymemes have also been used to move audiences to future dwelling places. Candidate Bill Clinton in 1992 offered his audiences "hope" and "change" for a better tomorrow. Candidate Barack Obama in 2012 built on that dream by saying "yes we can" achieve it. In each case, the audience was left to fill in the missing premise of what that future would look like. Enthymemes can also move us back in time, as with "Make America Great Again." A nostalgic past can be evoked as the audience looks back to what they may believe was a better time. Thus, enthymemes are a powerful way to take an audience to a home situated in the future or in the past. And whichever they choose will determine what call they are following.[46]

Aristotle on Form

Ethos, pathos, and logos are powerful tools for the speaker, especially for those who would build a house for their audiences, a place where they could issue a call of true eloquence. However, these artistic proofs need a home of their own if they are to be properly suited to the audience and the occasion. So Aristotle set out three pragmatic, elementary forms of public address to help the speaker adapt to the situation at hand. The highest minded was epideictic, a ceremonial form of public address that had for its subject matter virtue and vice in the form of praise and blame. The audience members were observers having their virtues reinforced and their vices diminished in the present moment. The goal of the speech was to honor or dishonor the subject. The deliberative form of public address had for its subject matter such legislative matters as ways and means, war and peace, and national priorities. The audience sat as a legislative body looking to the future to achieve contentment. The forensic form was focused on guilt or innocence, and the audience sat as a judge or jury to look into the past to achieve justice.

Aristotle was wise enough to know that one form of public address could mask another. For example, in the present, you could praise someone for what they did to encourage such deliberative action in the future. The sermon is often epideictic in terms of praising certain virtues; it is forensic when it condemns sin; it is deliberative when it encourages parishioners to change their lifestyles in the future. Later in this study, we will examine examples of each of the forms to reveal how eloquence in the service of truth can function in epideictic, deliberative, and forensic situations.

Identification and Disclosure

Building on Socrates's injunction that the unexamined life is not worth living, and the Delphic injunction to know thyself, Sigmund Freud set about to help his patients figure out who they were. The process of becoming one's self would result in a kind of ultimate disclosure because it would guide the patient for the rest of his or her life. Freud knew that you can't know what you want or where you are going until you know who you are. You need to get to your authentic dwelling place before you can find the authentic dwelling place of others, where a powerful identification can take place. As we shall see, it is in those authentic dwelling places that the ultimate call—the call that lies at the heart of human existence—can be heard.

In the process of investigating the psyche, Freud discovered that there were different types of personas that people projected and with whom people identified.[47] The rhetorical critic Kenneth Burke broadened our vocabulary for homemaking when he called such identification "consubstantial," meaning to become one with another.[48] He also equated identification with persuasion, and reinforced it with "substantial" identification, which is a material identification, such as identification with a place or object. When we share an identification with a place or object, the process of sharing can lead to a surface type of identification of an other and create a comfort zone for communication. For example, if I run into someone who owns the same model of car that I do, I would be much more likely to strike up a conversation with that person as opposed to one who owns a different car. Sharing nationalities, zodiac signs, and hometowns can function in the same way; it is a kind of homemaking. We like to know where people came from, where they dwell, and what they do.

Inside the home, substantial identification provides a bridge between individuals. In terms of rhetoric, when employing substantial identification, a speaker seeks to concretize an idea to make it more real and to relate to an audience. It is a potent form of naming that can call to us. In the 1932 presidential campaign, Franklin Roosevelt claimed his opponent, President Herbert Hoover, was "frozen in the ice of his own indifference," thereby redefining his opponent in substantial terms. In current parlance, the federal government is often referred to as a swamp, thereby redefining it as a place that should be drained. In both of these cases, substantial identification is used to name and presence something.

Consubstantial identification is even more powerful. It can be achieved by displaying a persona that resonates with audience members. Instead of alienation it seeks unification. It opens the audience to the speaker's disclosure of self and message. There are five basic kinds of personas that are useful to homemaking. The first is one who cares for others. Big brothers and sisters are common personas in this category. The second is one who wants to be taken care of. Children, the homeless, and the sick are common in this category.[49]

The next three are "narcissistic" in Freud's terms; in these cases, "in place of the ego itself, someone as nearly as possible to resembling" the ideal person is substituted.[50] The first narcissistic persona is one who has a love for a past self. Seeing himself as a perfect child in the past, he falls in love with his student. This personality type seeks a perfect past or part of themselves from which they feel disconnected. This personality is nostalgic; it wants to return to a former home to perfect itself. The next persona is one who falls in love with the perfected vision of themselves. This personality type is likely to perfect and defend the status quo; they like where they dwell. The next persona is one who has a love for a future self. Seeing herself as a teacher in the future, the student falls in love with her professor. This personality type hopes to dwell in a perfected utopia in the future. In each case, whether anaclitic or narcissistic, a person externalizes the ego-ideal by identifying with it in another person.[51] Freud explains why identification is more potent than ethos and how it plays into pathos: "Identification is the original form of emotional tie with an object.... [T]he assimilation of one ego to another one, as a result of which the first ego behaves like the second in certain respects, imitates it and in a sense takes it up into itself."[52]

Kenneth Burke saw this potency in identification when he understood communication to be "a generalized form of love."[53] As we have seen, identification is an attempt to overcome division, that is, alienation. It thus becomes a key tool for homemaking. When the attempt is shared with an audience, the audience identifies with the motives of the speaker and a unity is achieved.[54] Previously, Aristotle told us that ethos was the most potent "proof" for a speaker. If, as Freud and Burke assert, identification is more potent than ethos, then identification becomes the most potent strategy a speaker can use. It can be the ultimate form of dwelling together and thus provides an opening for disclosure of truth and the call.

Identification, Interpersonal Communication, and the Call of the Other

To delve into creative relationships in which the call is heard between two people, we need to pursue interpersonal eloquence and to examine how leading existentialists suggest dialogic eloquence can move us into authentic relationships (ultimate identifications) that lead to an understanding of the transcendent call and the creation of art that discloses new truths and perhaps God.

In 1966 Richard McKeon challenged rhetorical scholars to take a fresh look at invention.[55] In terms of interpersonal communication, the challenge was taken up by several scholars opening new pathways in rhetorical studies. John Stewart developed a new vocabulary for the examination of dialogic communication.[56] Roderick Hart, Dan Burkes, and Ron Arnett built on Stewart's original work to further explore the potentialities of dialogic communication.[57] Most important to what follows is Richard Johannesen's study of Martin Buber's and Karl Jaspers's notions of "presentness," "mutual equality," "empathetic understanding," "genuineness," and "positive regard" in their theory of interpersonal eloquence.[58] These are the elements of acknowledgment that we feature throughout this book to make the call more robust.

Buber and Jaspers further expand our vocabulary for assessing eloquence. They believed in a core self that can identify with another core self. These authentic selves can, if they work at it, hear the call that lies at the heart of human existence. To do this, the partners need a safe place in which to commune. They must take advantage of their freedom to develop an authentic sense of self and then to seek an other who has achieved the same sense of self. Thus, Buber and Jaspers deepen Kenneth Burke's theory of identification while also giving us standards for authentic interpersonal eloquence that lies beyond the banal and mundane, beyond common sense. It aims at the discovery of self and encourages a dialogue that can disclose transcendent truth between two people. Martin Heidegger agreed; he told us that when one finally hears the call of conscience, the responsible and caring thing to do is to reveal it to "authentic others" in dyadic communication.[59]

Buber's foundation is anthropological, poetic, and theological, which is what we might expect from a poetic rabbi. Jaspers, a Catholic, comes from a psychological perspective. He begins his second volume of *Philosophy* by claiming that "What we refer to in mythical terms as soul and God, and in philosophical terms as *Existenz* and transcendence, is not of this world."[60] He goes on to argue that since authentic discourse is often subjective and ambiguous, it is a disruption that invites investigation. It forces choices, and importantly, "Self-understanding begins with individual acts of choice."[61] For Jaspers, the process of reaching authentic dialogic eloquence includes four steps in the process of becoming: apprehending my material nature (understanding my body), cultivating my life (living a healthy life), understanding the mind (that enables me to communicate), and educating my soul (that develops my potential).[62] Like Freud and the Romantics, Jaspers encouraged self-discovery and self-development, the art of becoming.

Buber delineated a range of creative tension in language that can yield this kind of fruitful understanding of self. Too much ambiguity can be destructive; too little can retard growth because it doesn't allow for decision making: "The ambiguity creates the problematic of speech, and it creates its overcoming in an understanding that is not as assimilation but as fruitfulness."[63] Ambiguity interrupts our conventional wisdom causing us to search for new truths. Buber also realizes that there is another tension; it exists between the persona, that is, the projection of the psyche, and the authentic self, that is, authentic existence.[64] In dialogic relationships we can move one another from projected images (invented personas) to authentic being.[65] Such a breakthrough is essential for authentic identification and it is the result of an eloquence that opens us to the other.

Buber claimed that once authentic being is uncovered, individuals can restore primal I–Thou relationships: "In the beginning is relation as a category of being, readiness, grasping form, mold for the soul, it is the a priori or relation, the inborn Thou."[66] In the process of becoming, humans develop I–Thou relationships through identification and develop I–It relationships out of separation (alienation). I–Thou relationships are intimate and can result in growth and eventually transcendence. They are to be cultivated with an authentic eloquence that we will outline.

However, I–It relationships are necessary if we are to survive in the pragmatic world. They should be established only to the extent necessary: communication with the bank clerk, the grocery bagger, and the gas station attendant, essential though they are at times. As Buber tells us, "Every [human] lives the two-fold I."[67] The I–It pole of humanity is mostly a monologue, bound in time and space, and oriented subject to object; that is, the other is treated objectively, not as an authentic subject. The other is defined by "substantial identification." I–It relationships are necessary because they allow the categorization and objectification of experience so that a reliable and ordered world can be created to sustain an individual. They are necessary for survival.

The danger of such relationships is their tendency to institutionalize. Individuals may become so comfortable identifying with objectivity that they forgo dialogic risks and thereby lose the possibility of entering authentic I–Thou relationships. They stop the process of becoming. Worse, monologic relationships can lead to a propagandizing of others, an imposition of the subject's view onto the object. Thus, prejudicial common-sense notions can be reinforced at the expense of caring and tolerance. Still worse, individuals can flee into a general, collective mob or institution, such as the church or the university, where they can avoid responsibility and let the institutions make decisions for them. Here, Buber's warning parallels Soren Kierkegaard's disdain for the common sense of the "crowd" mentality, and Heidegger's disdain for the common sense of the "they."

Buber also pointed out that the individual can develop the view that he or she is supreme, a narcissistic solipsism that prevents engagement. In the age of computers, it is not difficult to find reinforcement for such strategies of isolation. Jaspers describes a similar problem not in terms of supremacy, but in terms of restraint: "Shyness, the cool preservation of distance under all circumstances, can never open the way from [human] to [human]."[68] Instead, Jaspers endorses taking the risk of acknowledging others: "For unless [the individual] squanders [him or herself], he [or she] can hardly ever succeed in existential communication."[69] Jaspers believes the subjective "I" has power, acts, and is therefore capable of creativity. This is not an easy proposition. It takes courage. Revelation of self to another allows the other to either treat the openness in a mutually exploratory way, to reject it, or to use it in a destructive way. And in the age of social media, the problem has been greatly magnified. Isolation has never been easier, nor has creating an inauthentic persona.

What Buber names an I–Thou relationship is different. It requires being open to change and taking the risk of speaking authentically with an other.[70] The risk includes the possibility of being hurt, of having your beliefs changed, and of finding new parts and potentialities of yourself. But before one can take that risk, one must become his or her authentic self; one must hear the call of conscience. Jaspers puts it this way: "self-penetrating elucidation" of self is a prerequisite to any authentic dialogue. He continues, "Speaking to me in conscience is a voice I am myself. . . . Conscience is the challenge that lets me soar and seize my being and feel it is true—and it is the bar that blocks my path when I might lose my being."[71]

After the call of conscience comes the connection with God: "Prayer is the individual soul's intercourse with God. . . . The mark of prayer is the real relation to God, who is conceived as personal, as listening, as effectively present," that is, as completing the individual.[72] Identification can then provide a personal ground that sets the stage for entering the world of the other. The individuals involved can only be rewarded if the dialogue is immediate, spontaneous, confrontational, direct, exclusive, creative, hospitable, responsible, and confirming. People in authentic dialogues are much more concerned with issues of self than people in the I–It world. Ideally the dialogue breaks down presuppositions and inhibitions and causes each person to become preoccupied with the being of the other. As Jaspers discovers, "I do not reach the point of communication by my own actions alone; the other's action must match it."[73] This requires acknowledgment, empathy, and disclosure. This empathetic imagining of the feelings of the other develops one's creative skills by forcing more sensitive linguistic choices.

Once they are dwelling in the home they have created, each member of the dyad must strive to release the potential of the other. That is, individuals help one another create and reinforce an authentic sense of self. Jaspers claimed that self-being is only real in communication with another self-being. It is the art of mutual discovery and vital to the process of becoming. Buber saw those who achieved this kind of transcendence in relationship as an essential WE: "By WE I mean a community [a dwelling place] of several independent persons, who have reached self and self-responsibility."[74]

There are many ways by which artists are inspired to create. Buber suggested how innovation could emerge from interpersonal eloquence: "only in dialogue can [humans] gain innovative insights."[75] Then they can create true art, which he believed was a reflection of God. This is Buber's version of Heidegger's "bringing forth."[76]

Heidegger went further when he claimed that art is the "happening of truth."[77] How is this possible? Heidegger emphasized that disclosing truth, a human being reveals itself as the "dwelling place" (ethos), the "site," the "clearing" or "opening" wherein Being (God) is disclosed and made meaningful. "Disclosedness," according to Heidegger, is the fundamental characteristic of Dasein; it denotes how human being is authentically related to Being (God). Human being is the witness of Being (God), the only creature capable of hearing and responding to a call that announces itself in the presencing of all that lies before us and that may then be disclosed to a certain degree in the interpretive workings of discourse or other symbolic activities (music, poetry, art).[78] Reflecting on the meaningfulness of this experience, we can and often do (as in times of personal crisis, for example) raise the question of what it means to exist. The question makes explicit our concern for Being (God). Only human being is concerned enough to do this—to ask the question, think it through to some extent, and then say something about what is thought.

We have seen that exploring our souls is an important step on the way to authentic relationships and so is acknowledgment of the other. Acknowledgment provides an opening out of such distressful situations of everyday life, for the act of acknowledging is a communicative behavior that grants attention to others and thereby makes room for them in our lives. With this added living space comes the opportunity for a new beginning. Our hospitality provides a "second chance" whereby one might improve one's lot in life. There is hope to be found with this transformation of space and time as people of conscience opt to go out of their way to make one another feel wanted and needed, to praise each other's presence and actions, and thus to acknowledge the worthiness of our existence. Offering positive acknowledgment is the moral thing to do.

We enter into authentic relationships in part to further develop our sense of self; it is part of the process of becoming. Sometimes we see our self in the other, as Freud has pointed out. Sometimes we enter these relationships to give shelter to the other, or to have the other shelter us. The relationship becomes a dwelling place, a safe space, a place of hospitality. Sometimes we enter these relationships in pursuit of the transcendent, which can then be reflected in the work of art.

In every case, each partner in the relationship achieves consubstantiality while retaining a sense of self. The I–Thou relationship retains the oneness of being through being with one another. Authentic identification functions to encourage and strengthen dialogic relationships; they in turn break through to a better understanding of self by forcing creative responses based on choices made in the conversation. And the creative choices further expand the understanding of the soul. That is to say, responses in a dialogue have the potential of being creative moments that disclose transcendent Being. Once transcendent Being has been contemplated, the artistic function is further strengthened within individuals, and their creative works can call to us.

Eloquence

We began the search for eloquence and the essential tools it provides for homemaking when we examined timing and expectation in terms of reaching the sublime with appropriate style. We then examined Aristotle's theory of judicious rhetoric in civic discourse in terms of ethos, pathos, and logos. We added identification in its many forms to the mix because it is so powerful. We stressed a dialogic eloquence (calling and listening) that we hope adds integrity and authenticity to Aristotle's theory of ethos and Kenneth Burke's theory of consubstantial identification. We hoped to show that authentic I–Thou relationships breed an eloquence of their own, a dialogic discourse of tolerance, spontaneity, candor, empathy, hospitality, and disclosure. The opening of the other begins with acknowledgment that is attuned to the emotional state of the other. It ends with disclosure of truth that is awesome and inspirational.

CHAPTER 3

Cheating Eloquence

n the last chapter, we pointed out that almost all rhetorical theorists agree
that eloquence can be used for good or evil. Plato's dialogue *Phaedrus* begins
with a speech of Lysias read by Phaedrus, who has nothing but praise for it.
Socrates quickly bursts Phaedrus's bubble, showing Lysias's speech to be no
more than the flattery of a seducer. Socrates then gives a speech of his own,
and again the impressionable Phaedrus is blown away. However, Socrates
confesses that the speech he gave might have been eloquent, but it was not
true to knowledge. Like Lysias's speech, Socrates's speech was ignoble. So
Socrates gives another speech that is true to knowledge, and shares that
knowledge with Phaedrus. This is the noble rhetoric of the call.

In this chapter, we examine two cases of ignoble eloquence to reveal how
it cheats and why it is so dangerous. In each case we see the home that the
speaker builds and how the speaker calls his audience into that home. In
the first case, President George W. Bush uses Manichaean rhetoric dividing
the world into good and evil, light and dark to translate his call into a call to

arms. In the second case, candidate and then president Donald J. Trump uses the rhetoric of the cult to gather a plurality of voters into his home. In each case, various elements of eloquence are employed within these frameworks to make their calls manifest.

Bush and the Manichaean Call

"It's easy to mock the simplicity of the George Bush view of the world. Some of it does indeed appear Manichaean," said Prime Minister Tony Blair.[1] In the presidential election of 2000, George W. Bush did not carry the popular vote, and many questioned the legality of the electoral count based on the controversial Supreme Court ruling in *Bush v. Gore*.[2] Subsequently, the president intensified his brand of civil religion and constituted a supportive public.[3] His chief speechwriter, Michael Gerson, an evangelical Christian who was hired from the *Wall Street Journal*, employed a Manichaean style to achieve this end.[4] For example, the president's First Inaugural Address issued a call based on references to biblical texts, including the image of an angel riding in the whirlwind and guiding the storm that is America's story, a passage reminiscent of the Book of Revelation.[5] Bush envisioned America not only as a "rock in a raging sea," but "a seed upon the wind." He claimed its citizens would not ignore "the wounded traveler on the road to Jericho"; they would respond to his call.

After the attack of 9/11, President Bush engaged in a series of rhetorical events. In his address to the nation from the Oval Office, he was stoic; in his eulogy at the National Cathedral Bush was appropriately somber as he called the nation to mourn. However, the intensity of his Manichaean style was not fully felt until he delivered his call for action to a joint session of Congress on September 20. For the first time during the crisis, the president made his call more robust. He defined the enemy in a detailed way and aligned that enemy with the forces of darkness. The neoconservative mission of spreading democracy was allied with the forces of light. The Manichaean dialectic between good and evil was established: Neutrality was eschewed; nations that harbored terrorists would be considered enemies. There was no middle ground. The crisis and the way he dealt with it were immediately followed by Bush's approval rating shooting to 93 percent, a 43 percent gain from the time of his first Inaugural. Bush had successfully built a Manichaean home and welcomed a plurality of voters into it. He was reelected in 2004, carrying not only the Electoral College but the popular vote. Bush was the first sitting Republican president since Calvin Coolidge to make net gains in Congress for his party in a run for a second term. Bush won the election by a margin of 60,693,281 to 57,355,978—that is, more than a three million vote difference and about ten million more votes that Bush received in 2000.[6] A majority of men AND women voted for Bush. However, less than two years later in the 2006 State of the Union Address, Bush turned away from this brand of civil religion, dropping the Manichaean style. Reality had broken into his home. The president had not been true to knowledge; he had used a cheating eloquence. And so, he moved to pragmatic rhetoric to try to shore up support for his programs and consequently made his call to action much less robust.

George W. Bush's use of Manichaean rhetoric is compatible with his Methodist orthodoxy; political events early in his and his father's careers may have increased his sensitivity to the Christian right and its rhetorical preferences. In 1978, Bush ran for Congress from the district in west Texas that centered on the city of Midland. He was challenged in the primary by a member of the Christian right even though George H. W. Bush in the summer of 1978 had met with a leading clergyman from Midland in an effort to gain support for his son and to dissuade the Christian right from fielding a candidate.[7] The Christian right rejected Bush's advice, and though his son won the primary, he lost the general election, in part because the Republicans had been divided by the primary campaign. As an advisor to his father's run for re-election in 1992, George W. Bush witnessed Patrick

Buchanan's challenges to his father in various primaries. Buchanan's ability to rally the Christian right weakened Bush in the primaries and enhanced skepticism of the president's commitment to the Christian right's agenda. Thus, when George W. Bush ran for governor of Texas and then president of the United States under the guidance of Karl Rove, he embraced the Christian right and touted his own religious conversion and commitment. He claimed that he had heard the call of Christ, though the timing of such a call is suspicious because it aided his political ambition. Nonetheless, the Manichaean call effectively associated Bush with fundamentalist religious themes.[8] During the December 14, 1999, Republican primary "debate," Bush listed Jesus as his favorite philosopher.[9] Upon winning the presidency, he began faith-based initiatives. After the presidential election, as we have seen, the Inaugural revealed that Bush would reinforce his civil religion by adopting a Manichaean style.[10]

In this case study, we focus on this Manichaean version of civil religion that can be found in many contemporary texts popular with the Christian right.[11] The Manichaean call can be characterized in the following ways. First, it takes an uncompromising view of the world that divides all things and people into two and only two houses—good/evil (light/dark, ignorant/wise, up/down, heaven/hell).[12] Second, it is ideological rather than pragmatic; thus, it is uncompromising in the pursuit of moral excellence. Third, it claims to deal with serious life-and-death or material-versus-spiritual issues. Fourth, it often seeks to simplify problems, hence in America the attraction to frontier metaphors of good guys and bad guys, an instance of cheating eloquence. Fifth, it is capable of lacking detail and employing false dichotomies, another instance of cheating eloquence. Sixth, it engages in direct, confrontational rhetoric. Seventh, due to its dialectical nature, the Manichaean style is more likely than other styles to rely on narratives with heroes, villains, and good and evil nations and forces. Eighth, it can be effective in the short term, but may prove troublesome if compromised. And even in the short term, Robert Ivie has shown that a Manichaean rhetorical style may undercut efforts to present rational arguments or to transcend the good-versus-evil juxtaposition, again an instance of how it cheats.[13]

Bush's Manichaean Appeals

By the time of his first Inaugural, Bush's Manichaean light-dark contrast not only simplified complex issues and incited supporters, it also led to political polarization and public mobilization. Then absolute horrifying awe, the attack on the Twin Towers and the Pentagon. Suddenly, the Manichaean call took on weight and worked to frame the president's policies in a more attractive mantle. For example, six days after the 9/11 attack, Bush returned to the White House from Camp David after meeting with his national security advisors. He told waiting reporters that "This crusade, this war on terrorism. . . . would rid the world of evil doers."[14] Bush's September 20, 2001, speech to a joint session of Congress is a masterful example of essentializing a conflict in terms of good versus evil.[15] To paraphrase Robert Hariman, by that time, Bush had produced a "coherent repertoire of rhetorical conventions" that came to characterize his call to action.[16] For example, in his State of the Union Address of 2002, he characterized North Korea, Iran, and Iraq as an "axis of evil."[17] In the State of the Union Address of 2003, Bush referenced the sinners of the Second World War:

> Throughout the 20th Century, small groups of men seized control of great nations, built armies and arsenals and set out to dominate the weak and intimidate the world. In each case, their ambitions of cruelty and murder had no limit. In each case, the ambitions of Hitlerism, militarism, and communism were defeated by the will of free peoples.[18]

An offshoot of this Manichaean style, as Mark West and Chris Carey point out, was a cowboy style that took no prisoners; for example, the president wanted Osama Bin Laden "dead or alive."[19] In 2003, Bush would form a posse of nations to hunt down the terrorists and confront an evil dictator, Saddam Hussein. Often when using the Manichaean style, Bush overrode the generic norms of the State of the Union by imposing a narrative structure on it.[20]

During his run for president in 2004, Bush disregarded the common sense that one should run toward the middle after the primary season closes. Instead, he presented himself as an unapologetic religious conservative and continued to use apocalyptic calls to solidify his base and his image. He opposed human stem-cell research and a woman's right to an abortion. His conservative nominees to the Supreme Court were approved.

After his successful run in 2004, he reinforced his Manichaean call in the 2005 Inaugural. He condemned "ideologies that feed hatred and excuse murder . . . and raise a moral threat."[21] He told his audience that "they bear the image of the Maker of Heaven and earth." He personified his call as the "soul of a nation [that] finally speaks." The Manichaean divide was clear: "There is no justice without freedom, and there can be no human rights without human liberty." The light and dark metaphors reappeared: "We have lit a fire . . . in the minds of men. . . . [O]ne day this untamed fire of freedom will reach the darkest corners of our world." He referred to the truth "of Sinai, the Sermon of the Mount, the words of the Koran, and the varied faiths of our people." This strategy was so successful that Bush did not need to veto any piece of legislation until after his State of the Union Address of 2006.[22] In short, from his Inaugural of 2001 to the State of the Union Address of 2006, Bush's Manichaean style had brought a majority of voters into his house. However, by early 2006, the president's approval rating had slipped below 40 percent. What had happened?

By the time Bush delivered the State of the Union Address to a joint session of Congress on January 31, 2006, reality had ripped holes in the home that Bush built. Though no weapons of mass destruction had been found, the war in Iraq had been underway almost three years and was on the brink of degenerating into a civil war.[23] The scandal at the Abu Ghraib prison revealed in 2004 had compromised the United States' moral standing around the world. The war in Afghanistan, which had been underway since 2001, still saw four thousand Taliban loyalists dominating southeast Afghanistan. Pockets of Al Qaeda units had sprung up in various countries outside of the Middle East. They helped topple the pro-Western warlords in Somalia, who would not be restored to power until 2007.[24]

On the domestic front, things had gone no better for the president. After winning the election in 2004 by turning out his constituted public, including enthusiastic supporters from the religious right, he immediately claimed he intended to spend the "political capital" he had earned in the election.[25] The president began by launching sixty days of conversations on Social Security, which were to consider such options as raising taxes and/or the retirement age, and allowing younger workers to put part of their payments into private accounts. The discussions led to attacks by the Democrats and the AARP that were followed by a decline in his support.[26] Some in the news media claimed that the administration had mishandled relief for victims of Hurricane Katrina, which smashed into the Gulf Coast and breached levees in New Orleans on August 29, 2005.[27] National Guard troops did not enter the city until September 2. Michael D. Brown, the director of FEMA, whom the president had praised on his first tour of the area, came under increasing criticism for not responding effectively to the crisis.[28] In October 2005, the failed nomination of Bush's White House counsel, Harriet Miers, to the Supreme Court further eroded his credibility.

Like the foreign policy context, the domestic one may have induced the president's advisors to move him toward accommodation and away from the more divisive Manichaean style. They knew that the 2006 State of the Union Address presented the president with the opportunity to make a call that would rescue his flagging popularity and his agenda. Bush and his advisors faced several opportunities and challenges: Should he continue to ground his rhetoric in civil religion, particularly in its Manichaean form? Or did this speech present an opportunity to depart from his confrontational and religious style in order to reach out to the opposition party and/or independent voters?

In January 2006, the news media, the president, and the Congress battled to set the national agenda. On January 25, for example, the president visited the National Security Agency to highlight national security issues, on which his ratings were highest. On January 26, during the press conference, Bush tested themes he would present to the Congress and the world five days later in the State of the Union Address.[29] He claimed that "We have a responsibility to lead" the world. He defended his administration's "terrorist surveillance" program, called for the renewal of the Patriot Act, and promised to protect the "civil liberties of our people." However, he only used Manichaean rhetoric when he alluded to the "dark ideology" of America's enemies.

The agenda battle spilled into the confirmation process for Samuel Alito, the president's nominee to the Supreme Court following the Miers debacle. During Bush's presidency, partisanship had intensified in the confirmation process; it had even worked its way into nominations to the lower courts.[30] In fact, Bush focused his radio address of January 28, 2006, on the Alito nomination. Senators confirmed the nomination mainly along partisan lines just before the State of the Union Address. With the earlier appointment of John Roberts as chief justice, conservatives believed that Alito's confirmation gave them a majority in favor of restricting abortion rights, a key plank in Bush's civil religion.[31]

However, outside events often intervene to shuffle national priorities. The day before the State of the Union Address, for example, Coretta Scott King died, an event that underlined civil rights issues and the fact that National African American History Month was nigh. These were not unrelated to the context, because following Hurricane Katrina, allegations of racism regarding the distribution of aid to New Orleans were hanging over the Bush administration.

President Bush laid out the broad themes of the call to the nation with his writers and then revised it with them in the days leading up to the State of the Union Address.[32] Bush insisted on an informal speech with short sentences. But was a departure from the zenith of his reliance on a Manichaean style in the 2005 Inaugural at hand? That would be a risky turn given that State of the Union addresses are most effective when they review the programs that support the major goals annunciated in Inaugurals.[33] The weekend before the address, the president reviewed various sections of the speech at Camp David. Bush then rehearsed the speech in the White House theater in the days leading up to the address.[34] In short, the president was very likely aware of the shift away from the Manichaean style in the new call to the nation.

Bush began by acknowledging the passing of Coretta Scott King and in the next paragraph reminded the Congress that the Capitol was where they had gathered in times of "national mourning."[35] He also established a dialectic between "two parties, two chambers, and two elected branches," but instead of using a Manichaean frame for the dialectic—for example, that it would be a struggle to the death, or a fight between good and evil—he minimized it by saying there "will always be differences and debate." The shift may have jolted his core supporters; at the very least, it disappointed them. In the next few paragraphs, the president addressed issues that were certainly part of his civil religion, but he did not discuss them in Manichaean terms: "We seek the end of tyranny in our world." In its place, America seeks to establish democracies, a key plank in the neoconservative agenda. The president pointed out that in 1945 there were only 24 "lonely democracies," but today "there are 122." Furthermore, "we are writing a new chapter in the story of self-government," one that included women voting across the Middle East. Democratization of the world was emphasized over the war on a specific enemy.

A few sentences later, he condemned nations that had not embraced his neoconservative vision, including Syria, Burma, Zimbabwe, North Korea, and Iran. This led to a brief resurrection of Manichaean rhetoric: "radical Islam—the perversion by a few of a noble faith into an ideology of terror and death." He isolated and illustrated this evil group by accusing Osama Bin Laden of "mass murder." These forces of darkness seek to "seize power in Iraq" and use "the weapon of fear" around the world. He supported his claim with examples of the school children murdered in Beslan and the commuters killed in London. "We will not surrender to evil" because we "love our freedom, and we will fight to keep it." Applause greeted this juxtaposition, which the president reinforced by claiming the United States would stay on the offensive on such major fronts as Afghanistan and Iraq.

Continuing in this vein, the president claimed that "Our work in Iraq is difficult because our enemy is brutal."[36] Those who had died fighting for democracy "live in the memory of our country." Then came a passage in the speech that would haunt the congressional elections later in the year and be contradicted in the State of the Union Address of 2007.[37] Bush claimed that "As we make progress on the ground, and Iraqi forces increasingly take the lead, we should be able to further decrease our troop levels." (In 2007, he would call for a 21,000-troop increase, known as the "surge.") The president's compromise on "troop levels" in January 2006 undercut not only the urgency of the war on terrorism but the Manichaean tone of the preceding paragraph.

In the next segment of the speech, the president softened his civil religion when he talked about its compassionate side. He began with Africa, where "Americans believe in the God-given dignity and worth of a villager with HIV/AIDS, or an infant with malaria, or a young girl sold into slavery." The president then called for backing our allies in a bipartisan appeal that invoked Franklin Roosevelt, Harry Truman, John Kennedy, and Ronald Reagan. If this bipartisan praise did not remove all doubt about retaining the Manichaean style, the next bipartisan ploy did. When Bush talked about Social Security, he compared himself to former President Clinton, noting that they both became eligible for Social Security in 2006. While the line drew a laugh, the use of humor undercut the serious Manichaean persona he had projected in earlier speeches. This lighthearted and bipartisan play also opened the audience to questioning the president. For example, when Bush mentioned his "conversations" on Social Security, Democrats hooted loudly, rebuking the president. Such disrespect for his call had not greeted the president in any of his previous State of the Union addresses.

Ignoring that reaction, he continued with his domestic agenda: "Here at home, America also has a great opportunity." The next segment of the speech was devoid of the Manichaean style altogether; the president was all business: "I will set out a better path: an agenda for a nation that competes with confidence; an agenda that will raise standards of living and generate new jobs." Perhaps because he intended to talk about material things—"small businesses . . . tax relief . . . non-security discretionary spending"—he or his writers decided the Manichaean tone would be inappropriate. These were not matters of faith, nor were they matters of life and death. Maybe that is why the domestic section included so much Washington "inside the Beltway" jargon: "Mandatory spending," "earmark reform," "cost of entitlements," "medical liability reform," "advanced energy initiative," "nano-technology." The speech had gone from an inconsistently characterized struggle regarding foreign threats to a laundry list of programs that Bush believed provided a "better path" on domestic affairs. With little development and a staccato delivery, the president called for tax relief, elimination of government programs, a line-item veto, open markets, immigration reform, affordable health care (not grouped with Social Security, where it would have made more sense), portable coverage, development of alternative energy programs, incentives for innovation, funding for the physical sciences, research and development tax credits, and increases in the number of math and science teachers.

After showing that violent crime, welfare cases, and abortions had declined, he argued that "these gains are evidence of . . . a revolution of conscience." And yet, Bush warned that there was work to be done because the "direction of our culture" revealed deterioration of our basic institutions. He pointed to unethical conduct of public officials and "activist courts that try to redefine marriage." However, again refusing to embrace the Manichaean style, the president claimed that "our culture" was not "doomed." The muddled nature of the speech can also be seen in the lack of frontier metaphors that had seemed an authentic part of his Texas roots. Bush claimed that "we will never surrender to evil," without providing the vivid descriptions of it that had marked his previous speeches.

Instead Bush returned to his bipartisan thread by calling for more ethical conduct by both parties, a thought that would have been more logically grouped with the passage on American cultural decline. From there he jumped to how his "hopeful society" would deal with HIV/AIDS. With no transition, the president moved into his conclusion, claiming he faced an "ideological conflict we did nothing to invite." The lines that follow are so abstract in comparison to his previous Manichaean crispness that they are almost meaningless: "Sometimes it can seem that history is turning in a wide arc, toward an unknown shore. Yet the destination of history is determined by human action, and a very great movement of history comes to a point of choosing." The passage places human action above divine providence, creating more distance from the Manichaean persona he had projected from the bully pulpit in the past. In his conclusion, he relied on his moderated civil religion to call on Americans to exercise their courage: "We will renew the defining moral commitments of this land." Without telling his audience what those commitments were, he ended his address by saying, "And so we move forward—optimistic about our country, faithful to its cause, and confident of the victories to come. May God Bless America."

In immediate reactions to the speech, pundits generally considered it to be realistic or somber. Former presidential advisor and CNN commentator David Gergen noted the bipartisan cast of the speech, while David Sanger, White House correspondent for the *New York Times*, commented on the shift in energy policy. Available poll data, while subject to other variables, certainly indicate that the public was unmoved by the speech. There were no noticeable improvements in Bush's approval ratings. Before the speech his decline in popularity with the public in general was matched by similar declines among his strongest support group. Baylor University, in conjunction with Gallup, took a poll in the fall of 2005 that revealed that nearly 40 percent of evangelicals surveyed did not agree that the Iraq war was justified, and that 38 percent no longer had a high level of trust in the president.[38] In short, while Bush may have maintained support from Evangelicals, it was not nearly as enthusiastic as it had been up to 2004. After the 2006 State of the Union, the polls by *Time Magazine* proved typical and showed that Bush was unable to reenergize his support from independents.

CHEATING ELOQUENCE | **71**

The pre–State of the Union poll gave the president a 41 percent approval rating, with 55 percent disapproving and 4 percent undecided; after the speech, the changes were barely perceptible. The approval rating was 40 percent; the disapproval rating was 54 percent, with the rest undecided. Whether you examine the Fox News polls or the Pew polls, the result is the same. The speech had no measurable effect. These reactions were typical of those immediately following the speech. However, they fail to reveal deeper strategies and more telling problems with an address that contributed to its compromising the Manichaean style. And it is here that we see Bush cheating eloquence.

False Dichotomies

The cheating of eloquence is revealed in several tactics. The most obvious of these was the reliance on the fallacy of false dichotomies and being false to knowledge, not revealing what he knew to be true. The president had become so notorious for using the fallacy of false dichotomies that the tactic was satirized in a *Doonesbury* cartoon of August 6, 2006.[39] The opening line of the cartoon is attributed to Bush and reads, "So do we stay the course or do we cut and run?" Compare that to these lines from his State of the Union Address seven months earlier: "We will choose to act confidently in pursuing the enemies of freedom—or retreat from our duties in the hope of an easier life. We will choose to build our prosperity by leading the world economy—or shut ourselves off from trade and opportunity." Neither of these "choices" included all of the possibilities, but they did reduce a complicated situation into a simple one for the viewing public, a tactic common in Manichaean rhetoric.

> President Bush was not the first president to use this fallacy, nor would he be the last. However, he was more open to this fallacy than most presidents because of his traditional reliance on Manichaean rhetoric. The foreign

policy section of the speech was built around a false dichotomy between terrorism or democracy, and between "dictatorship" or "liberation." Only six months after the speech, the world would learn that terrorists could be elected to office in democratic regimes. The militant representatives of Hamas in Palestine and Hezbollah in Lebanon were duly elected into their respective parliaments.

Regarding the domestic front, Bush established a false choice between surveillance to ensure security and the failed security system of the pre-9/11 years. Realizing that some had questioned his authority, Bush claimed to have "authorized a terrorist surveillance program" based on his constitutional powers. He further rationalized his choice citing past presidents and the federal courts ruling in his favor. Simplifying the situation, the president said, "If there are people inside our country who are talking with Al Qaeda, we want to know about it, because we will not sit back and wait to be hit again." However, Bush did not acknowledge that under his program, library records, university research, and purely domestic phone records had been examined.

Bush established another false dichotomy between those who would retreat into isolationism, centralization, and anti-immigration policies and those who would take his "better path." That path was a compromise that included building a fence along the Mexican border and providing work permits to aliens. His path also included tax reduction even in the face of mounting budget shortfalls, which the president chose not to acknowledge in his speech. He did propose cutting 140 programs that were not performing up to standard, but he did not detail a single one of them. He asked for a line-item veto to reduce pork barrel spending but provided no example of a program he would cut.

Finally, at the end of the next to last paragraph of the speech, the president described several historical examples of choices that great men faced. Lincoln could have accepted "disunity" but instead chose to free the slaves. Martin Luther King Jr. could have "stopped at Birmingham or at Selma." Oddly and out of balance with the Lincoln example, Bush left it to the audience to fill in the rest of the narrative in King's case. Bush concluded rather vaguely, "We must decide: Will we turn back, or finish well?" The choice ignores several other alternatives.

While the Manichaean call has proven effective at constituting an audience of loyal supporters during a crisis, the Manichaean call may not be suitable for political compromise in the long run, particularly regarding domestic issues and consensus building. When a country is attacked by an external force, it is less difficult to demonize the attackers than when one is simply dealing with a domestic policy dispute. Crises provide opportunities to call a people into being, and Manichaean rhetoric is very effective at doing that. Starting with his first Inaugural and particularly in his September 20, 2001, address to a joint session of Congress, Bush relied on a Manichaean call. However, Manichaeanism is not something that one can turn on and off because it lends itself to the constitutive dimension of rhetoric, as opposed to the instrumental, which is often needed in terms of compromise and consensus among various groups.

The dilemma Bush faced during the construction of his 2006 State of the Union Address was how to retain some elements of the Manichaean style when it came to addressing the war on terror, and how to move to a more instrumental style when addressing other issues without seeming inauthentic. Unfortunately, the Manichaean call does not lend itself to combination with less dramatic rhetorical styles. Withdrawing from the Manichaean call is problematic because once this call is invoked, speakers use a very serious persona to constitute an audience that exists in a quasi-religious sphere where compromise is unacceptable. Good contends with evil; the forces of light battle the forces of darkness. Foreign policy threats lend themselves to this style because they deal with life-or-death struggles. However, while some domestic issues such as abortion, capital punishment, and stem-cell research concern mortality, most other domestic issues do not. Thus, once one makes an uncompromised and uncompromising call, it is difficult to return to pragmatics at ground zero and expect the audience to follow. However, that is often what is required in State of the Union addresses, which by their nature cover a panoply of issues. Inflation, taxes, and the proper funding of schools are not life-or-death issues and, therefore, do not lend themselves to Manichaean rhetoric. If policymaking is the art of compromise, then in general it does not lend itself to uncompromising rhetorical styles. That may explain why the president shifted from Manichaean to pragmatic rhetoric in his 2006 State of the Union Address. However, that shift may have been unacceptable to an audience that Bush had welcomed to a Manichaean home. Furthermore, moving from the Manichaean to the pragmatic frame may have indicated to some that Bush's Manichaean home was a sham—ignoble rhetoric that was as false to knowledge as Socrates had been in his first speech to Phaedrus.

The story of Bush's administration reminds us that history provides tough lessons about the damage an ignoble speaker, whether ignorant, manipulated, or sinister, can do. However, Bush's capture by his neoconservative advisors, particularly Vice President Cheney, reminds us of a statement by Franklin Roosevelt: "Presidents do make mistakes, but the immortal Dante tells us that divine justice weighs the sins of the cold-blooded and the sins of the warm-hearted on different scales."[40] History will have to provide divine justice for a much more recent use of Manichaean rhetoric, the acceptance speech at the Democratic National Convention by former vice president Joe Biden. We cite the speech because it proves that the Manichaean style is alive and well. Biden used "light" or "bright" twelve times; he used "dark" or "darkness" seven times. The dialectic between these forces constituted "a battle for the soul of the nation." And clearly for Biden, "an ally of lightness," Donald Trump was the Dark Prince, who had "cloaked America in darkness." Thus, Biden provides a transition from the Manichaean to the fascist. The Trumpian examples we next explore are clearly cold-blooded interruptions that called on good people to intervene.

Fascist Rhetoric

Adolf Hitler produced an interruption to the Democratic Weimar Republic with his fascist rhetoric. Weimar was built on the ashes of World War I and was meant to turn Germany into a democratic republic after the tragedy of being run by a kaiser. By 1933, the republic had operated for thirteen years; however, it suffered from massive inflation, especially during the Depression, and the weight of war reparations. Still Hitler's rise to power is all the more frightening when you realize that Weimar Germany was the leading country in the world in terms of physics, engineering, and many of the arts. Its educational establishment was second to none.

In an essay entitled "The Rhetoric of Hitler's Battle," the literary critic Kenneth Burke explores Hitler's call. Burke's goal was to alert us to new forms of rhetoric that were dangerous and needed to be combated. In fascist rhetoric, appeals to emotion and nationhood replace rational arguments; lies, distortions, and exaggerated stories replace carefully worked out policies; dictatorship replaces deliberation; invaders and/or immigrants become scapegoats. In the 1930s fascist rhetoric spread to America. It was in Father Coughlin's radio broadcasts from the Chapel of the Little Flower in Detroit. Charles Lindbergh received a medal from Herman Goering in Berlin and then returned to the United States to lead America First rallies to keep America out of war, and hence not to combat fascism. Pearl Harbor ended such talk.

Later, fascist rhetoric came back with a vengeance in 1950, when Senator Joseph McCarthy claimed that subversives were undermining American security. McCarthy's right-hand man through his four-year reign of terror was Roy Cohn. In the 1970s, Cohn served as Donald Trump's lawyer. The United States then experienced a McCarthy-like interruption with the election of Donald Trump in 2016. His rhetoric included the America First appeals of McCarthy and Lindbergh, and the anti-immigrant appeals of xenophobic senators of the 1930s. Among media critics, historians, and comics, President Trump has been labeled a fascist. The side-by-side videos of Trump and Benito Mussolini jutting out their jaws and nodding approval to national populist rallies are disconcerting. Whether in tweets or on the stump, Trump's attacks on the news media mirrored fascist regimes. His fascist style is also marked by bragging, branding, bar talk, and the big lie, each of which we explore in more detail below.

However, with regard to cheating eloquence, we are quick to note that there is a difference between fascist rhetoric and fascist action. The speeches of President Franklin Roosevelt provide case in point. In his First Inaugural Address in 1933, Roosevelt threatened to "ask for . . . broad executive power to wage a war against the emergency, as great as the power that would be given to me if we were in fact invaded by a foreign foe." Luckily, Roosevelt did not have to make good on his threat; Congress gave FDR the power he sought, and the New Deal was born. At the end of the 1936 campaign, FDR announced a Second New Deal in a rabble-rousing speech not only to his audience in Madison Square Garden, but to those assembled in the surrounding streets listening to loudspeakers. A frightening moment came when FDR said, "I should like to have it said of my first Administration that in it the forces of selfishness and of lust for power met their match." He was interrupted by cheering and regained control of the audience by shouting "Wait a minute, wait a minute . . . I should like to have it said of my second Administration that in it these forces met their master." A demonstration ensued that nearly turned into a riot.

However, FDR was not a fascist; with the exception of the Japanese internment and his attempt to pack the Supreme Court, his record on protecting civil rights and minorities is well established. For example, in 1941 he called for freedom of expression and religion, and freedom from want and fear "everywhere in the world." He became a heroic orator who held the American home together through the Depression and protected it from attack during World War II. Roosevelt's public addresses were often judicious and show us why fascist rhetoric should be differentiated from fascist action.

Donald Trump had hinted at running for president several times before he sat down as a guest of the *Washington Post* at the White House Correspondents' Dinner of 2011 in Washington, DC. Seated among the media elite and some of the most powerful politicians in the nation, the evening turned sour for Trump as he was lambasted by the host, comedian Seth Myers. At one point, he referred to Trump's presidential ambitions as a "running joke." Soon after, President Obama came to the lectern and continued the attack. A few days earlier, during an interview with Anderson Cooper on April 25 on CNN, Trump had asserted that Obama's birth certificate could not be found in Hawaii, stoking the fires of the "birther movement." The president recalled that he had released his birth certificate in 2008 and then said, "Now he can get back to focusing on issues that matter. Like did we fake the moon landing? What really happened at Roswell? And where are Biggie and Tupac?" It was a horrible embarrassment for Trump and a call to action. He vowed to support whoever ran against Obama in 2012, and when Mitt Romney won the Republican nomination, Trump was quick to supply funding. Trump was disappointed with Romney's loss and immediately trademarked Ronald Reagan's phrase "Make America Great Again" for his own use in the 2016 campaign. Trump had heard the call and was off and running for president. We could not know then that he would win the Electoral College, survive an impeachment trial, and after losing his reelection bid, urge an attack on the house of the people, the Capitol of the United States.

Awed by Donald Trump

The words "shock and awe" blanketed social media websites as Donald Trump worked his way toward winning the 2016 presidential election. Awed supporters were ecstatic! Awed members of the opposition were horrified! Indeed, in how he acted, spoke, and tweeted during the campaign, Trump showed himself to be "unbelievable," "stunning," an "amazing" agent of change, someone who transcended and moved his supporters beyond the objectionable and detested ways and means of the political, social, economic, and moral rule of an Afro-American president who, according to Trump, warranted five years of lying accusations about his citizenship. Trump was something more, something radically different than what people expected from a presidential candidate—who normally would be willing to abide by the traditional rules of decorum when debating the opposition. In short, Trump's unbelievability made him "awesome."

Reading responses to a survey conducted by the *Washington Post* to learn why its readers voted for Trump, one discovers a host of reasons that informed Trump's unbelievability.[41] For example, Trump "spoke the truth about political correctness"; he is against Obamacare; he wants to "deport illegal immigrants"; he is a "critic of the mainstream media"; he will make America "affordable, safe, and prosperous"; it is "time we had a businessman with strong executive skills leading our nation back to capitalism"; he will "nominate conservative Supreme Court justices"; he will not "tap-dance" around "our national debt, our failure to contain Iran and North Korea, and our long-term unemployed citizens"; he supports the "military" and "law enforcement"; he supports the argument that "the part of America that grows your food, produces your energy, and fights your wars believes the country needs a course correction"; he "is sincere in his love of country"; and he is "willing to be open" and "transparent." There is also much said about how a vote for Trump was related to a strong dislike and distrust of Hillary Clinton because of such matters as her possibly felonious actions as secretary of state, her pro-abortion and gay rights stance, her predicted Supreme Court judicial appointments, her WikiLeaks and personal email scandals, questions about the unethical financial activities of the Clinton Fund, and how she was conceived as a representative of the political elite and status quo.

The awe-inspiring Trump also carried a lot of baggage. For example, he had a long racist history:

I've got black accountants at Trump Castle and at Trump Plaza—black guys counting my money! . . . I hate it. The only kind of people I want counting my money are short guys that wear yarmulkes every day. Those are the kind of people I want counting my money. Nobody else. . . . Besides that, I've got to tell you something else. I think that the guy is lazy. And it's probably not his fault because laziness is a trait in blacks. It really is. I believe that. It's not anything they can control.[42]

And then there was Trump inflating his ego as a saintly murderer as he revved up his audience at a campaign event in Sioux City, Iowa: "I have the most loyal people, did you ever see that? I could stand in the middle of 5th Avenue and shoot people and I wouldn't lose voters."[43] He seemed to invite assassination with a false claim about Clinton's position on the Second Amendment: "Hillary wants to abolish, essentially, the Second Amendment. . . . By the way . . . if she gets the pick of her judges, nothing you can do, folks. Although the Second Amendment people, maybe there is, I don't know."[44] The National Rifle Association tweeted its support, saying "Donald Trump is right," and that if Clinton is elected president, there is "nothing we can do."[45] The scenario of assassination continued. Trump suggested that the Secret Service agents who guard Clinton voluntarily disarm to "see what happens to her" without their protection.

And then there was the scandal of Trump University. And then there were ongoing sexist and racist remarks by Trump and supporters like the Ku Klux Klan and other white supremacists about woman, Hispanics, Muslims, Jews, and anybody who threatened Trump's worldview. By October 24, 2016, nearing the end of his first run for president, Trump had insulted 281 politicians, celebrities, publications, and countries.[46] And his ego, which his critics found nauseating, never ceded center stage: "I am the only one who can make America great again"; "I am the most successful person to run for president"; "People love me. And you know what, I've been very successful. Everybody loves me";[47] "I will be the greatest job producer God has ever created."[48] Trump had an almighty vision of himself.

That vision opened Trump to support that has no equal in religion when it comes to honoring a person's sublime status. Segments of the Evangelical community, with a population of over 80 million devotees, saw fit to interpret their awe-inspiring candidate in a way that was itself awe-inspiring: they acknowledged Trump as being a gift from God. The Reverend Jeremiah Johnson knew about Trump's heavenly status because God personally told him as much: "I was in a time of prayer several weeks ago when God began to speak to me concerning the destiny of Donald Trump in America. The Holy Spirit spoke to me and said, 'Trump shall become My trumpet to the American people, for he possesses qualities that are even hard to find in My people these days.... I am going to use him to expose darkness and perversion in America like never before.'"[49]

For Evangelicals, having God speak directly to you is the ultimate experience of awe. A more everyday way of stating the matter is offered by Wendy Taylor: "I get more Trumped up as it goes along. He flies in with his jet, he's meeting everybody—it's just powerful. We are blessed to have him running for the presidency. He's a gift from God. No, he's not perfect, but what politician is?"[50] Two "Trumpette" sweatshirt-wearing supporters, Sandee and Noreen (last names not given), put it this way: Trump is a "god that's gonna come down and help us all.... Yeah, he is ... Jesus, then Trump."[51] The Christian scholar Michael Brown felt strongly that Trump was fated to be president by the "sovereign intervention of God."[52] Former member of the House of Representatives Michele Bachman maintained that "God lifted up Trump to be the leader" of the conservative movement.[53]

Trump confirmed these claims in an interview with the Christian Broadcasting Network. He said he had heard from pastors that his nomination was a "divine calling," but noted he didn't want to think of it that way because it's "too big of a burden": "I think I'm not perfect, because I think I'm less perfect than some people, but I have certain abilities that are good, like, being able to do things, and I think I'll be able to do things that will be really great for the evangelicals and others and they understood that. . . . Many of my friends and many political experts warned me that this campaign would be a journey to Hell. They said that. But they're wrong, it will be a journey to Heaven because we will help so many people."[54] In the Evangelical tradition, people who lead such journeys are a gift from God, for they practice Christ's command for his followers to do "greater works."

Trump, the Republican messiah, preached that he was on a journey to do just that. And a messiah need not be perfect; rather, he needs only be a professed or accepted leader of some hope or cause, who is expected to save people from an extremely troubling situation. Trump joined the company of other such god-appointed and flawed individuals as Cyrus (a pagan kind), Elijah (suicidal), Noah (a drunk), David (a murderer), and Saul of Tarsus (a persecutor of the Christians).

For Clinton supporters (minus the many thousands of African American, Hispanic, and white middle-class individuals who originally backed President Obama), the verdict was in: Trump was repulsive, brutish, psychologically unstable, a pathological liar, and thus unsuited to be president. The journalist Mark Goulston offers an economical statement of the verdict: "The values and virtues of reflection, thoughtfulness, contemplativeness, patience, hearing another person out, considering what someone says before interrupting and rejecting it have been eclipsed by fanning the flames of conspicuous consumption and immediate gratification."[55] Past Republican presidential candidate Mitt Romney forecast this judgment when, speaking on behalf of the GOP establishment and, he hoped, the citizenry of the American public with good sense, he showed no restraint in his assessment of Trump: "Donald Trump is a phony, a fraud. His promises are as worthless as a degree from Trump University. He's playing the American public for suckers. . . . His domestic policies would lead to recession. His foreign policies would make America and the world less safe. He has neither the temperament nor the judgment to be president."[56]

Trump was more like the anti-Christ than a messiah. One could say, drawing inspiration from Francis Collins's argument that the human genome is the language of God, that Trump qualifies as a cancerous mutation in God's plan. Trump did not help his case during an interview with Christian Broadcast Corporation consultant David Brody. The interview took place as the men stood outside on Trump's Palos Verdes coastal golf course in California. Brody asked: "Who is God to you?" Trump's answer is self-centered and banal:

> Well, I say God is the ultimate. You know you look at this? Here we are on the Pacific Ocean. How did I ever own this? I bought it 15 years ago. I made one of the great deals they say ever. I have no more mortgage on it as I will certify and represent to you. And I was able to buy this and make a great deal. That's what I want to do for the country. Make great deals. We have to, we have to bring it back, but God is the ultimate. I mean God created this [points to his golf course and nature surrounding it], and here's the Pacific Ocean right behind us. So nobody, no thing, no there's nothing like God.[57]

One might expect (hope) that a presidential candidate would be more eloquent, more rhetorically sublime, when explaining what God means to him. Authentic, inspiring, positive awe is a truth-telling process. Trump does not possess the character and the talents that facilitate this process. The journalist Jack Shafer offers a comical assessment of Trump's stunning lack of eloquence:

> Donald Trump isn't a simpleton; he just talks like one. If you were to market Donald Trump's vocabulary as a toy, it would resemble a small box of Lincoln Logs. Trump resists multisyllabic words and complex, writerly sentence constructions when speaking extemporaneously in a debate, at a news conference or in an interview. He prefers to link short, blocky words into other short, blocky words to create short, blocky sentences that he then stacks into short, blocky paragraphs.[58]

Shafer bases his depiction of Trump on what Longinus describes as "the proper choice of words and the use of metaphors and other ornaments of diction."[59] Trump is not the model orator, the Cato's fabled "good man speaking well" about a topic that for believers is the ultimate source of awe. He is out of touch with the rhetorical sublime—although his discourse could be credited with being awe-full, bad beyond belief. Yet, as Schafer goes on to point out, this deficiency was also a significant asset for Trump: "Trump's rejection of 'convoluted nuance' and 'politically correct norms,' mark him as authentic in certain corners and advance his creed as a plain-spoken guardian of the American way. By not conforming to the standard oratorical style, he distinguishes himself from the pompous politician. Less is more when you're speaking Trumpspeak."[60]

One does not have to be a gift from God to be a source of awe. Just being *unbelievably* different from the norm can be enough. From a religious standpoint, an earlier noted insight is affirmed: there is *awe*, and then there is awe. Trump possessed this second, negative awe because, in addition to everything else, he talked like many of his supporters do. The higher degree of awe proved problematic. Although Trump's vice-presidential selection Michael Pence sought to rectify the situation with God's help: "I believe in grace," Pence said. "I've received it. I believe in it. I believe in forgiveness."[61]

The Evangelical community nevertheless realized that accepting Trump as a gift from God cast a negative reflection on the community's professed reputation for inspiring wise religious judgment and high moral standards. In Paul Pearsall's terms, the problem was that of favoring and promoting "the dark side of awe": how it can be used not for the sake of cultivating open-mindedness, but rather as a manipulative tool for deceiving and misleading others. "Instead of having our consciousness broadened by awe's assurance that we can never know all the answers, it becomes constricted because we believe an authority figure has found the answer for us and that we don't have to do any more deep thinking for ourselves."[62] Recall that awe works to diminish self-centeredness. Using awe as Trump did is "sinful." Some Evangelicals urged their brethren to see the light. Erick Erickson, head of the Christian conservative website *The Resurgent*, makes the point with a sublime use of storytelling.

> Donald Trump is God's anointed candidate. How do I know this? Because good and devout Christians keep telling me this. One sent me a letter this week declaring Trump a miracle from God to restore the church in America. Many others told me that my wife would not have lung cancer if I was not fighting God's will and, most assuredly the cancer will go away if I support Trump.

Finding such advice offensive, Erickson suggests a more "Christian" approach to respect God's ways: "Christians, fear the Lord, not the future. If you feared the Lord instead of the future, you would not be making such foolish declarations about Donald Trump.... If Hillary Clinton wins ... you who think Trump is God's anointed will, I hope, repent and acknowledge God's will was still done.[63] Erickson wrote these words five days before the election.

Having covered Trump's last campaign rally in Grand Rapids, Michigan, the night before the election, the editors of the Rightforever webpage wrote this: "Donald Trump glows like never before, strength, power and intelligence in one piece—ready to give us HOPE. A place to remember. The place where the new American revolution has been announced! We expected 'calm waters,' but the 'republican messiah' made us, shaking and trembling, our hearts are full of pride, our eyes are full of tears." Two days after the election, evangelist Franklin Graham declared: "Hundreds of thousands of Christians from across the United States have been praying. This year they came out to every state capitol to pray for this election and for the future of America. Prayer groups were started. Families prayed. Churches prayed. Then Christians went to the polls, and God showed up."[64]

Eighty-one percent of white Evangelicals voted for Trump.[65] As far as we know, no definitive data exists indicating the percentage of Evangelicals who voted for Trump because he is a gift of God. We suggested above how he could make that claim, despite his flaws. The becoming nature of positive awe and God are the key. But his flaws still pose a problem. I Shall Be What I Shall Be does not preclude suffering as part of the process. On the contrary, in the Judeo-Christian tradition, suffering is an esteemed educational tool for teaching us not only what not to do when acknowledging God's presence in our lives but also to develop the stamina and courage to see ourselves through whatever God defines as a temporary moment of despair, depression, fear, and anxiety. For God's sake and ours, we are tested in adverse ways so that we are better able to promote with our thoughts and actions God's charge of perfectibility. I Shall Be What I Shall Be. Trump may be a gift of God, but the gift is more of an emetic than a growth hormone. In the Kabbalistic tradition (the basis of Judaism, Christianity, and Islam), this type of gift is an earthly example of I Shall Be What I Shall Be desiring, "in the beginning," to "purge" and cleanse Itself of the powers of poor judgment.[66] Trump dramatized what we need to rid ourselves of, if we are to progress with God. I Shall Be What I Shall Be allows for setbacks in progress as a way of making us wise about how important such progress is. The darkness of awe perhaps has ended at last, but we are doomed to repeat it if we do not admit that its four-year reign was rhetorically sustained.

Trump's Rhetorical Call

"Make America Great Again" called voters to Trump's home.[67] It worked because it is so incomplete, so enthymematic. Note that there are several missing premises: America is not great in the present; America was great in the past. This compound enthymeme's missing "past" implies a "before" that allowed Trump supporters to fill in their favorite past; that is, to return to a dwelling place they would prefer to the one they occupied. It was a rhetoric of powerful rightist nostalgia. America was great before women were permitted to have abortions, before same sex marriages were legal, before rampant homelessness plagued our cities, before technological confusion overwhelmed us, and so forth. Stephen Miller, Trump's Goebbels, used this enthymeme to great effect at the end of Trump's acceptance speech at the Republican Convention of 2016. Each day of the convention had a make-America-something-again theme. Trump then brought the convention and his speech to a close using these themes. We have placed the enthymematic calls in brackets:

> To all Americans tonight, in all of our cities and in all of our towns, I make this promise: We Will Make America Strong Again [Like it was in the 1950s? 1960s? 1970s?]. We Will Make America Proud Again [Like it was in the 1980s?]. We Will Make America Safe Again [Like it was before 9/11?]. And We Will Make America Great Again [Like it was in the 1980s?]. God bless You and Good Night.

Thus, without condemning any policy by name, Trump cobbled together a coalition of disgruntled voters that got him enough electoral votes to be elected president. For his audience, Trump conjured up a common-sense nostalgia that served his purposes. It was clever rhetorical choreography.

In his Inaugural Address, Trump described a dystopian America. It is not difficult to see why. He needed America to be in bad shape so that he could save it. That rescue began when Trump used Ronald Reagan's strategy of placing heroes in the gallery so that he could include epideictic moments in his State of the Union addresses. But instead of a few, Trump placed many heroes in the gallery in order to acknowledge and identify with them. In his State of the Union Address for 2019, Trump took the strategy to another level, citing more people in the gallery than any president ever had in a speech that lasted one hour and twenty minutes. The recognition of these heroes forced members of Trump's opposition to applaud, or face what might look like a callous disregard for America's heroes. These heroes also underlined a point Trump was making or displayed as a virtue. In this way, Trump appeared to allay hostility toward him. Two Jewish guests in the gallery included Herman

Zeitchik, who was part of the Normandy invasion, and Joshua Kaufman, whom Zeitchik helped liberate from Dachau in 1945. This moving narrative not only demanded acknowledgment from the president's audience but also was part of his continuing effort to court the Jewish vote, which included moving the American Embassy from Tel Aviv to Jerusalem. The president also mentioned the Tree of Life Synagogue shooting in Pittsburgh to cement his persuasive appeal.

This State of the Union Address also announced the opening of the president's reelection campaign. He began with a long list of accomplishments, some of which he had not produced. And then came the 2020 campaign's most important piece of branding: America will never be a socialist country. The cameras moved to a grumpy Senator Bernie Sanders slumped in his seat, then switched to a baffled Representative Alexandria Ocasio-Cortez, the very symbol of the leftward drift in the Democratic Party.

Just as Trump defused his opponents with gallery guests, he also used cross-party appeals. For example, he somewhat hypocritically referred to America as a "nation of immigrants." He embraced prisoners' rights and condemned racism in the justice system. And then near the end of the speech, Trump launched a patriotic appeal to American civil religion by recounting America's greatest moments, including the abolition of slavery, the D-Day success, and the building of the interstate highway system. Trump's clear nostalgic vision contrasted with the Democrats' confusing, postmodern amalgam of identity politics and guilt-tripping socialism. Trump's vision revealed that for the 2020 campaign, he was turning from his Nixonian negativism, as seen in his Inaugural Address, to the optimism of Ronald Reagan's "It's morning in America," which was mocked in a commercial attacking Trump in May 2020 that was funded by moderate Republicans, some of whom had been "Never Trumpers." They put together the Lincoln Project, which proved effective in undermining some of Trump's appeal. They made clear that Donald Trump broke with convention and engaged sham enthymemes to capture and retain his presidency. The Lincoln Project, more than any other group, revealed that these three tactics characterized

Trump's fascist rhetoric: his hateful, misogynistic, and bellicose *bar talk*, *braggadocio*, and *branding*.

By bar talk, we mean that Trump said things from his political pulpit that one would normally only hear after a few drinks in the privacy of an underlit bar—a kind of racist, anti-feminist "common sense." For example, in his announcement of his candidacy on June 16, 2015, Trump scapegoated undocumented immigrants who were "bringing drugs" and "crime" into the country. He claimed that some were "rapists."[68] Trump said he would prohibit Muslims from immigrating to America. He would bomb ISIS even if that meant killing civilians. He called for a wall on the Mexican border that he would force Mexico to fund. When Trump canceled a rally in Chicago at Illinois State University on March 11, 2016, demonstrators clashed with his supporters. Two days later in Bloomington, Illinois, Trump encouraged retaliation, a common fascist action: "If you see somebody getting ready to throw a tomato, knock the crap out of them. . . . Just knock the hell—I promise you I will pay for the legal fees."[69] His nationalistic, xenophobic, paranoid (invasion of aliens) speeches were reminiscent of the Populism of the 1890s and 1950s. On March 2, 2019, in a two-hour rant before the Conservative Political Action Conference, Trump said that members of Congress who opposed him "hate our country." You can almost hear him ordering another round of drinks in a bar or calling his brown shirts to action.

His bellicose bar talk often extended to women. It reveals that Trump was closer to Aristotle's "grazing animals" than to his virtuous choice maker. In his toxic masculinity, Trump engaged in a disgusting attack on Megan Kelly's anatomy after the first Republican Primary debate. In response to remarks Cher made about him, Trump responded, "I knocked the shit out of her" on Twitter.[70] He claimed the *New York Times* columnist Gail Collins had "the face of a dog."[71] His comments about Carly Fiorina's looks and Rosie O'Donnell's temperament are well known; less well known is his long history of sexism.[72] A day after she stood by her husband on the podium at the Democratic Convention, Trump attacked Ghazala Khan, the mother of a soldier killed in Iraq. His off-the-record interview with Billy Bush claiming that Trump liked to grab women by the genitals was the most obscene utterance by a presidential candidate in American history. Countless other examples show that Trump is less interested in his audience's happiness than he is in his own gratification and popularity. However, in terms of virtue, that such a corrupted soul could win the presidency says more about the health and home of the American body politic than it does about him. That after four years of his sophistry, an even larger number of voters could support him tells us that paranoid populism is alive and well in America.

Bar talk also often engages in prejudice. In 2016, Trump mockingly imitated a handicapped reporter during the campaign.[73] A rhetorical marker of racism in Trump's discourse is the way he refers to minorities. He calls them "the Blacks," "the Hispanics," "the Mexicans," and "the Muslims."[74] In a tweet, he repeated false white-supremacist claims that blacks committed 81 percent of the homicides of whites.[75] When a judge of Hispanic descent was put in charge of the Trump University fraud case, Trump said the judge could not be objective because he was "Mexican." The judge was born in Indiana. Trump went on to claim that a Muslim judge could not be objective if ruling on his case.[76] In June 2020 Trump re-tweeted a white demonstrator yelling "white lives matter" to a group of counter-protestors.

A carryover from Trump's business practice was his braggadocio, which often incorporated big lies. He regularly claimed to be a hugely successful businessman and negotiator; his tax returns show otherwise. The author of *The Art of the Deal* claimed he could out-negotiate anyone; just tell that to the North Koreans and the Chinese. On February 4, 2016, in Exeter, New Hampshire, Trump echoed the campaign rhetoric of Pat Buchanan from 1992 and 1996 by claiming that "Christianity is under siege."[77] Buchanan returned the favor and claimed that Trump was the future of the Republican Party.[78] On Super Tuesday, March 1, 2016, Trump crowed, "We have expanded the party."[79] He regularly claimed that "no one" had done more for gays or women than he had. "No one" had studied trade agreements more than he had. Following the Orlando massacre of June 11, 2016, he tastelessly bragged in a tweet about "being right about radical Islamic terrorism ... I called it."[80]

He bragged that he knew more about war than his generals and more about foreign policy than his secretaries of state. After his acceptance speech of 2016 and two days after Texas senator Ted Cruz refused to endorse him, Trump bragged, "Whether you're a senator from Texas or any of the other people that I beat so easily and so badly, you gotta go for Trump."[81]

One can't imagine Ronald Reagan saying any of these things. And though Reagan was sometimes prone to exaggeration, Trump's outrageous claims are highly inaccurate. For example, in his 2020 State of the Union Address, Trump claimed the economy was "the best it's ever been." In fact, the growth rate of the economy was about half of what it was in the late 1990s. During the 2020 pandemic, Trump speculated that drinking disinfectant might cure Covid-19. At his first presidential reelection campaign rally, he called for closing down testing for the virus because it was producing false infection-rate data. During the 2016 presidential campaign, *PolitiFact* found that only 2 percent of his claims were accurate, only 7 percent were mostly true, 15 percent were half-truths, 16 percent were mostly false, 42 percent were false, and 18 percent were "pants on fire" false. By comparison, the aggregate total for Hillary Clinton on the false side of the ledger was 29 percent.[82] Normally, Clinton's score would open her to charges of mendacity; however, Trump's score so overshadowed hers that her distortions received much less coverage in the media. It is also true in both cases that elements using social media have so corrupted the news-gathering process that voters had a difficult time locating a credible news source, particularly when "cable news networks" conflated editorial opinion with hard news broadcasts.

During the 2016 primaries, Trump's bravado garnered him much more free media coverage than his Republican opponents, which in turn attracted large audiences to watch the ensuing rhetorical fireworks. Twenty-four million people watched the first Republican debate.[83] The final Republican debate of 2015 was watched by 18 million people, and the debate of March 3, 2016, was watched by nearly 17 million people.[84] These numbers translated into turnouts in Republican caucuses and primaries that vastly exceeded the previous record numbers of 2000.[85] The same was true of Republican convention coverage. All networks showed a marked increase in viewers over 2012, including for the acceptance speech, the longest in memory at 75 minutes.[86] In the general election, Hillary Clinton outspent Trump on advertising by a two to one margin; however, Trump got 50 percent more news-media coverage than Clinton, negative though it often was. Flash forward to 2020: Trump ran around 8 million votes ahead of his 2016 turnout and still managed to lose the election.

A third major characteristic of Trump's rhetoric is branding, a labeling that issues a call. Trump had become wealthy in part because of it. His name appears on every building he has constructed. The tower on the Chicago River bears his name in 20-foot letters. During the presidential campaign, Trump engaged in positive and negative branding. As we have shown, his positive branding relied on familiar slogans to evoke an enthymematic nostalgia, such as making "America great again." After he became the presumptive nominee, he claimed that his foreign policy would put "America First," recalling Charles Lindbergh's pre–World War II isolationist views.[87] In his acceptance speech, Trump reasserted the slogan: "The most important difference between our plan and that of our opponents is that our plan will put America First."[88] On July 3, 2020, Trump turned the tables on those who accused him of fascism by accusing them of the same ideology: "Our nation is witnessing a merciless campaign to wipe out our history, defame our heroes, erase our values, and indoctrinate our children."

During the 2016 campaign and his presidency, he also used negative branding to devastating effect. He regularly referred to Jeb Bush as a "low energy" candidate. In Fort Dodge, Iowa, Trump labeled Ben Carson, his nearest competitor at the time, as "pathological."[89] In the debate of February 25, Trump referred to Senator Cruz as "lyin' Ted" and a "basket case." Senator Rubio became "little Marco."[90] These labels seemed to stick as each of his opponents fell by the wayside. When Trump emerged as the presumptive nominee, he referred to Clinton as "crooked Hillary." The same fate befell her as it did his primary opponents.[91] Once president, he continued his negative branding. Ridiculing her claim to have Cherokee blood, Trump referred to Senator Elizabeth Warren as Pocahontas. The House Speaker became "nervous Nancy." The head of the impeachment, Congressman Adam Schiff, became "shifty Schiff." When it came to global warming, President Trump labeled scientists as "perennial prophets of doom . . . foolish fortune tellers" at the Davos, Switzerland, economic conference.[92]

Perhaps Trump's worst and most revealing distortion came after the march in Charlottesville that resulted in death and destruction. After the clash between white supremacists and Antifa marchers, Trump claimed there was "blame on both sides" and that there were "very fine people on both sides," thereby welcoming racists into his dwelling place. This was not a one-time slip of the tongue. In the first presidential debate with former vice president Joe Biden, Trump was asked to condemn the Proud Boys right-wing group. Instead, he told them to "stand back and stand by," and then he condemned the Antifa group instead.

On the day the present manuscript was sent into production, Trump's run ended with the inauguration of a new president in January of 2021. However, his run had lasted four years, almost exactly the same time as Senator McCarthy's juggernaut in the early 1950s. Trump had survived an impeachment trial. And in the 2020 House races not a single Republican incumbent had been defeated. The Democrats failed to switch a single state legislature, which means that Republicans will reapportion and redistrict a majority of House seats.

Fascist rhetoric is dangerous; it overwhelms with the negative awe of hate speech: dehumanizing rhetoric, incitement to violence, and division. The Anti-Defamation League reported that in 2018 and 2019 the incidence of white supremacist propaganda increased by 120 percent.[93] In this environment some of us anticipated that Trump's fascist rhetoric would lead to fascist action,[94] which resulted in his being impeached twice. The first case was based on the fact that in a phone call with the president of the Ukraine, Trump asked—in return for releasing aid to the Ukraine—for an investigation of Hunter Biden, the son of his most likely opponent in the 2020 election. When an investigation was undertaken by the House of

Representatives, he obstructed justice by refusing to send documents to the House and by refusing to let any of the members of his administration testify. Thus, he vastly expanded executive privilege. He interfered in the election again in the New Hampshire primary of 2020 when only days before, he told his independent supporters who were eligible to vote in the Democratic primary to vote for the weakest candidate.

There were other fascist moments of awe. Trump vowed to bring back torture as an instrument of war. He appointed Gina Haspel as director of the CIA even though she was accused of overseeing the torturing of prisoners of war. Trump released Edward Gallagher from jail prior to his trial. Gallagher was a Navy Seal who was accused of war crimes by his troops; he was later convicted of posing for a photo with an Islamic State fighter's corpse. Trump then pardoned Gallagher and overturned a Defense Department order removing Gallagher's status as a Seal and restored his rank after the trial. Trump diverted $7.2 billion from the defense budget to the fund for building his wall at the Mexican border, only to have the courts overrule his use of the funds for that purpose. In his 2020 State of the Union Address, he debased the Presidential Medal of Freedom, the highest civilian award one can receive, by awarding it to Rush Limbaugh. After his Senate trial was over, Trump tweeted that he believed the Roger Stone sentencing recommendation of his prosecutors was too severe. The attorney general then revised the letter to include no recommendation on sentencing; the four prosecutors for the government promptly resigned. During the riots following George Floyd's murder, Trump sent federal agents to protect federal buildings from rioters in Seattle and Portland, even though state and local officials did not request them. The federal troops in Portland escorted protesters into unmarked vehicles. Perhaps most disturbing was the claim by Trump's lawyers in a case before the Supreme Court in which the district attorney for New York's Southern District sought Trump's financial records. In *Trump v. Vance,* they argued that the president is immune from any criminal proceedings and does not have to surrender any documents that are subpoenaed.[95] The attorney for the Southern District investigating Trump's lawyer Rudy

Giuliani was fired by Attorney General Barr. In August 2020, Trump crossed the separation-of-powers line when he ordered the Federal Emergency Management Agency to extend the lapsed unemployment stipend by providing $300 a week in relief. This is clearly the prerogative of the Congress, as is the deferral of collecting payroll taxes, another of Trump's executive orders. After his election defeat, he tried to scuttle a Covid-19 relief package his secretary of the treasury had negotiated in Trump's name. Then came the egregious use of the presidential pardon. He had already commuted the felony sentences of Phoenix sheriff Joe Arpaio in 2017, and Roger Stone, one of his campaign advisors, and Michael Flynn, his national security advisor, in 2020. In a flurry of pardons on his way out of the White House, he pardoned his son-in-law's father, Charles Kushner, an admitted felon; he pardoned former congressmen Chris Collins (guilty of insider trading), Duncan Hunter (guilty of misappropriating campaign funds), and Steve Stockman (guilty of cheating a charity). Worst of all, Trump pardoned four Blackwater contractors to the military who were convicted of killing fourteen unarmed Iraqi civilians. These contractors did immense damage to the United States' international reputation, not to mention the commission of murder. Their pardons undercut seven years of prosecutorial work, thereby committing the worst abuse of power in the history of the presidency.

Amidst the chaos caused by his refusal to accept the results of the election in 2020, Trump launched a series of legal challenges to undermine the election. They all failed, even at the level of the Supreme Court where three of his own appointees ruled against him. Worse yet, after the 2020 presidential election was certified and despite the fact that two recounts confirmed Georgia's vote for Biden, Trump called the Republican secretary of state there and asked him to "find 11,870 votes" that would flip Georgia into the president's column of electors. Heroically, the secretary of state resisted the president's hour of cajoling.

Then a handful of Republican senators and 140 House members challenged the results of the election when it was certified by the Congress on January 6, 2012. That moment was disrupted by a Trump-induced act of sedition, perhaps the most awesome of all fascist activity. In the morning, addressing demonstrators, Rudy Giuliani and Donald Trump Jr. preceded the president, thus establishing a context for the president's remarks. Giuliani urged the demonstrators to enter into a "trial by combat," and, in our opinion, skated very close to the line of culpability for the deaths that occurred later in the day. Donald Trump Jr. addressed the Congress, warning legislators "we are coming for you." Trump then encouraged the demonstrators to march on the Capitol: "We are going to walk down Pennsylvania Avenue. . . . We will never give up. We will never concede. It will never happen. You don't concede when there's theft involved. Our country has had enough. We will not take it anymore." He urged his followers to "fight" for their country but did not follow them to the Capitol.

Five people died, including a Capitol policeman, and many were injured in the melee that followed as Trump's supporters broke into the People's House, trashing the floor of the Senate and many congressional offices in the midst of a pandemic. One demonstrator made his way into Speaker Pelosi's office and sat in her chair. He left a note behind: "We will never back down." Another took her podium and paraded with it through the Capitol Rotunda. The nation was shocked. Even some Republican members of the Senate and the House, including Representative Liz Cheney, called for Trump's removal from office. On January 13, 2021, with only a week left in his term, the House impeached Trump for the second time. The single article of impeachment charged the president with incitement to insurrection.[96]

The majority of Trump supporters don't act like racists or fascists. There are several reasons why a sizable minority continued to support Trump even after his first impeachment.[97] Some citizens believed Trump provided a vehicle for attaining their version of contentment no matter how much virtue he lacked or how much vice he displayed. They were on a journey to a conservative or populist home, and they did not care who the landlord was. Or perhaps they are afraid of losing their way of life, their home, and they sought help from anyone who would protect them, no matter how vile. Others may have been confused by the transformation of society, the increase in diversity, and/or the online revolution. Some didn't see his vices as faults at all, which speaks volumes about their own. In this way, Trump was a barometer of his audience's ethos, a corrupting influence in the now less-perfect Union. It is important to note that while former vice president Joe Biden and his running mate, Senator Kamala Harris, drew more votes than any other ticket in American history, President Trump and Vice President Mike Pence drew the second most votes in history. In the post-Trump era, one hopes that as it continues to mend, the Republican Party will engage in moral rectification and listen to the voices of its better angels, such as the courageous members of the Lincoln Project. One hopes that civility can be restored, critical thinking endorsed, and authentic spirituality embraced, but it will take powerful eloquence to achieve those goals.

Conclusion

It is a long descent from Plato's noumenal world to George W. Bush's war-torn world and to the presidential propaganda of Donald Trump. Both befouled their nests. If we do not restore the quest for truth, if we do not become judicious in our assessment of what we are told, we are doomed to a common sense based on fallacious reasoning and lies. Part of the problem stems from the unforeseen circumstances generated by the personal computer/cellphone world of social media. It is a case of the good turned bad.

The personal computer is a tool capable of advancing ethical behavior in that it is especially attuned to the challenge-response function of the call that lies at the heart of human existence and that makes itself known in our everyday being with others. No technology in the history of humankind (with the exception of language) allows for and facilitates acknowledgment more than the personal computer and its offspring. Now regularly available on the personal computer or smartphone or tablet, cyberspace offers itself as an awesome transformation of space and time, an immense and easily accessible dwelling place for people to meet, possibly feel at home with others, and thereby know together what is going on in their lives. People can provide information and, perhaps more importantly, a caring response to others. Moreover, the "virtual communities" found in cyberspace can help revitalize the spirit of civic republicanism while overcoming the loneliness of the Covid-19 era.

As Robert Bellah and his colleagues remind us, in the tradition of civic republicanism "community means a solidarity based on a responsibility to care for others because that is essential to living a good life." Moreover, civic republicanism, emphasizing as it does the importance of developing a rhetorically competent citizenry, maintains that the authenticity of "public life is built upon the . . . languages and practices of commitment that shape character. These language and practices establish a web of interconnection by creating trust, joining people to families, friends, communities, and churches, and making each individual aware of his reliance on the larger society. They form those habits of the heart that are the matrix of a moral ecology, the connecting tissue of a body politic."[98]

The downside of all this good, however, is that on social media, and in the dwelling place of cable media, a citizen can find affirmation for the most outrageous claims, let alone common sense. Barack Obama was born in Africa. Global warming is a hoax. Most immigrants commit crimes. The Ukraine engaged in interference with the 2016 presidential campaign. There is a deep state undermining the Trump administration led by a Q-Anon conspiracy. Biden stole the election of 2020. Even on reputable cable programs, editorial and ideological commentary has bled into the news side, where once there was a solid wall of separation. Many viewers believe that Anderson Cooper, Tucker Carlson, Sean Hannity, Don Lemon, and Rachel Maddow, to name just five of the most prominent, present objective news when in fact they are merely giving their opinion of what is going on. The call of the truth has been corrupted. There is no one who has inherited the mantle of Walter Cronkite as the most trusted man in America. If we can't know what premises are true, how do we construct arguments that come to true conclusions? How can we be judicious in our decision making? The restoration of critical thinking is essential.

However, the impact of social media has had other serious consequences for an informed house of consensus. Big newspaper chains, cable news, and the internet are driving local independent newspapers into bankruptcy. More than two thousand have stopped publishing since 2004. The number of people employed by newspapers declined by almost 50 percent between 2008 and 2017.[99] At the same time, advertising revenues declined from $45 billion to $18 billion. Magazines were hit even harder. For example, *Newsweek*'s circulation went from 4 million to 100,000.

Furthermore, the slogan "cut the cable" has been embraced across the country. Though, as we have shown, cable has its problems, those excluding cable from their homes substitute even worse alternatives—streaming services, Facebook, and Twitter—to get their "news." On such sites, one can find "influencers," famous people's sites, or pages that have an unusually persuasive effect on their followers. Advertisers pay influencers to "push" their products in various ways. The insidious practice has found its way into political campaigns. In the 2020 primary season, former New York mayor Michael Bloomberg ran humorous messages promoting his candidacy for president on sites followed by millions of young people.[100] Bloomberg also spent millions and millions of dollars of his own money on the campaign, using a loophole in the law that does not restrict the spending of personal wealth on one's own campaign. Once eliminated, he turned to spending millions of his funds to help Joe Biden in his presidential race. Entrepreneurs Andrew Yang and Tom Steyer were also among those who used their own fortunes to advance their candidacies in the last cycle.

We had come to rely on the free marketplace of ideas to produce the truth. It was postulated before and during the Enlightenment by such thinkers as John Milton and John Locke. It was made part of the political system with the incorporation of the First Amendment into the Constitution, and by Justice Oliver Wendell Holmes's specific reference to a free marketplace of

CHEATING ELOQUENCE | **99**

ideas. But as we have shown, it has been destroyed in our own time by at least two salient factors. First, *access* to the marketplace has been monopolized by conglomerates that can easily overwhelm dissenters for whom access is not free. Thanks to Section 230 of the Communication Act of 1996, entities such as Facebook and Twitter are NOT classified as public forums and are thus not subject to the First Amendment. Instead they are entirely governed by their corporations and can reject any posting they please. Worse yet, they have it both ways. As designated common carriers, they cannot be held liable for what is posted on the services, unlike newspapers and television stations.

Second, artificial intelligence is generating fake voices that affirm false opinions in subliminal ways to influence various audiences over social media. In the Brexit and Trump elections of 2016, artificial intelligence, relying on algorithms, turned out millions of voters who had never voted before, which might have been a good thing had they been motivated by the truth. However, they were targeted by a barrage of falsehoods adjusted to their prejudices.[101] For many in our society, the tendency and the temptation are to seek affirmation even though it may come out of a cesspool of lies and distortion. We have lost our sense of community and critical thinking, which is evident in the divisiveness pervading the nation. The body politic has been polluted and there is no authentic dwelling place, no place one can trust to be true. No one understood this better than President Trump. He regularly circumvented the news media by tweeting to his choruses.

It is certainly time to reflect on the call of our first president, who in his farewell address issued a stern warning:

> [Political parties may] become potent engines, by which cunning, ambitious, and unprincipled men will be able to subvert the power of the people and to usurp for themselves the reins of government, destroying afterwards the very engines which have lifted them to unjust dominion.... [D]isorders and miseries which result gradually incline the minds of men to seek security and repose in the absolute power of an individual; and sooner or later the chief of some prevailing faction, more able or more fortunate than his competitors,

turns this disposition to the purposes of his own elevation, on the ruins of public liberty. . . . [He] agitates the community with ill-founded jealousies and false alarms, kindles the animosity of one part against another [and] opens the door to foreign influence and corruption. . . . That way lies despotism.[102]

For the rest of the book we will focus on examples of true eloquence. We will turn to speakers and other artists who have heard a call of conscience, are inspirational, and seek to build a decent place to dwell. These speakers and other artists provide examples of those who want to heal themselves, their audiences, and their nation. They engage in a heroic and noble task of homemaking. They use eloquence in service of truth. They evoke a positive sense of awe that leads to the call of the sublime.

CHAPTER 4

Epideictic Eloquence

A ristotle described one of the genres of public speaking as epideictic. The speech consists of praise and/or blame and has for its goal establishing what is honorable in the present for its audience. To accomplish this task, the speech needs to display virtues and condemn vices. This chapter explores epideictic calls delivered by Senator Barack Obama in his quest for the presidency and as president. He certainly understood the necessity of eloquence. President Barack Obama put it this way in his Inaugural Address: "To those who cling to power through corruption and deceit and the silencing of dissent, know that you are on the wrong side of history, but that we will extend a hand if you are willing to unclench your fist. . . . There is nothing so satisfying to the spirit, so defining of our character than giving our all to a difficult task."[1]

Obama and the Speech on Race

At this point in his candidacy, Barack Obama intended to create a dwelling place where activists could help to improve a wretched world. Up until the day he delivered "A More Perfect Union," Obama never directly addressed the issue of racial inequality in America and proceeded as if nothing was unique about his historical campaign. Instead, Obama chose the moral high ground. Then his campaign was disrupted.

The speech was delivered in Philadelphia on March 18, 2008, and was considered by many media commentators and political pundits to be a masterpiece of contemporary eloquence, a guiding light for the development of civic virtue. The speech has come to be known as "The Race Speech."[2] The eloquence of the speech is directed toward the creation of openings that will encourage collaborative deliberation about racism in America and what is needed to eliminate or at least lessen the severity of this hateful disease.[3]

The interruption that called for the speech was a controversy surrounding Obama's former African American pastor and current supporter Reverend Jeremiah Wright, who was videotaped using incendiary language during a church sermon to express his negative views about American injustice and racism in this country and throughout the world. Clips from the tape were aired on the three major television networks (ABC, CBS, NBC), cable TV outlets (CNN, MSNBC, FOX), and YouTube. Wright maintained that the United States "caused" the hellish history-changing event of 9/11.[4] Attacks from the radical right on Wright's character incited political and racial tension in the country and placed Obama in the position of being guilty by association.

Although Obama is specifically concerned with the racist white-non-white divide that pervades this country and infects our sensibilities, his discourse is meant to speak to any group of people who know the pain and suffering of social death. President Abraham Lincoln dealt with the problem over 150 years ago when he first argued for the creation of a more perfect union. Obama continues the good fight. Racism marginalizes the other, commends social death, and, if necessary, would have its followers exterminate the other altogether. Racism is a hellish world of thought if you are the race that is hated. In terms of identification, Obama's character as it develops is a function of how, among other things, he brings to mind in imaginative ways these essential characteristics of human being as he addresses practical happenings of the day that demand his attention.

Obama began his presentation with the words "We the people, in order to form a more perfect union"—words from the Constitution originally intended to establish for a people an openness towards future changes in their way of being. Obama then recalled how our country's founders created that document, which, sadly, remained "stained by this nation's original sin of slavery." Still, the document "had at its very core the ideal of equal citizenship under the law" and "promised its people liberty, and justice, and a union that could be and should be perfected over time." What was needed to fulfill this promise "were Americans in successive genera- tions who were willing to do their part—through protests and struggle, on the streets and in the courts, through civil war and civil disobedience and always at great risk—to narrow the gap between the promise of our ideals and the reality of their time." Obama is such an American. A rhetoric of perfection is on his mind:

> I chose to run for the presidency at this moment in history because I believe deeply that we cannot solve the challenges of our time unless we solve them together—unless we perfect our union by understanding that we may have different stories, but we hold common hopes; that we may not look the same and we may not have come from the same place, but we all want to move in the same direction—towards a better future for our children and our grandchildren. This belief comes from my unyielding faith in the decency and generosity of the American people. But it also comes from my own story.

Racism and its effects sound a "call of conscience": a need to know (*scientia*) with (*con*) each other.[5] Obama's speech amplifies the call. We cannot solve the challenges of our time "unless we perfect our union" by engaging first in the civil, communicative, and rhetorical activity of collaborative deliberation so to understand what these challenges truly are. "Different stories" will be at work in the conversation.

Thus, Obama shows us how narrative can enhance epideictic speeches, an important sophistication for those who would call others to the truth. When done well, the telling of stories is a rhetorically powerful activity in that it caters to who we are as *homo narrans*, creatures who use storytelling as a primary way of creating and enhancing our understanding of the world and our relationships with others. Stories enable us to use discourse in narratives that are congruent with the temporal structure of existence, its beginning (past), middle (present), and end (future).[6] We like stories that admit coherence, that display fidelity with our everyday hopes and dreams, and that, even if sad, are still instructive and make us feel good when all is said and done. A good story is almost always more effective than a good argument.

Obama begins his personal story by noting that he is "the son of a black man from Kenya and a white woman from Kansas." He "was raised with the help of a white grandfather who survived a Depression to serve in Patton's Army during World War II and a white grandmother who worked on a bomber assembly line at Fort Leavenworth while he was overseas." However, Obama embodies otherness: "I've gone to some of the best schools in America and lived in one of the world's poorest nations. I am married to a black American who carries with her the blood of slaves and slaveowners—an inheritance we pass on to our two precious daughters." His larger family, "of every race and every hue, [is] scattered across three continents." In acknowledging this otherness, Obama not only provides openings for others to identify with his existence but also extends a compliment to his homeland that serves as a life-giving gift of acknowledgment: "For as long as I live, I will never forget that in no other country on Earth is my story even possible." The story, admits Obama, does not make him "the most conventional candidate. But it is a story that has seared into my genetic makeup the idea that this nation is more than the sum of its parts—that out of many, we are truly one." Obama seeks to be with and for his audience. For the competent and eloquent speaker, an audience is not set at a distance in the rhetorical situation; rather, it is acknowledged, engaged, and called into a space of practical concerns. Obama is what was termed elsewhere a "homemaker."[7] He wants to construct a dwelling place for collaborative deliberation and the display of virtue. He wants his fellow Americans to know that in their communicative struggle to ascertain the truth of some disputed matter and to advance their community's ethos and moral consciousness, both the self and others are responsible for making sure that the life-giving gift of acknowledgment and the openness it fosters are cultivated and shared as much as possible. All of this is what Obama imagines as he shares his story.

He speaks of heroic behavior performed by common folk. He speaks of the genius and goodheartedness of our ancestors in their creating a document that opens people to the possibilities of democracy, encourages acknowledgment, equality, and collaborative deliberation, all for the purpose of having us engage in the cultivation of conscience. The activity entails a joint adventure in homemaking, in constructing a dwelling place where we can know and feel at home with others. Like all homes in which we take pride, this one needs upkeep. Taking care of such business is a well-tested way of feeling good about our future prospects. Practice makes perfect. The American Dream is a reality, a dream that was enhanced by our victory in a noble war. His grandparents both helped out in the effort. He comes from good and caring genetic stock. He lives in a country where racism is not as bad as it used to be. Not as bad, but certainly still here wounding our dignity as a great people. Knowing Obama's story, we are faced with a contradiction, an interruption: no matter how much the generosity of our country has grown, it still seems "unbelievable" that an African American could rise through the ranks to become the first black president of the United States—that, in fact, a black man could embody the American Dream. His supporters saw it as a move toward perfection; his detractors did not. The situation could not help but admit a call for moral consciousness, imagination, judgment, and action.

The Interruption of Reverend Wright

Standing in his way of dealing with the problem of racism in this country was his association with the controversial pastor and activist Reverend Jeremiah Wright. Wright's activist days go back to the 1950s and 1960s. Wright's assessment and activities of the situation were aligned with the thinking of such Black Power advocates as Malcolm X. The black church has long served as a dwelling place, a home where its members could receive this gift. Reverend Wright had more than forty years of experience in this giving and receiving activity when he was recorded in his church denouncing American capitalism, militarism, and racism. Obama was a member of Wright's church. In his speech, Obama admitted that the reverend employed "incendiary language to express views that have the potential not only to widen the racial divide, but views that denigrate both the greatness and the goodness of our nation; that rightly offend white and black alike." Obama had already condemned in unequivocal terms Wright's behavior. Obama notes, however, that for some people, nagging questions remain. "Did I know [Wright] to be an occasionally fierce critic of American domestic and foreign policy? Of course. Did I ever hear him make remarks that could be considered controversial while I sat in church? Yes. Did I strongly disagree with many of his political views? Absolutely—just as I'm sure many of you have heard remarks from your pastors, priests, or rabbis with which you strongly disagreed."

Wright was a reason for people to close the door on Obama, to refuse to be open-minded and open-hearted to his message. But guilt by association was a bogus charge. Obama was more than willing to acknowledge Wright's "profoundly distorted view of this country—a view that sees white racism as endemic, and that elevates what is wrong with America above all that we know is right with America; a view that sees the conflicts in the Middle East as rooted primarily in the actions of stalwart allies like Israel, instead of emanating from the perverse and hateful ideologies of radical Islam." Such acknowledgment was negative for Wright but positive for his white detractors. Obama sounded a counter-call, if you will, an interruption of the rhetorical pattern of his former pastor, and in doing so, constructed a dwelling place for people to know together that, like Obama, they had legitimate reasons for distrusting Wright and his associates. Obama was no longer an associate, but he also was not a mere detractor. On the contrary, in one of many emotional moments in his speech, Obama acknowledged that the wrongs of the reverend are not all "that I know of the man." Obama's clarification of this point is noteworthy:

> The man I met more than twenty years ago is a man who helped introduce me to my Christian faith, a man who spoke to me about our obligations to love one another; to care for the sick and lift up the poor. He is a man who served his country as a U.S. Marine, who has studied and lectured at some of the finest universities and seminaries in the country, and who for over thirty years led a church that serves the community by doing God's work here on Earth—by housing the homeless, ministering to the needy, providing care services and scholarships and prison ministries, and reaching out to those suffering from HIV/AIDS.

With these words Obama reconstructs Wright as a person who deserves some positive acknowledgment, which also provides relief for those African Americans who knew Wright to be more than simply a reverse racist and who would object to Obama's critique and the negative implications it had for the black community. Without the strong support of this community, Obama could not win the election. He continues his acknowledgment of the important role that Wright played in Obama's youth and maturing dreams. Obama recalls the experience of his first service at Wright's church:

People began to shout, to rise from their seats and clap and cry out, a forceful wind carrying the reverend's voice up into the rafters. . . . And in that single note—hope!—I heard something else; at the foot of that cross, inside the thousands of churches across the city, I imagined the stories of ordinary black people merging with the stories of David and Goliath, Moses and Pharaoh, the Christians in the lion's den, Ezekiel's field of dry bones. Those stories—of survival, and freedom, and hope—became our story, my story; the blood that had spilled was our blood, the tears our tears; until this black church, on this bright day, seemed once more a vessel carrying the story of a people into future generations and into a larger world. Our trials and triumphs became at once unique and universal, black and more than black; in chronicling our journey, the stories and songs gave us a means to reclaim memories that we didn't need to feel shame about . . . memories that all people might study and cherish—and with which we could start to rebuild.

Wright helped Obama recognize a religious and racial history that, operating in unison, could bring together whites and blacks, Muslims, Christians, and Jews, as well as other races and religions. In this consubstantial identification, otherness would be welcomed for the greater good of the country. Wright's teachings broke ground for cultivating Obama's imagination—his social and political vision. A pastor's rhetoric offered Obama a dwelling place where he could develop a moral character worthy of high praise. "And this," says Obama, "helps explain, perhaps, my relationship with Reverend Wright." Obama continues:

As imperfect as he may be, he has been like family to me. He strengthened my faith, officiated my wedding, and baptized my children. Not once in my conversations with him have I heard him talk about any ethnic group in derogatory terms or treat whites with whom he interacted with anything but courtesy and respect. He contains within him the contradictions—the good and the bad—of the community that he has served diligently for so many years. I can no more disown him than I can disown the black community. I can no more disown him than I can my white grandmother—a woman who helped raise me, a woman who sacrificed again and again for me, a woman who loves me as much as she loves anything in this world, but a woman who once confessed her fear of black men who passed by her on the street, and who on more than one occasion has uttered racial or ethnic stereotypes that made me cringe. These people are a part of me. And they are a part of America, this country that I love.

Blacks and whites can identify with Obama's imaginative vision of God and country. Lincoln had said it before, but this time the saying showed something more: Obama was acknowledging racism in an unprecedented way. He was bringing whites and blacks together by praising and blaming them for doing the same right and wrong things to each other. The old and unethical tactic of scapegoating "the other" was cast aside. Obama knew that the heroes in his story were also antiheroes in the eyes of others. And he knew that these others did not have it all right. And he knew that these others were embarrassed to admit it in most public situations. And so, by answering one interruption with another, Obama spoke up for the citizens of the United States, thereby making it easier for them "to do the right thing." Spike Lee, the African American award-winning filmmaker, director, and political activist, had earlier sounded this rhetorically configured call in such films as *Do the Right Thing* (1989). Filmmakers have more leeway than presidential candidates. However, Obama took a chance and decided to put everything on the table in a bold, imaginative, candid, and rhetorically competent way. He brought into the open and displayed facets of racism that, up to now, were too uncomfortable for people to talk about. He discovered a way (with words) that helped them feel more at home with themselves and others. His rhetoric is epideictic in the fullest sense of the term: it sounds an eloquent interruption that brought people to tears with such well-spoken words as "I can no more disown [Reverend Wright] than I can disown the black community. . . . These people are a part of me. And they are a part of America, this country I love." It was an amazing rhetorical moment, and it was far from over. He was only on page 5 of an 11-page speech.

Obama's audience is the common man understood as those true-blooded, good-hearted, albeit imperfect, Americans who want to do the right thing for their country and others as well. Race, says Obama, "is an issue that I believe this nation cannot afford to ignore right now. We would be making the same mistake that Reverend Wright made in his offending sermons about America—to simplify and stereotype and amplify the negative to the point that it distorts reality." The reverend thus returns as an interruption to Obama's goals, but an interruption that can now be used as an instrument for sounding the call on behalf of Obama and his fellow Americans. In his badness, Wright is good. In his goodness, Wright has said bad things. Wright is neither more nor less than a common man; we all share "contradictions" in our character, our ethos, and our dwelling places and homes. These contradictions are part of our lived bodies. Wright's lived body continues to be a text for describing the country's racial problems. And thus, once again, Obama returns to a positive take on Wright, one that indicts the country that Wright scorned:

> But we do need to remind ourselves that so many of the disparities that exist in the African American community today can be directly traced to inequalities passed on from an earlier generation that suffered under the brutal legacy of slavery and Jim Crow. Segregated schools were, and are, inferior schools; we still haven't fixed them, fifty years after *Brown v. Board of Education*, and the inferior education they provided, then and now, helps explain the pervasive achievement gap between today's black and white students.

Obama helps his audience identify with blacks by reminding them about the hardships that blacks faced with legalized discrimination, and that they still face with lack of economic opportunity. Obama reminds his listeners of the same horrible things that Reverend Wright helped to bring to Obama's mind. Maintaining his eloquent trajectory, Obama also makes the point with the help of William Faulkner: "The past isn't dead and buried. In fact, it isn't even past." Obama continues his strategy of seeming contradiction as he offers the following positive remark about what he has just been saying: "What's remarkable is not how many failed in the face of discrimination, but rather how many men and women overcame the odds; how many were able to make a way out of no way for those like me who would come after them." But then Obama returns to the negative: anger, tragedy, and immorality. For the men and women of Reverend Wright's generation, the memories of humiliation and doubt and fear have not gone away; nor has the anger and the bitterness of those years. That anger may not get expressed in public, in front of white coworkers or white friends. But it does find voice in the barbershop or around the kitchen table. At times, that anger is exploited by politicians to gin up votes along racial lines, or to make up for a politician's own failings.

As he moves back and forth from positive to negative, Obama assumes a dialectical approach to his topic and subtopics. From the standpoint of argumentation theory, the approach is rational and dignified, as old as Socrates, and still a respected and much needed practice for today's dismaying times.[8] Obama is offering an imaginative narrative that progresses as he constructs, deconstructs, and reconstructs his material. He builds, tears down, and then rebuilds his white and black characters, and calls into question friends and nonfriends such that they might begin to see the light, the truth of the situation at hand: racism!

Obama's treatment of his topic is thus imaginatively aligned with and attuned to the ontological workings of human existence. He is making us feel at home by dismantling worlds of prejudice, exposing us to the awesomeness of being backed up against life and being (our most original home), and then instructing us in an eloquent way about how the problem can and must be remedied. Obama's eloquence is thereby given ontological purchase. His discourse speaks to us of who we are as creatures who inhabit worlds of know-how; are open to the call to truth; have the heart and mind to acknowledge, respond, and stay open to this call; and with this response and openness continue to build dwelling places where we can know together with others matters of importance and what should be done about them.

Obama's dialectical narrative creates paradoxes throughout his speech. For example, he next shines another negative light on Wright—one that, in truth, is applicable to a much larger audience: "The fact that so many people are surprised to hear ... anger in some of Reverend Wright's sermons simply reminds us of the old truism that the most segregated hour in American life occurs on Sunday morning." Alas, we are all common folk with good and bad habits that contradict each other. We pray and we are prejudiced. And we oftentimes have good reasons for this prejudice. Obama explains this judgment with a positive account of the "anger" that "exists within segments of the white community." He continues by identifying white listeners:

> Most working- and middle-class white Americans don't feel that they have been particularly privileged by their race. Their experience is the immigrant experience—as far as they're concerned, no one's handed them anything, they've built it from scratch. They've worked hard all their lives, many times only to see their jobs shipped overseas or their pension dumped after a lifetime of labor. They are anxious about their futures, and feel their dreams slipping away; in an era of stagnant wages and global competition, opportunity comes to be seen as a zero-sum game, in which your dreams come at my expense. So, when they are told to bus their children to a school across town; when they hear that an African American is getting an advantage in landing a good job or a spot in a good college because of an injustice that they themselves never committed; when they're told that their fears about crime in urban neighborhoods are somehow prejudiced, resentment builds over time.

True to form, Obama follows this affirming explanation of white resentment with a negative jab at its posture:

Like the anger within the black community, these resentments aren't always expressed in polite company. But they have helped shape the political landscape for at least a generation. Anger over welfare and affirmative action helped forge the Reagan Coalition. Politicians routinely exploited fears of crime for their own electoral ends. Talk show hosts and conservative commentators built entire careers unmasking bogus claims of racism while dismissing legitimate discussions of racial injustice and inequality as mere political correctness or reverse racism.

Acknowledgment and Perfection

Another positive remark ends the first part of his speech and serves as a transition:

And yet, to wish away the resentments of white Americans, to label them as misguided or even racist, without recognizing they are grounded in legitimate concerns—this too widens the racial divide and blocks the path to understanding. This is where we are right now. It's a racial stalemate we've been stuck in for years.

The stalemate defines a controversial world of know-how, a specific state of objective uncertainty that reveals an interruption. Acknowledgment, not just recognition, is needed. Otherness deserves respect. We must remain open to others in order to remain true to the fundamental self that we all are. Human being is a process of disclosure, an epideictic event of openness that constantly demands personal responsibility, courage, and ever-developing moral sensibilities. We are perfectly incomplete as a species, and we ought to know and admit it. What would life be like if no one acknowledged our existence, if no one identified with us, not even we ourselves?

Obama is telling us a story about how we are backed up against life and being, against the objective uncertainty of our existence. His imagination is hard at work. Concerned thought and action are called for. Obama holds to a "conviction rooted in [his] faith in God and [his] faith in the American people—that working together we can move beyond some of our old racial wounds, and that in fact we have no choice if we are to continue on the path of a more perfect union." Obama would lead us on this path of perfection. Obama believes it is our destiny:

> For the African American community, that path means embracing the burdens of our past without becoming victims of our past. It means continuing to insist on a full measure of justice in every aspect of American life. But it also means binding our particular grievances—for better health care, and better schools, and better jobs—to the larger aspirations of all Americans—the white woman struggling to break the glass ceiling, the white man who's been laid off, the immigrant trying to feed his family. And it means taking full responsibility for our own lives—by demanding more from our fathers, and spending more time with our children, and reading to them, and teaching them that while they may face challenges and discrimination in their own lives, they must never succumb to despair or cynicism; they must always believe that they can write their own destiny.

Here Obama again speaks both positively and negatively about the African American community. They certainly deserve equality for who they are, but they know in their hearts that their community is weakened and tarnished by a stereotype that is all too true: far too many black men are not there for their families. All of this must change. In making this point Obama returns to a negative assessment of Reverend Wright:

> The profound mistake of Reverend Wright's sermons is not that he spoke about racism in our society. It's that he spoke as if our society was static; as if no progress has been made; as if this country—a country that has made it possible for one of his own members to run for the highest office in the land and build a coalition of white and black, Latino and Asian, rich and

poor, young and old—is still irrevocably bound to a tragic past. But what
we know—what we have seen—is that America can change. That is the true
genius of this nation. What we have already achieved gives us hope—the
audacity to hope—for what we can and must achieve tomorrow.

Following the pathway of his speech, we are led to believe that we can
build a more perfect dwelling place for ourselves and others. There are
many more positive goals to achieve. Obama makes the point by remaining
negative, although this time, perhaps in the name of equality, he turns to
the white community for examples:

> In the white community, the path to a more perfect union means acknowl-
> edging that what ails the African American community does not just exist in
> the minds of black people; that the legacy of discrimination—and current
> incidents of discrimination, while less overt than in the past—are real and
> must be addressed. Not just with words, but with deeds—by investing in
> our schools and our communities; by enforcing our civil rights laws and
> ensuring fairness in our criminal justice system; by providing this generation
> with ladders of opportunity that were unavailable for previous generations.
> It requires all Americans to realize that your dreams do not have to come
> at the expense of my dreams; that investing in the health, welfare, and
> education of black and brown and white children will ultimately help all
> of America prosper.

Positive and negative, back and forth, Obama's dialectical journey
continues. Its practical end, Obama makes clear, "is nothing more, and
nothing less, than what all the world's great religions demand—that we do
unto others as we would have them do unto us. Let us be our brother's keeper,
Scripture tells us. Let us be our sister's keeper." Obama instructs us on the
virtuous life that religion worships and that, empirically speaking, is rooted
in the ontological workings of our spatial and temporal existence, in our
complete incompleteness. The epideictic call summons us to make choices.

What we should not choose, argues Obama, is "a politics that breeds division, and conflict, and cynicism." Nor should we treat "race only as spectacle, as we did in the OJ trial or in the wake of tragedy, as we did in the aftermath of Katrina or as fodder for the nightly news." Making such choices adds to the problem of race continuing to be seen as a "distraction" to certain close-minded, common-sense worlds of know-how. Change, however, requires us to go deeper into the problem of race so that we can understand its real character. "And to do this we must, for example, talk about the crumbling schools that are stealing the future of black children and white children and Asian children and Hispanic children and Native American children. This time we want to reject the cynicism that tells us that these kids can't learn; that those kids who don't look like us are somebody else's problem. The children of America are not those kids, they are our kids, and we will not let them fall behind in a 21st century economy. Not this time."

The phrase leads Obama to his strongest appeal for identification and acknowledgment:

> This time we want to talk about how the lines in the Emergency Room are filled with whites and blacks and Hispanics who do not have health care, who don't have the power on their own to overcome the special interests in Washington, but who can take them on if we do it together. . . . This time we want to talk about the men and women of every color and creed who serve together, and fight together, and bleed together under the same proud flag. We want to talk about how to bring them home from a war that never should've been authorized and never should've been waged, and we want to talk about how we'll show our patriotism by caring for them, and their families, and giving them the benefits they have earned.

Put simply, and much less eloquently, Obama's path for a more perfect union redirects us away from the path of the failed policies of the Bush administration: the ultimate negative for an African American presidential candidate who desires change. Obama closes his speech with a dialectical turn toward the positive. He tells another story that he told earlier that year at a celebration of Dr. Martin Luther King Jr.'s birthday. Combining narrative and identification, praise and blame, the story achieves epideictic eloquence:

There is a young, twenty-three-year-old white woman named Ashley Baia who organized for our campaign in Florence, South Carolina. She had been working to organize a mostly African American community since the beginning of this campaign, and one day she was at a roundtable discussion where everyone went around telling their story and why they were there. And Ashley said that when she was nine years old, her mother got cancer. And because she had to miss days of work, she was let go and lost her health care. They had to file for bankruptcy, and that's when Ashley decided that she had to do something to help her mom. She knew that food was one of their most expensive costs, and so Ashley convinced her mother that what she really liked and really wanted to eat more than anything else was mustard and relish sandwiches. Because that was the cheapest way to eat. She did this for a year until her mom got better, and she told everyone at the roundtable that the reason she joined our campaign was so that she could help the millions of other children in the country who want and need to help their parents too. Now Ashley might have made a different choice. Perhaps somebody told her along the way that the source of her mother's problems were blacks who were on welfare and too lazy to work, or Hispanics who were coming into the country illegally. But she didn't. She sought out allies in her fight against injustice. Anyway, Ashley finishes her story and then goes around the room and asks everyone else why they're supporting the campaign. They all have different stories and reasons. Many bring up a specific issue. And finally, they come to this elderly black man who's been sitting there quietly the entire time. And Ashley asks him why he's there. And he does not bring up a specific issue. He does not say health care or the economy. He does not say education or the war. He does not say that he was there because of Barack Obama. He simply says to everyone in the room, "I am here because of Ashley." "I'm here because of Ashley." By itself, that single moment of recognition [and acknowledgment] between that young white girl and that old black man is not enough. It is not enough to give health care to the sick, or jobs to the jobless, or education to our children. But it is where we start. It is where our union grows stronger. And as so many generations have come to realize over the course of the two- hundred and twenty-one years since a band of patriots signed that document in Philadelphia, that is where the perfection begins.

Compared to the eloquent and powerfully persuasive language preceding it, one might be tempted to gloss over or dismiss this closing story as being too simplistic or a mere pandering for votes. This would be a mistake. Ashley's story is nothing if not an interruption that speaks for the importance of identifying with others, of being open to their presence and circumstances, and of bringing them together to dwell in collaboration so that they can figure out how to do the right thing. The story is offered to help us feel good about ourselves. Ashley is a hero whose deeds we are at least good enough to appreciate, if not replicate. The rhetorical theorist and critic Robert Wade Kenny has a nice way of stating what is going on here: "We can call the world and even ourselves into question because we can imagine better. And as we hold out the possibility of a better life, we choose our ethos."9

Feeling good about oneself certainly makes life easier. What would you think of others who had no idea about what the story "means," or who could care less about the worth of the story, or who maintained that the story was boring, inappropriate, the invention of some too soft-hearted liberal? These are the people that will make the reaching of Obama's goal a Herculean task, if not a Sisyphian one, for those who would walk with him on his path. Obama and his supporters are up against worlds of know-hows that are hard pressed to change their righteous ways. Social death is alive and well in the debate over race. Whites and African Americans suffer marginalization.

A feeling of homelessness is palpable and that is why identification works so well. Although unpleasant, feeling homeless nevertheless exposes us to our most original home: the openness and objective uncertainty of our spatial and temporal existence, the place where we are when backed up against life and being, owing to some crisis in our lives where being shows itself for our consideration, where the universe becomes conscious of itself, and where we supposedly can be in the presence of God. Obama's speech seems intended to move us to the very heart of our existence and its otherness. We are creatures who want to feel complete. God is a perfect solution to our incompleteness. By way of dialectical steps, Obama walks hand in hand with God in his speech. He abides by the Scripture: "Walk before me and be thou perfect" (Gen. 17:1) The story of Ashley offers us a parable that calls us into question. "Where are you?" "Here I am," says Ashley. And "I am here" too, says an elderly black man, "because of Ashley." The story of Ashley offers us a model of heroism. Ashley stands out from the crowd in a praiseworthy way. Experiencing heroism is an emotional (e.g., anxious, joyful) experience. The Latin for emotion is *emovere*, "to move out of" the confines of some physical or psychological habitat (e.g., one's ego). The story of Ashley is meant to move us to another way of feeling at home with others, another place where being with others in a generous manner is much welcomed. The potential struggle of getting along well with one's neighbors is worth the effort. The struggle helps develop our moral character and consciousness.

Obama reaches out to touch us with a story about a young girl eating mustard and relish sandwiches so that she can save money for her seriously ill, unemployed, and uninsured mother. The description is vivid and real; its eloquence invites the audience to smile, cry, sympathize, and empathize at the same time. The story is truth in its most raw form. And the truth is awesome. In the pure and simple case of the mustard and relish sandwiches, there is beauty in the ordinary nature of the request and in the mental picture it evokes. The sandwiches are, themselves, a beautiful interruption of worlds of know-how that lack experience with such hardship.[10] Obama wants to change these worlds. Ashley already did. Obama displays her beauty; hence, the eloquence of his speech. By identifying with Ashley, his audience identifies with him. The story of Ashley is perfect for Obama's purposes. It brings Obama's imaginative vision and dialectical narrative to a positive point where the problem of race is dealt with and transcended at the same time. The white Ashley is a hero, but so is the elderly black man who received and answered Ashley's call and perhaps will share it with others.

A more perfect union now manifests itself with whites, blacks, and other forms and types of otherness. Obama did not run on the issue of race, but stories about racism serve him well. Nobody is blameless in these stories (until we learn about Ashley and the elderly man). Obama's imaginative way of constructing and deconstructing his narrative makes sure that we know as much. The narrative serves social, political, psychological, and religious identifications: do unto others what you would have them do unto you. Share and receive. Keep the process going. This is how we remain open to others. A more perfect union is possible only to the extent that openness is a defining characteristic of our being, our ethos, our dwelling place here on earth.

The Eloquent Eulogy

All of these elements came together again after a major disruption in the fiber of the nation. On January 8, 2011, Jared Lee Loughner took his semi-automatic Glock to a shopping center in Tucson, Arizona, where U.S. Representative Gabby Giffords was to speak at a rally of supporters. When Giffords came forward, Loughner pulled out his gun and shot Giffords in the head, killed six others, and wounded eighteen more.[11] The event was a major disruption ready for a timely speech appropriately constructed to make a call for unity and reconciliation.[12] In times of trauma, that call has been made in what Karlyn Kohrs Campbell and Kathleen Hall Jamieson explore as a "national eulogy." Usually relying on the grand style of oratory, these calls for national unity transform the president into a sort of high priest of national values.[13]

On January 12, 2011, President Barack Obama came to the University of Arizona to lead a nationally televised service. The time was ripe for a speech of healing. The expectation was that the president would eulogize the dead, the wounded, and the first responders, giving him an opportunity to praise virtue and condemn vice.[14] Obama started by rebuilding a dwelling place for his audience by calling on them to unify in prayer: "I have come here tonight as an American who, like all Americans, kneels to pray with you today and will stand by you tomorrow." He then acknowledged the "hole torn in your hearts," the disruption that calls us to a "holy place where the Most High dwells." Thus, in his opening paragraphs, Obama tells his audience that he is not only talking about our present condition, but our future and hopefully its transcendent nature.

Using plain language, Obama reconstructed what happened into a scene where government of, by, and for the people was functioning. He used the example of each of the dead to advance a virtue that could perfect our Union. District Judge John Roll represented service to the nation over his distinguished career on the bench. Seeking unity, Obama pointed out that Roll was appointed to the court by a Republican president and that Roll was on his way home from a Catholic mass when he stopped to attend the rally for Giffords, a Democrat.

George and Dorothy Morris exemplified family values: "They did everything together." Phyllis Schneck served the same values by tending to her children and her grandchildren. Though a Republican, she had befriended Giffords when Scheck retired to Tucson from the East. In the same vein, Dorwan and Mavy Stoddard grew up together in Tucson, raised separate families, and then seventy years later, when widowed, came together to renew their adolescent bond. In his retirement, Dorwan helped fix his church and the dwellings of its constituents. Gabe Zimmerman, one of Giffords's staff members, embodied the virtue of caring for others. "As Gabby's outreach director, he made the cares of thousands of her constituents his own, seeing to it that seniors got the Medicare benefits that they had earned, that veterans got the medals and the care that they deserved, that government was working for ordinary folks." In short, he made this world a better place. Nine-year-old Christina Taylor-Green believed she was blessed to lead the life she led. She exemplified the virtue of charity. "And she'd pay those blessings back by participating in a charity that helped children who were less fortunate." Thus, by making each of the dead present, Obama displayed a virtue by which audience members could perfect themselves and the nation.

To this point in the eulogy, Obama had let the characters and the narrative speak for themselves by using the plain style of speech. Their example was shown through his eloquence. But as he turned from the dead to the living, he began to use more stylistic devices to make his ideas more present, his call more robust. In the next paragraph, he began its four sentences with the phrase "Our hearts," echoing the repetition so common in the black pulpit he had so often witnessed in his lifetime. Then in telling the story of his visit to Gabby Giffords earlier in the day, he repeats the phrase "She opened her eyes for the first time" four times. It was the news the audience was thrilled to hear. It was a sublime moment of awe.

But Obama was not finished. He returned to plain language to describe the heroic conduct of the people on hand who tried to stop the carnage. They displayed selfless courage. And here we see again one of Obama's favorite rhetorical moves from the negative to the positive: "These men and women remind us that heroism is found not only on the fields of battle. They remind us that heroism does not require special training or physical strength. Heroism is here, in the hearts of so many of our fellow citizens, all around us, just waiting to be summoned." As he brings the first responders to life, he brings heroism to life, again showing the way to perfection.

Obama used this moment of heroism to pivot to his deliberative agenda. To honor the dead and to extend the work of the heroes, we need to reevaluate our gun control laws. Smartly, Obama recognized how divisive the issue can be. So, he proposed that we "pause for a moment and make sure that we're talking with each other in a way that heals, not in a way that wounds." Relying on Scripture, Obama acknowledged that there is evil in the world and we must deal with it if we are to perfect our Union. He then returned to the figure of repetition: "We should be willing to challenge old assumptions in order to lessen the prospects of such violence in the future.

But what we cannot do is use this tragedy as one more occasion to turn on each other. That we cannot do. That we cannot do." Here Obama refutes the "common sense" of painting those who oppose us as aliens and calls on us to open ourselves to communication with those with whom we disagree.

Obama again acknowledged the tragic disruption and the necessary and understandable questions death always raises. We are always living unto death and we need to ponder the temporality of that condition: "So sudden loss causes us to look backward—but it also forces us to look forward; to reflect on the present and the future, on the manner in which we live our lives and nurture our relationships with those who are still with us." The home to which Obama invites us is one of self-actualization, responsibility, and caring. He asks us to abjure our material accretions and focus on loving others.

That sentiment serves as a bridge from the past (and past tense) to the present (and present tense) to make the victims present and again display the values they represent. The two married couples reinforce our love for our families. Judge Roll represents fidelity to the law. Gabby Giffords represents public service. Christina represents all our children in their curious and trusting ways. Obama used the moment to claim that we can perfect ourselves, "we can do better." The way forward is to heed his call for unity and civility: "Those who died here, those who saved life here—they help me believe. We may not be able to stop all evil in the world, but I know that how we treat one another, that's entirely up to us." We can perfect ourselves in the face of evil by treating one another with respect; that is the responsible thing to do.

Obama's peroration brings Christina back to life again. He summarizes her short life and asks his audience to see the world through her eyes. And then comes a closing sublime moment where Obama lifts his audience to heaven: "If there are rain puddles in Heaven, Christina is jumping in them today. And here on this Earth—here on this Earth, we place our hands over our hearts, and we commit ourselves as Americans to forging a country that is forever worthy of her gentle, happy spirit."

Conclusion

With these mainly epideictic speeches, Obama reminds us of Emerson's understanding of the rhetor as hero: He stands "with forward foot, in the attitude of advancing. . . . His speech is not to be distinguished from action. It is action." Obama demonstrates the "power [of imagination] to connect his thought with its proper symbol, and so to utter it"; he thereby also demonstrates his "love of truth and . . . [the] desire to communicate it without loss." The eloquent orator creates openings for others to see and to dwell in. The eloquent orator is a homemaker, creating places devoted to encouraging openness to others. It is a very dignified vocation. Salvation from loneliness and escape from social and biological death are possible when the happening of acknowledgment is encouraged by some rhetorically competent, dignified, and heroic individual who is willing to take the time to construct a dwelling place for others where some degree of peace of mind, happiness, and hope is possible.

CHAPTER 5

Deliberative Eloquence

Perhaps there is no purer example of deliberative oratory than the call to battle. It can resonate through the generations inspiring later generations. One case involved a fictional re-creation of such a call that was then used almost five hundred years later to encourage the same nation to fight on in the face of an evil foe.

In 1415, the Dauphin of France issued a diplomatic interruption when he insulted Henry V of England, who then crossed the English Channel, restarting the Hundred Years' War. Capitalizing on the element of surprise, Henry was at first successful with his month-long siege of Harfleur, near the mouth of the Seine. When the French rallied, Henry attempted to retreat to Calais, a port held by the English. But the French blocked his way. Henry was forced to march inland, cross several rivers, and then turn back west hoping to regroup in Calais. But again, he was blocked, and on St. Crispin's Day Henry was forced to face an army twice the size of his own on a field near Agincourt. Three events would reveal that Henry V had a keen sense of timing that would allow him to carry England to victory. The first was the superior firepower of the longbow, developed by the English, and the effective use of short-range archers. The second was the muddy field on which the battle was fought; the night before the battle had seen downpours. The French cavalry and foot soldiers were weighted down by their heavy armor and found it difficult to maneuver. The third was Henry's call to battle, a display of courage and nobility that inspired his soldiers to fight as they never had before. Instead of waiting for the French army to charge him, Henry decided to charge them, taking them by surprise. At the end of the day-long battle, Henry had lost about six hundred men; the French had lost about six thousand, many of them noblemen.

Shakespeare immortalized Henry's speech in his play *Henry V* (1599), which inspired Elizabethan England to resist her enemies and unite behind her queen. Laurence Olivier used the same speech in his 1944 movie version of *Henry V* to inspire the British people during their hour of need in World War II.[1] Thus, the initial call of Henry V echoed through history as an example of the Greek rhetorician Gorgias's opportune moment to inspire and Aristotle's deliberative form. And no wonder. Earlier, at Harfleur, Henry had carried the day by urging his men "once more into the breach." Now, before the battle of Agincourt with all eyes on him, Henry again found an opening for inspiration. Turning disadvantage to advantage, he told his men that being outnumbered is a blessing because it affords them the opportunity to achieve a victory more glorious than most. They can become memorialized heroes. In a moment of acknowledgment, he allowed those who would not seize this moment to leave because he did not want such men by his side. And then he switched to the affirmative, making the spiritual and the relational present for his troops: "This day is called the feast of Crispian: / He that outlives this day and comes safe home, / Will stand a tip-toe when the day is named, / And rouse him at the name of Crispian. / He that shall live this day, and see old age, / Will yearly on the vigil feast his neighbors, / And say, 'Tomorrow is Saint Crispian': / Then will he strip his sleeve and show his scars. . . . / We few, we happy few, we band of brothers." A heroic interruption that made soldiers into heroes.

What Shakespeare and Laurence Olivier seemed to realize was that the speech of inspiration needs an audience ready to be led, in this case, into battle. Whether it was the beleaguered English at Agincourt or the English people suffering from V-2 rocket attacks during World War II, they needed to hear the call not only to survive but to march into battle. No call, no survival. No survival, no victory over Nazism. In each case, patriotism, love of country, was crucial to the leader's success.

Daniel Webster

There is a case in American history that deserves our attention. In January 1830, Senator Robert Hayne of South Carolina issued an interruption to Senate decorum and to the peaceful accommodation that had flowed from the Compromise of 1820. Hayne alleged that there was a conspiracy between Northern and Western states to confine slavery to the South. Under the tutelage of the political philosopher of states' rights, Vice President John C. Calhoun, Hayne constructed a speech that attempted to remake the North-West alliance into a South-West alliance. Said Hayne, "The very life of our system is independence of the States." He offered revenue to the western farmers, not seeking more revenue for the federal government in terms of imposing tariffs that sent up the cost of imported goods. At that moment, Senator Daniel Webster came into the Senate having completed a case before the Supreme Court in the bowels of the Capitol.

When Hayne finished, it was late in the day, and Webster requested time for a response the next day. Speaking from three pages of notes, Webster issued a counter-interruption. It argued that Hayne's doctrine of states' rights was not only a product of Calhoun's brain, but would result in unprecedented harm to the Union, Webster's transcendent home for the nation. Webster also pointed out that it was not the Northern or Western states that sought to preclude slavery from the new states. It was the Northwest

Ordinance of 1787 that preceded the Constitution and prohibited slavery from the territories of the United States, and hence, the states that were formed out of them. Webster sensed that slavery was the Achilles' heel of Hayne's position, and sought to draw him out on the issue. Webster went on to allege that the real goal of South Carolina was disunion (disruption) in general and "nullification" of federal policy in particular. (The Nullification Doctrine had been laid out by Calhoun in 1828.) Webster claimed that the nation had been moving toward "consolidation" since the time of President Washington. Consolidation meant to perfect the American home by "whatever tends to strengthen the bond that unites us and encourages the hope that our Union may be perpetual." Webster established his and the nation's ethos as "unionist."

Hayne chose to reply to Webster's attack. Attempting to burnish his image with a literary allusion, Hayne compared Webster's imagined South-West conspiracy as a ghost: "Has the ghost of the murdered coalition come back, like the ghost of Banquo, to 'sear the eye-balls' of the gentleman, and will it not 'down at his bidding'? Are dark visions of broken hopes, and honors lost forever, still floating before his heated imagination?"[2] Encouraged by Calhoun's nod from the chair as president of the Senate, Hayne let fly with a full-throated defense of slavery and its spread to the new states in the West. He dramatically grabbed at his heart and said that Webster's attack had "rankled" there. Hayne said that Webster "had discharged his fire in the face of the Senate," and he was grateful he had the opportunity "to return the shot." Literally issuing an interruption, Webster stood and yelled from his desk, "I am ready to receive it." Hayne replied that Webster had "pour[ed] out all the vials of his mighty wrath upon my devoted head" and was "making war on the South." Hayne claimed that the South had made less money on slave labor than the North made in its inhuman factories. Hayne claimed that slavery actually benefited the nation as a whole because it produced cheap cotton for the northern mills operating in Webster's home state of Massachusetts. Hayne then attacked Webster for supporting the Hartford Convention of

1812, which considered secession from the Union. Nothing could be more damaging to Webster's reputation as "the defender of the Union."

Hayne concluded by returning to Calhoun's Nullification Doctrine; if a state did not like a federal law, it did not have to obey it. He cited the Tenth Amendment and Jefferson's Virginia and Kentucky Resolutions of 1798 to support his point. Hoping he had finished on the high road, Hayne returned to his seat. Webster was ready with a second reply that would take the afternoons of January 26 and 27 to complete. Anybody who was somebody in Washington could be found in the Senate gallery. Webster was dressed immaculately in a dark blue coat with shiny brass buttons, a cream-colored vest, and a white cravat; in full regalia, he played to the galleries. His highly stylized lines acknowledged and pleased the bonneted ladies in the gallery. His lines of argument were pressed home to his colleagues on the floor.

One of the most impressive strategies of Webster's speech was his acceptance of Hayne's organization of arguments in Webster's refutation. He was going to acknowledge and defeat his opponent on his opponent's home ground. Webster's patented fugal form of argument was evident; he refuted Hayne's argument, and then returned to it to extend his argument again and again. He began the speech using one of his favorite sublime metaphors: The Senate debate was like a storm-tossed sea. He would guide the ship of state to safe harbor: the Union, the home he was building.

Chasing Hayne from the field, Webster denied what he was actually doing, the trope of apophasis allowing him to expose what Hayne was really about:

> I will not accuse the honorable member of violating the rules of civilized war—I will not say that he poisoned his arrows. But whether his shafts were, or were not, dipped in that which would have caused rankling, if they had reached [their target], these were not, as it happened, quite strength enough in the bow to bring them to their mark. If he wishes now to gather up those shafts, he must look for them elsewhere; they will not be found fixed and quivering in the object at which they were aimed.

Webster smiled as the galleries and his supporters broke into peals of laughter. If that were not enough, Webster's correction of Hayne's understanding of Banquo's role in *Macbeth* left his reputation in tatters.

Hayne disposed of, Webster could advance his more substantive arguments on land use and slavery. He explained how the tariff system had funded an American infrastructure that benefited every state. He showed how the Founders forbade slavery's spread. He used substantial identification to associate his positive ideology with Massachusetts, his home state, and his dystopia with Hayne's state of South Carolina, knowing full well that neither of its senators would vote with Webster. Massachusetts and the West displayed national unity; South Carolina displayed disunion. Here epideictic praise of virtue (union) and blame of vice (disunion) are concealed within the deliberative dialectic. The South would reduce the Union to "four and twenty masters, of different wills and different purposes." If the states were supreme, how would federal courts be able to issue decisions that applied to them?

And then he concluded, and it was like a coda to a symphony, an awesome moment that sought to heal the Senate and the nation by making preservation of the Union a transcendent call:

Would to God that harmony might return! . . . When my eyes shall be turned to behold for the last time the sun in heaven, may I not see him shining on the broken and dishonored fragments of a once glorious Union; on States dissevered, discordant, belligerent; on a land rent with civil feuds, or drenched . . . in fraternal blood! Let their last feeble and lingering glance rather behold the gorgeous ensign of the republic, now known and honored throughout the earth, still full high advanced, its arms and trophies streaming in their original luster, not a strip erased or polluted, not a single star obscured, bearing for its motto, no such miserable interrogatory as "What is all this worth?" nor those words of delusion and folly, "Liberty first and Union afterwards"; but everywhere, spread all over in characters of living light, blazing on all its ample folds, as they float over the sea and over the land, and

in every wind under the whole heavens, the other sentiment, dear to every
American heart—Liberty and Union, now and forever, one and inseparable!

This sublime moment was a transcendent disclosure of the truth. It aided
the nation in its process of becoming a more perfect Union. School children
were required to memorize these words, and thirty-one years later they
could be heard from the lips of Union soldiers going into battle to preserve
the Union and end slavery.

The 1850 Compromise

But before the war, Webster would again be called upon to save the home
the Founders had built. The interruption began in 1846 when President
Polk provoked a war with Mexico. The U.S. victory increased the size of the
nation by 20 percent; in the name of "manifest destiny," Polk had expanded
the nation from sea to shining sea. In 1849, he was succeeded by the Whig
nominee General Zachary Taylor, "old rough and ready," a "hero" of the
Mexican American War. He had won major battles at Monterey, Buena
Vista, Palo Alto, and Resaca de la Palma. However, the election of 1848 also
had created a deadlock between the Whigs and the Democrats. It took 64
ballots to select a Speaker in the House of Representatives. The Senate was
split among Democrats, with a bare majority against Whigs and Free Soilers.[3]
However, party affiliation was not what would produce an impasse; more
important was whether the senator came from a slave state or a free state,
and on that issue, the Senate was evenly divided.

By January 1850 a number of issues had arisen from the recent acquisition
of territory from Mexico. Each issue constituted an interruption to normal
business. First, the president attempted to circumvent the Senate's authority
to admit states into the Union. Taylor encouraged Deseret (now Nevada and
Utah) and California to organize for statehood as free states. The gold rush of
1849 had made the former Republic of California a lucrative holding. Bonds

that had underwritten Texas's war effort needed to be funded. The western boundary of Texas was in dispute. Slave states demanded a fugitive slave law to get their "property" back. Northern states not only wanted the slaves to be freed but sought to end the slave trade in Washington, DC.

Senator Henry Clay of Kentucky rose in the Senate and spent most of February 5 and 6, 1850, laying out an omnibus bill to end the crisis. His speech is an example of rhetoric attempting to achieve a pragmatic result. Clay was confident in his cause; after all, he had engineered the Compromise of 1820. He had been the nominee of his party for president twice. That's why he was given a preeminent position in the speaking order when it came to the crisis of 1850. As Clay issued his call for compromise, the senators listened in rapt attention, acknowledging his place in the leadership. Clay would replace earlier legislation with a provision that each state would determine its own status, slave or free, based on "popular sovereignty" in that state. Hence, Clay would admit California without making a predisposition as to slavery; its geography would determine if slavery would work there.[4] Clay would grant the Territory of New Mexico its claim to lands east of the Rio Grande River. To compensate Texas for this loss of territory, Clay would fund Texas's bonds. Clay's legislation would end the slave trade in the District of Columbia but permit ownership of slaves there and where permitted by states. He would have fugitive slaves returned to their owners.

It soon became clear that Clay had spoken too soon and missed his mark. The majority of senators were not ready to save his reconstructed home. His speech was not an example of fitting timing, though as we shall see, it contained all the elements necessary for compromise. Clay's speech is a good example of *kosmos* (form) not being enough to achieve persuasion; *kairos* (timing) is essential also. Clay's failure can be seen in the actions that followed. Slave states called for a convention in June to discuss secession from the Union. Though a slave owner himself, the president claimed he would hang all "traitors," meaning those who would foment secession. Another telling moment in the crisis came on March 4 when the very ill John C. Calhoun of South Carolina came to the floor of the Senate to hear his speech read into the record by a colleague. It was a major interruption, not unlike Hayne's of 1830. The speech denounced Clay's bill and the president's plans for statehood. Ominously, Calhoun offered no other solution to states' rights. He would build twenty-four homes, reducing the Union to a confederation. The dialectic was electric: slave states versus free states; union versus secession.

The next major speech came on March 7; it was delivered by Webster. Realizing the time for compromise in the Congress had not come, Webster did not speak to his colleagues in their acrimonious dwelling place. He realized that the Senate had yet to hear from the young lions who needed their turn to roar. Abolitionists like William Seward of New York, an ally of the president, would lay out his agenda and attack the Clay compromise on March 12. Senator Stephen A. Douglas of Illinois would endorse popular sovereignty as the only way out of the logjam. Southern senators would rally around Calhoun's rationalization of slavery, especially when he died at the end of March. So, on March 7, Webster addressed moderates in the North and South in an effort to create an atmosphere of compromise in the public in the hope that they would then exert influence on the elected representatives in the House and Senate. Once again, he sought to make the Union a dwelling place for compromise. He realized that abolitionists were a minority even in the North, and that slave owners were a minority even in the South. So, he carved them away from his compromise. While he was denounced by abolitionists and slave owners, he struck a chord with bondholders and those wishing to preserve the Union. Thus, he strove to deduce a synthesis from the dialectic that he could invoke when the time was right.

The debacle continued into the summer of 1850. Disheartened, Clay retreated to his hemp plantation in Kentucky. And then events conspired to create an opportune moment for compromise. After drinking bourbon and cream that covered pitted cherries, he ate the cherries as he celebrated the Fourth of July. President Taylor then contracted cholera morbus and died five days later. Millard Filmore, a protégé of Webster, became president and immediately appointed Webster secretary of state. He was quickly confirmed by the Senate and then gave a farewell address on July 17, seizing the moment to lay out a plan for his version of compromise. While it had most of the elements of Clay's original proposal, it called for the formation of shifting majorities to adopt each part of the proposal as a single piece of legislation rather than as an omnibus bill as Clay had suggested. Moderates were to swing between the more ideological Northern or Southern voting blocs to achieve the necessary majorities for each part of the compromise.

Webster's stroke of genius was to shift between transcendence and pragmatism whenever they suited his purpose. If an issue was divisive, he asked for compromise. It would be necessary to swallow a bitter pill to save the nation. And saving the nation was not only important for prosperity; a war would cost many lives. Thus, he endorsed the Fugitive Slave Act. If an issue had more consensus, he elevated it to the spiritual level. Paying of the Texas bonds won the support of Texans and northern bondholders. Supporting this legislation would save the Union. On support for the Union, Webster had impeccable credentials extending back to 1830 when he had issued his call for "liberty and union, one and inseparable, now and forever." He had heard the call of Union then, and he heard it again in 1850. Translating the call for his colleagues, on July 17, 1850, he concluded, "No man can suffer too much, and no man can fall too soon, if he suffer or if he fall in defense of the liberties and constitution of his country."5 That was the dwelling place into which Webster moved his audience. Now all that was left was some housekeeping.

While assuming the office of secretary of state and drafting messages for President Filmore, Webster worked tirelessly in the House and the Senate to pass the Compromise of 1850. Senator Douglas became the floor manager of the legislation in the Senate following Webster's instructions of July 17. On September 6, the first legislation passed the House. By September 20, the compromise legislation was signed by President Fillmore, and the citizens of the District of Columbia celebrated with fireworks, bonfires, and demonstrations of relief. They gathered in front of Webster's townhouse a block from the presidential mansion and cheered until he joined the celebration.

Having been educated in classical rhetorical theory at Dartmouth, Webster understood Gorgias's notion of fitting timing. Once he sensed that an impasse had been reached, he tried to re-create the Union as a dwelling place for compromise, first for the nation at large and then for the Senate. Once events created an opportunity to break the logjam, he seized the moment and laid out a plan to overcome the difficulties. He sold that plan using his rhetorical skill to appeal to transcendent and pragmatic values. However, we would be remiss if we did not note that Webster had a keen power of observation when it came to assessing his primary audience, the Senate. He realized that allowing a certain amount of role playing would be necessary before the fitting time for a compromise would be realized. All the major players needed to lay their cards on the table before the game could end. That the final legislative resolution was almost identical to Clay's original proposals is a testament to this phenomenon. Clay had the right answer at the wrong time. Webster used dialectical reasoning to provide the right answer and the right time. His judgment calls led the Senate to affirm his compromise.

Furthermore, Webster realized that the drama had to play out over time. It was fortuitous for the compromise that the president died, that Webster's protégé became president, that Webster became secretary of state, and that he was able from that post to coordinate the final compromise. There is also something to be said for the role of exhaustion in this category of speeches of "fitting timing." In many cases, when a political body reaches a stalemate, it is exhaustion on both sides that overcomes the logjam. Then again, as with Webster, if incentives for both sides can be found, then success is all the more likely. The role of acknowledgment in all of this should not be underestimated. Webster acknowledged that Texans wanted their boundaries fixed, their runaway slaves returned, and their bonds paid off. He acknowledged that Northerners wanted "popular sovereignty" in the West and an end to the slave trade in the District of Columbia. His genius was to deploy a strategy of shifting majorities, swinging between the dialectical sides with single up-and-down votes that allowed each side to have some of the things they wanted.

The Compromise of 1850 was not perfect. The Fugitive Slave Act was the height of immorality, ignoring the calls of conscience issued by such abolitionists as Harriet Beecher Stowe and Frederick Douglass. However, on this occasion, Webster was not trying to perfect the Union, he was trying to save it. Had no compromise been reached, Southern states might well have seceded from the Union, fomenting a civil war that the North was ill-equipped to win. The Compromise of 1850, flawed though it was, delayed the inevitable war for a decade during which time the North was able to prepare for such an eventuality.

Webster died in the fall of 1852 having failed to obtain the nomination of his party for president. He would not live to see the home he had built, the Union, ripped asunder over the slave issue. He would not hear the voices of Northern soldiers charging into battle uttering his words of true eloquence from 1830 when he stood against slavery: "Liberty and Union, now and forever, one and inseparable." Many corrections that perfected the Union followed: Amendments to the Constitution acknowledged that black men were citizens, not property, and the same acknowledgment was extended to women; other amendments provided equal protection under and due process of the law; social programs helped the aged and the poor; wars sought to make the world safe for democracy. However, as we shall see in ensuing chapters, we do not yet dwell in a perfect union. There is much work still to be done.

Ronald Reagan's Last State of the Union Address

Presidents George Washington and John Adams delivered their State of the Union addresses to a joint session of Congress, acknowledging it with their presence. However, Thomas Jefferson, who was somewhat uncomfortable with public-speaking situations because of his stammering, decided that as part of his revolution, he would write his State of the Union as a message to Congress from a distant president. The new tradition continued through the administration of William Howard Taft, whose Inaugural read like a State of the Union Address and whose State of the Union addresses were epically detailed. President Woodrow Wilson, as part of his progressive agenda, decided that acknowledging the Congress in person as had Washington would be a major improvement in relations with Congress, which the Democrats had conquered in the 1912 election. And ever since, presidents have trudged up Capitol Hill to deliver their annual State of the Union Address in person.

Many scholars have written about State of the Union addresses. Their work is summarized and advanced by Karlyn Kohrs Campbell and Kathleen Jamieson in their book *Deeds Done in Words: Presidential Rhetoric and Genres of Governance*. Campbell and Jamieson make clear that these addresses are often a hodgepodge of programs that reflect the input of many executive departments. They "vary greatly" and often catalog "unrelated concerns or policies."[6] They also point out that "In the State of the Union Address, presidents revive principles to which they committed their presidencies," most of the time in their Inaugural addresses.[7]

Delivered on January 26, 1982, Reagan's first State of the Union Address followed a terrible tragedy in Washington. On January 13 an Air Florida jet with too much ice on its wings began to falter after takeoff from Washington's National Airport. (Ironically, now Washington's Reagan Airport.) The plane slammed into the 14th Street Bridge spanning the icy Potomac River at rush hour, crushing cars and pushing others into the frigid water below. Becoming a hero, Lenny Skutnik dove into those freezing waters and rescued several survivors. During his address, Ronald Reagan praised Skutnik's display of heroism. When Skutnik rose from his seat next to the First Lady to acknowledge the applause, the House was no longer divided, and Americans could take pride in the virtue of one man that showed forth. Ronald Reagan made that happen and a new tradition was established. It would continue through every State of the Union Address of every president to the current time, as we have seen.

On the morning of January 25, 1988, members of Congress and the administration awoke to exciting possibilities. That night President Reagan would deliver his final State of the Union Address. The venue would provide the last chance to dress up and cheer the old man in his best venue. Reagan's State of the Union addresses had become legendary for their conversational delivery, openness, clarity, style, and originality. Reagan had set a high bar for his addresses and rarely failed to achieve it. There were several important components of the scene into which the address would be injected. First, it was again election time in an America that was moving toward the Iowa caucuses. The vice president of the United States was the leading candidate on the Republican side and was favored to succeed over such rivals as former White House chief of staff Alexander Haig, Senator Bob Dole, and Delaware governor Pete Dupont. Leading Democrats included Massachusetts governor Michael Dukakis and New Jersey senator Bill Bradley.

When the election year began, CBS News decided to provide its viewers with profiles of these candidates. Several segments had run by January 25, 1988, the date of the State of the Union Address. Dan Rather, the anchor and managing editor of the *CBS Evening News*, believed that evening would be an excellent time to run a profile of Bush, since later in the evening he would be sitting behind Reagan as the president addressed the joint session of Congress. Negotiating what Bush and Rather would talk about and how the profile would be constructed became contentious. Roger Ailes, Bush's media consultant and eventually president of Fox News, demanded that the interview be live and unedited. The producer of the *CBS Evening News* agreed. Ailes demanded that like other candidates, Bush be asked about both domestic and international issues. The producer agreed. Finally, Ailes demanded that the interview not center on the Iran-Contra scandal, but a question or two on that topic was not ruled out. The producer agreed.[8] Thus, at 6:30 p.m., eastern standard time, the *CBS News with Dan Rather* went on the air live as the vice president sat in his office in the Old Executive Office Building with Roger Ailes behind the camera waiting for the interview.

Bush and Ailes were infuriated by what followed. First, there was a long story about Bush's involvement in the Iran-Contra deal and particularly the involvement of his aide, Hugh Gregg, who had been with Bush since his days as director of the CIA. Ailes warned Bush that he was about to be ambushed, but not to throw the first punch. Ailes told Bush to counterpunch.

After a commercial break, Rather began the live interview with Bush. He started with Iran-Contra, and Bush stuck by his story that he was out of the loop on the proposal. Rather pointed out that former secretary of state George Schultz claimed that Bush was in the room when the arms swap was discussed with the president. Bush denied the claim and requested that Rather move on to other issues. Rather refused and began questioning Bush about Hugh Gregg's involvement in the affair. Bush bristled and said that like other candidates who had been the subject of these profiles, he wanted to talk about domestic issues. Instead, Rather became more aggressive on the arms scandal. Bush then said to Rather, "How would you like it if someone just focused on one thing you did in your career? How would you like it if all people remembered was when you walked off that set in Miami?" Bush was referring to an incident in which Rather became peeved when a sporting event on CBS went overtime and Rather refused to wait to start the news and walked off the set. Rather looked stunned but pushed on, "Mr. Vice President, I think you'll agree your qualifications for president. . . . are much more important than what you just referred to." He then asked Bush to participate in a full press conference on the issue. Bush responded that he had done eighty-six news conferences since March of 1987. Rather responded, "I gather the answer is no. Thank you very much for being with us." Turning away from the monitor on which Bush's face could be seen, Rather said, "We'll be back in a moment," cutting Bush off. It did not take long for the infamous interruption to make the rounds of Washington. It became a national sensation that for some proved CBS was liberal and biased against Republicans in general, and Bush in particular.[9] The event provided the immediate context for Reagan's State of the Union Address and undoubtedly increased its viewing audience.

Three hours later, the president arrived in the House Chamber to more than the usual huzzahs and cheers. Even though the House and Senate were now in the hands of the Democrats, civility demanded that Reagan be given his due during this last State of the Union Address. As he moved up to the dais, Reagan handed a copy of his speech of the Speaker of the House, Tip O'Neal, and another to Bush, both of whom sat behind a high desk that was behind Reagan. He began by acknowledging the long tenure of his presidency but said, "Let's leave that to history: we're not finished yet. My message to you tonight is, put on your work shoes—we're still on the job." The line brought the house down and all seemed relieved to see that the "Great Communicator" was up to the evening. Reagan was not about to go quietly into this good night. He was going to offer an interruption of his own. Reagan reasserted his philosophy and turned to his first use of an inartistic proof: "Chinese philosopher, Lao-tzu, said, 'Govern a great nation as you would cook a small fish; do not overdo it.'" The line won more applause, but more importantly signaled one of Reagan's most important inventions for the State of the Union Address. His effective use of inartistic proofs had included live bodies in the House gallery such as Lenny Skutnik. What, one wondered, would Reagan pull out of his hat tonight?

The epideictic tone continued for a few more paragraphs emphasizing individualism and the people granting rights to the government, not the other way around. This platform was used to support a spirit of bipartisanship, a key plank in Reagan's home. Reagan said he hoped it would pervade the Congress. He also had shown authenticity on bipartisanship, which gave him added credibility. For example, he had worked with Speaker O'Neal on several legislative projects, and it was common for legislation to be written and sponsored by members of each party. In short, it was a time when the Congress was a comfortable and welcoming dwelling place. Reagan sought to perfect that home. Further enhancing his ethos, Reagan recounted the achievements of his administration in terms of jobs created, rising income, and the expansion of international democracy. He touted a strong, rebuilt defense that featured his Strategic Defense Initiative, a program that was aimed at spending the Soviets into the ground, though Reagan would not admit to that part of the program in this speech.[10] He then claimed that for all these reasons the state of the Union was healthy.

After this introduction, Reagan announced that his speech would be organized around "four basic objectives," each attempting to perfect the American home. The first focused on strengthening the economy. The second emphasized social programs, particularly schools. The third focused on global strategies for economic development and the spread of democracy. The fourth objective was to enhance national security. This was an important and effective move since it consolidated his speech in understandable blocks instead of covering 51 issues in 51 minutes, which is too often the case with State of the Union addresses. Reagan made sure the audience always knew where he was and where he was going in his State of the Union addresses. For example, after reiterating that he wanted to work hard to make his last year his best, he cited his guiding principles. He then turned to economic growth as the vice president and the Speaker could be seen turning pages and following along behind the president. Reagan's underrated use of statistics could be seen in this section as he wove evidence into the speech: "We have had a balanced budget only 8 times in the last 57 years. For the first time in 14 years, the federal government has spent less in real terms last year than the year before. We took $73 billion off last year's deficit. . . . The deficit itself has moved from 6.3% of the Gross National Product to only 3.4%." As he often did, Reagan then concluded his litany of statistics with a punch line: "I can assure you, the bipartisan leadership of Congress, of my help in fighting off any attempt to bust our budget agreement. And this includes the swift and certain use of the veto."[11]

Two paragraphs later, Reagan launched another litany that was prologue to the most unconventional interruptions of this or any other State of the Union Address. Reagan pointed out that only ten of ninety-one appropriation bills had made it to his desk on time. To plug the budget gap, Reagan claimed, "Last year, of the 13 appropriations bills due by October 1st, none of them made it. Instead, we had four continuing resolutions lasting 41 days, then 36

days, and two days, and three days. And then along came these behemoths."
Suddenly, everyone's attention, including that of the television camera,
was drawn to tall stacks of paper sitting near the president. He moved over
and lifted one up and brought it back to his lectern: "This is the conference
report—a 1,053-page report weighing 14 pounds." He plopped the stack down
to much laughter and picked up another one. "Then this—a reconciliation
bill six months late . . . 1186 pages long, weighing 15 pounds." He plopped
it down and picked up another stack, again to continuing laughter and
cheers. "The long-term continuing resolution—1057 pages long, weighing
14 pounds." He plopped it down and then continued, to much laughter,
"That was a total of 43 pounds of paper and ink. You had three hours—yes,
three hours—to consider each one, and it took 300 people at my Office of
Management and Budget just to read the bill so the government wouldn't
shut down. Congress should not send another one of these. . . . and if you do,
I will not sign it." The House Chamber erupted with applause and cheers.
This passage is signature Reagan taken to new heights: the use of a litany of
statistics, visually illustrated by heavy inartistic proofs, and concluded with
an effective punch line. Nothing after that point in the speech would get as
much attention.

The president continued by calling for a line-item veto and was cheered
by Republicans but only politely applauded by Democrats. However, Reagan
effectively supported this call with another litany of inartistic proofs that
listed what we now call earmarks, amendments to bills that provided special
projects to congressional districts. Reagan called for education and welfare
reforms. On welfare, Reagan uttered this epideictic line contributed by
speechwriter Peggy Noonan: "There are a thousand sparks of genius in 50
states."[12] True to his conservative calling, Reagan used his appeal to endorse
more responsibility for states and less for the federal government. On the
issue of drugs, Reagan returned to his patented use of inartistic proofs. And
again, he was unconventional. The interruption went this way: "The war
against drugs is a war of individual battles, a crusade of many heroes—including . . . someone very special to me. . . . Nancy, much credit belongs to

you, and I want to express to you your husband's pride and your country's thanks." The audience cheered as the First Lady stood. Then Reagan added a personal touch. He said to his wife: "Surprised you, didn't I?" That tender moment served as an effective segue into family issues and values, again mixing in epideictic moments to support deliberative objectives. Reagan's agenda was self-described as Judeo-Christian and even called for a "school prayer amendment." To enforce his philosophy, Reagan called for the quick approval of Judge Anthony Kennedy to the Supreme Court along with twenty-seven nominees to the federal bench. Reagan's success in placing conservatives on the federal bench may be his longest-lasting legacy.

Reagan moved to international matters beginning with trade agreements. These would eventually lead to the North American Free Trade Agreement negotiated by President George H. W. Bush, just as Reagan's defense spending would lead to the fall of the Soviet Union under Bush. He called on the Senate to approve his INF treaty and claimed to be within reach of a missile reduction treaty with the Soviet Union. He called for continued support for his Strategic Defense Initiative, which the media had dubbed "star wars" in 1983. Their attempt at ridicule had backfired; a public enamored of George Lucas's films adopted the phrase and supported the program.

Reagan argued that progress was being made in Latin America's march toward democracy. His proof played right into the Iran-Contra scandal, which had been the subject of Dan Rather's scathing attack on Bush. Having won over the audience, Reagan could now help Vice President Bush: "The Sandinista regime knows the tide is turning and the cause of Nicaraguan freedom is riding at its crest. Because of the freedom fighters . . . the Sandinistas have been forced to extend some democratic rights, negotiate with Church authorities, and release a few political prisoners." Reagan then called on Congress to "sustain the freedom fighters," clearly indicating that the Iran-Contra crisis was behind him. In fact, Reagan claimed that we could be for Nicaragua what foreigners like "Lafayette, Pulaski, and Von Stuben" were to the American Revolution. There was no apology for any actions he or his vice president had taken. And no reference to the attack by Rather.

Reagan then called for support of the Mujahedeen in Afghanistan and for the removal of all Soviet troops from that nation.[13] As he moved to his conclusion, Reagan once again turned to inartistic proofs: Jacob Shallus of the Pennsylvania General Assembly, who wrote the preamble to the Constitution, and Abraham Lincoln, who elevated its goals in his Gettysburg Address. Reagan closed by taking his audience outside of the House Chamber and down to the Potomac where they could see the lights of Washington, DC, reflected in the river. It symbolized his "shining city on a hill."

Conclusion

Reagan demonstrated a mastery of the use of diverse inartistic proofs running from the citation of a Chinese philosopher through myriad statistics to physical props and finally to his wife. These proofs held the attention of the audience, provoked cheers, and explain in part the success of his State of the Union Address. Reagan's acknowledgment of heroes emphasized the virtues he sought to reinforce.

Clearly, deliberative eloquence can achieve great things. Webster's deliberative interruptions constructed a home that united and sustained the nation in 1830. He then saved that house from being divided in 1850. Reagan maintained an aura of comfort and cooperation even as he chided Congress for its budgetary indiscretions in 1988. Obviously, Reagan and Webster did not always achieve perfection in their deliberative utterances, but they did help to perfect the home they came to live in.

CHAPTER 6

Forensic Eloquence

I n the Gospel of Mark, there comes a moment when Jesus is confronted by the Jewish scribes. These were important men who copied the sacred scrolls and interpreted them for their people. In so doing, they were the architects of the house of Judaism. Jesus had engaged in casting out devils, and the scribes judged him guilty of a high crime; he was the anti-Christ because only the prince of devils could cast out devils. Jesus defended himself by pointing out that if the prince of devils cast out devils then he was the head of a house divided against itself, and "A house divided against itself cannot stand."[1] Jesus would later argue that the same was true of Judaism; if it divided it could not stand. These were heady words at a time when the Jews were under the thumb of the Roman Empire and divided among themselves between Pharisees and Sadducees, not to mention smaller, more rebellious sects who, like Jesus, threatened the peace with Rome. As a rabbi and the self-proclaimed messiah, Jesus hoped to perfect this house by uniting it behind a major reform that threatened the common sense of the Jewish leaders. Jesus emphasized intent over effect, a loving God, and faith over the strict laws of the Pharisees. He utterly failed in that task but brought forth with the help of his disciples a new faith that provided a new house to countless believers around the world.

In 1858 as he accepted the nomination of his party for the U.S. Senate, Abraham Lincoln stood up in Springfield, Illinois, having heard the call of conscience. He condemned slavery. In the course of his address, he echoed Jesus, saying, "A house divided against itself cannot stand." Lincoln's house was the Union. To perfect and save the Union, Lincoln would permit slavery only where it already existed but not allow it to spread into the territories and new states admitted to the Union. Lincoln utterly failed. He was not elected to the Senate, and when he was elected to the presidency two years later, seven Southern states seceded from the Union before he was inaugurated. The South had taken on an otherness; it was alienated from the North. The divided house had fallen. That interruption provided Lincoln with new opportunity to provide an address that was fitting. Lincoln took on the task of rebuilding the house that divided. He began in his First Inaugural Address by trying to prevent war and save the Union through reconciliation. His eloquence was readily apparent as was his call for his listeners to reach for the moral high ground: "We are not enemies, but friends. We must not be enemies. Though passion may have strained, it must not break our bonds of affection. The mystic chords of memory will swell when again touched, as surely they will be, by the better angels of our nature." His truly eloquent call was rejected by the South, and a horrific war ensued in which over half a million would die.

It was only after the battle of Antietam that Lincoln felt confident enough in eventual victory that he issued his limited Emancipation Proclamation. After Gettysburg, Lincoln felt secure enough to make another call to rebuild the Union. In November 1863, in perhaps the shortest and most eloquent speech of his presidency, Lincoln called for a house of, by, and for the people that shall not perish from this earth. In March 1865, he delivered his Second Inaugural Address and, at the end, described the forgiving and caring nature of the dwelling he sought for his people: "With malice toward none, with charity for all, with firmness in the right as God gives us to see the right, let us strive on to finish the work we are in, to bind up the nation's wounds, to care for him who shall have borne the battle and for his widow and his orphan, to do all which may achieve and cherish a just and lasting peace among ourselves and with all nations." Lincoln was martyred a month later. His party ruled the country, divided between those who wanted to follow the path of mercy and those who wanted retribution for the terrible price they had to pay to save the Union. The otherness and alienation of the South was reinforced as it was divided into five military districts governed by five Union generals. This "Reconstruction" of the South would last until 1876; the backlash would put in place racial discrimination that lasts to this day. However, Lincoln's legacy survived in the amendments to the Constitution near the end of the war and following it. His Emancipation Proclamation was expanded into the Thirteenth Amendment, freeing all of the slaves. The Fourteenth Amendment provides equal protection under, and due process of, the law. The Fifteenth Amendment gives black men the vote. Jesus and Lincoln were rhetorically ineffective. They failed in the short run. However, their eloquence in the service of truth eventually prevailed and their sentiments inspire us still.

Earlier in this book, we examined Aristotle's construction of judicious eloquence; it was tempered by prudence and constructed on credible evidence and valid argument. One of the forms he described was forensic public address, which usually took place before a judge and/or jury. Its ultimate aim was justice and its subject matter was guilt or innocence. In this chapter, we provide three case studies of that form. In each case, the jury is the United States Senate and the speakers are senators wrestling with their consciences in public. They are also trying to bring civility to the Senate to make it a more perfect dwelling place for deliberative public address.

Senator Margaret Chase Smith

The meteoric rise, juggernaut, and fall that became known as the McCarthy era lasted over four years, from the winter of 1950 to the fall of 1954. McCarthy cheated eloquence by playing into national paranoia. In 1946 when Winston Churchill launched his Iron Curtain metaphor at Westminster College in Missouri, a Cold War began between the nations of the North Atlantic Treaty

Organization and the Soviet Union. Realizing the threat of subversion, President Truman called for government employees to take an oath of loyalty to the United States. In 1948, the undersecretary of state, Alger Hiss, was found guilty of perjury for testifying that he had not been a member of the Communist Party. In 1949, China fell to the Communist regime of Mao Tse Tung and the Soviet Union exploded their first atom bomb. In 1950, the UN, under the leadership of the United States, entered the Korean War, and Julius and Ethel Rosenberg were found guilty of espionage and sentenced to death.

It was simple for McCarthy to claim that while the Soviet Union constituted an external threat, subversives in the Department of State constituted an internal threat that had abetted the Communist expansion. Senator Joseph McCarthy revived the paranoid style of the Populists of the 1890s.[2] It didn't seem to matter to his audiences that the numbers McCarthy produced were erratic. In the first speech to gain national attention in the winter of 1950, McCarthy waved a hotel laundry list at a gathering of Republican women in Wheeling, West Virginia, and claimed that it held the names of 205 subversives in the State Department. In Salt Lake City, perhaps inspired by a Heinz ketchup bottle, he claimed there were 57 subversives in the State Department.

The tragic manipulation of the facts led to dire consequences. Professors who took the Fifth Amendment when asked about their past and/or present affiliations were fired even if they had tenure. Actors and writers who tried to exercise their First and Fifth Amendment rights when called before the House Un-American Activities Committee were blacklisted. Libraries were intimidated into removing books from their shelves that hinted at socialism, let alone Communism. Roy Cohn, McCarthy's lawyer and henchman, went on a tour of State Department libraries in American embassies and removed books he labeled as subversive.

While no one seemed able to stop McCarthy until he undid himself during the Army-McCarthy hearings, there were many who tried. One of the most heroic was Senator Margaret Chase Smith, a Republican senator from Maine. Shortly after her husband's death, she won a special election to her husband's seat in the House of Representatives in 1940. She was overwhelmingly reelected in the regular election of 1940 on a platform of military preparedness. She favored alliances and a bipartisan foreign policy in the face of the America First Movement. In 1947, she strongly recommended integration of the armed forces. She continued to serve in the House until her election to the U.S. Senate in 1948. In that primary, the Republican Party endorsed her opponent because she had crossed party lines on several crucial House votes. Nonetheless, she prevailed overwhelmingly in the primary and in the general election that followed. She thus became the first woman to be elected to both Houses of Congress. It was not long into her Senate term that she recognized the national paranoia and the threat that McCarthy posed. On June 1, 1950, on the way to the floor of the Senate, she crossed paths with McCarthy. He asked her if she were going to speak. She told him she was and that he was not going to like it. Standing in the Senate wearing her trademark rosebud on her lapel, she delivered what she called a "Declaration of Conscience." And so it was that Senator Smith became the first politician of note to challenge McCarthy, and she did so in her house and his, the floor of the United States Senate.

She got right to the point, addressing "a national feeling of fear and frustration that could result in national suicide."[3] The phrase was dramatic, stunning, and immediately got the attention of her audience. She claimed that her colleagues and the Truman administration were to blame because of their indifference to McCarthy's unconstitutional investigations. She continued to hold attention by saying her remarks would be brief and to the point, something rare in the Senate. Using repetition and personal identification, she spoke eloquently while condemning eloquence that cheated:

> I speak as briefly as possible because too much harm has already been done with irresponsible words of bitterness and selfish political opportunism. I speak as simply as possible because the issue is too great to be obscured by

eloquence. I speak simply and briefly in the hope that my words will be taken to heart. Mr. President, I speak as a Republican. I speak as a woman. I speak as a United States senator. I speak as an American.

She praised the Senate for having been a great deliberative body. However, she claimed that this house had been sullied: "Recently that deliberative character has too often been debased to the level of a forum of hate and character assassination sheltered by the shield of congressional immunity."4 She pondered the irony of being able to defame any citizen while on the floor of the Senate, but being unable to criticize a colleague without being called "out of order." Heroically, she made clear she was about to break that rule.

She had searched her soul, heard her conscience, and sought to have her colleagues follow suit. It was at this point that Smith pivoted into the forensic mode: "I think that it is high time that we remembered that the Constitution, as amended, speaks not only of the freedom of speech but also of trial by jury instead of trial by accusation." It is not those who shout the loudest that have the most respect for the right to criticize and to be criticized. They ignore the right "to hold unpopular beliefs . . . to protest . . . to original thought." Attacking the reputation of others simply because they disagree with us is to challenge the "soul" of the other. Invoking a phrase from 1984, which George Orwell published in 1948, she said such conformism was tantamount to "thought control." Using the refrain "the American people are sick and tired," Smith condemned "smear" tactics that in the current environment "cause nationwide distrust and strong suspicion that there may be something to the unproved, sensational accusations." She then appealed to her party, "the party of Lincoln," to behave honorably. She stated that because of the failure of the current administration, the Republicans had the opportunity to reunite the country without resorting to innuendo and fallacious reasoning. Using a reference to the Book of Revelation, she said, "But I do not want to see the Republican party ride to political victory on the Four Horsemen of Calumny: Fear, Ignorance, Bigotry, and Smear."

Smith then identified herself as she sought to widen her audience from the Senate and her party to women nationally: "As a woman, I wonder how the mothers, wives, sisters, and daughters feel about the way in which members of their families have been politically mangled in Senate debate—and I use the word 'debate' advisedly." Returning to address her fellow Republicans and using another refrain, "I am not proud of," she condemned the practices of her colleagues, including the use of "reckless and unproven charges that have been made on this side of the aisle." In a neat set of antitheses that encapsulated the crisis before her, Smith issued a call of conscience to both parties: "As an American, I do not want a Democratic administration 'whitewash' or 'coverup' any more than I want a Republican smear or witch hunt. As an American, I condemn a Republican Fascist just as much as I condemn a Democrat Communist. I condemn a Democrat Fascist just as much as I condemn a Republican Communist."

She then read from the "declaration" that had been signed by six other Republican senators and entered it into the record. In part, the declaration urged

1. Senators to put loyalty to country before loyalty to party.
2. The Truman administration to clarify the crisis the nation faced.
3. An end to "political exploitation of fear, bigotry, ignorance, and intolerance."
4. Senators to admit that they have played into the Communist game of confusing, dividing, and conquering our nation.
5. Senators to start "thinking patriotically as Americans about national security based on individual freedom."

Despite McCarthy's ensuing attack on Smith, she won the support of other senators and was praised across the nation in the media. Sadly, her heroic speech fell on deaf ears for the most part in the Senate and on the hustings across America where McCarthy prevailed. He often came to states whose members of Congress opposed him and his tactics in an effort to defeat them in primary and general elections. McCarthy continued to use fascistic rhetoric to manipulate the public for four more years, including scare tactics, guilt by association, big lies, scapegoating, and exaggerations of internal threats to America. He supported his assertions using cropped photos or phony "classified" information. It was fake news. But not to his supporters, who ignored an investigating committee that called McCarthy's charges a "fraud and a hoax perpetrated on the Senate of the United States and the American people."[5] McCarthy expanded his coalition to Chinese missionaries and the military dispossessed, who supported General MacArthur's frustrated attempt to take the UN "police action" into Red China. The coalition included Joseph P. Kennedy and other anti-Communist Democrats.[6] Intimidating even such liberals as Senator Hubert Humphrey, McCarthy was able to pass the Subversive Activities Control Act in 1950 and the McCarran-Walter Immigration Act in 1952 over President Truman's veto.[7] In that year, his rhetoric of purification was featured at the Republican Convention in Chicago:

> I say, one Communist in a defense plant is one Communist too many. One Communist on the faculty of one university is one Communist too many. One Communist among American advisors at Yalta was one Communist too many. And even if there were only one Communist in the State Department, that would be one Communist too many.[8]

McCarthy then appeared on campaign platforms with such prominent Republicans as Senators William Jenner, Karl Mundt, and Kenneth Wherry, the Senate minority leader. When Private David Schine claimed he had evidence of Communist infiltration into the Army, McCarthy seized on the opening. On February 18, 1954, "McCarthy exploded into a personal attack on General Zwicker, roughing him up verbally and humiliating him."[9] That led to McCarthy's alienation from President Eisenhower, an attack by Edward R. Murrow on CBS in March, and thirty-six days of Army-McCarthy Hearings that summer that halted the McCarthy juggernaut.[10] Joseph Welch, the attorney for the Army, heard the call of conscience when McCarthy attacked one of Welch's aides, claiming he had been a member of a Communist front organization. Looking directly at McCarthy and carried live on television, Welch broke through McCarthy's seemingly impenetrable veneer with true eloquence:

> Until this moment, Senator, I think I have never really gauged your cruelty or your recklessness. Fred Fisher is a young man who went to Harvard Law School and came into my firm and is starting what looks to be a brilliant career with us.... Little did I dream you could be so reckless and so cruel as to do an injury to that lad. It is true he is still with Hale and Dorr. It is true that he will continue to be with Hale and Dorr. It is, I regret to say, equally true that I fear he shall always bear a scar needlessly inflicted by you. If it were in my power to forgive you for your reckless cruelty I would do so. I like to think I am a gentleman, but your forgiveness will have to come from someone other than me.

While Roy Cohn sat beside McCarthy shaking his head, McCarthy renewed the attack. Welch again broke in, "Senator, may we not drop this? We know he belonged to the Lawyers Guild. . . . Let us not assassinate this lad further, Senator. You've done enough. Have you no sense of decency, sir? At long last, have you left no sense of decency?"

A four-year nightmare was over. In the fall of 1954, the Senate censored McCarthy; he became a pariah until his death in 1957 of cirrhosis of the liver. Unlike Margaret Chase Smith, McCarthy was rhetorically effective in the short run but condemned in perpetuity. Margaret Chase Smith pursued a stellar career in the United States Senate and was often referred to as its conscience.

Senator Susan Collins

On October 5, 2018, the public was witness to an example of the eloquence of fitting timing when the U.S. Senate took up the confirmation of President Trump's nomination of Brett Kavanaugh to the Supreme Court. The context of this particular confrontation cannot be understood unless it is contextualized in the recent history of the conflict between the parties over the nomination of judges. When President Lyndon Johnson decided to promote his friend Abe Fortas from associate to chief justice of the Supreme Court, it was discovered that Fortas had ruled in a case where he had a conflict of interest. Fortas resigned from the Court, but the event left a bitter taste in the president's mouth. In the next administration, President Nixon, in pursuit of his Southern strategy, nominated G. Harold Carswell to the Supreme Court. However, it was soon discovered that he had given a racist speech many years earlier. The nomination was withdrawn, and Nixon nominated Judge Clement Haynsworth of South Carolina to replace Carswell. During its investigation, the FBI found that Haynsworth had a minor conflict of interest in a case he had ruled on. That was enough to remove him from contention given the "Fortas standard." William Rehnquist was finally nominated and confirmed for the seat.

The next controversial nomination was that of Robert Bork, who sat on the D.C. Court of Appeals in 1987. Bork had published articles indicating that he was a strict constructionist reader of the Constitution. Before hearings even began, various groups led by Senators Joe Biden and Edward Kennedy announced their opposition. The problem for his opponents was that Bork had no conflicts of interest or other blemishes on his record. His only sin was being a conservative who defended his ideology in legal journals. When the Senate Judiciary voted him down, Republicans were incensed, arguing that Bork had been vetoed on ideological grounds, which had not happened before.

President George H. W. Bush faced the next challenge in the nomination process. Bush wanted to put a conservative on the Court but worried that he or she might face the same fate as Bork. Bush's solution was to nominate Clarence Thomas to the Court, a black man who had been raised in poverty in Pin Point, Georgia. Thomas was the head of the Civil Rights Commission with a solid record of attacking racial bias from that position. The Bush administration relied on the narrative of Thomas's life to persuade senators to support the nomination. However, after the first round of hearings, an aide to Senator Biden found an FBI report that had been overlooked. The report contained an accusation by Anita Hill that while in Thomas's employ, she had been sexually harassed by him. A new round of hearings was scheduled at which Anita Hill was treated to some very rough questioning. Then Thomas was called back to the stand, where he emotionally denied the charges and claimed to be a victim of a "high tech lynching." His nomination was barely approved as both sides condemned the tactics of the other.

Kavanaugh's hearing went through a process similar to Thomas's. His first set of hearings were uneventful. Then the leaking of a letter to the FBI led to a disruption. Was Kavanaugh truly a highly qualified nominee to the high court? Or was he a sexual harasser when intoxicated? A contentious second round of hearings before the Senate Judiciary Committee was convened. There Kavanaugh was accused of inappropriate behavior at a private party while he was in high school. On one side of the emerging dialectic was his accuser, Christine Ford, a professor of psychology at Palo Alto University and a research psychologist at Stanford University. She calmly told the story of being attacked by the then seventeen-year-old Kavanaugh while at a house party when she was fifteen. While witnesses were produced who claimed Ford had told them about the event, no witness of the event itself came forward. Her story was further weakened when the four people she alleged were at the party failed to corroborate her story.

Nonetheless, her charges reopened the hearing at which Kavanaugh came forward to defend himself and open the other side of the dialectic. However, instead of a reasoned and cool-headed statement that one might expect from a prospective justice, Kavanaugh gave a speech brimming with anger and condemnation in which he lost his composure at several junctures. In the question-and-answer session that followed, he often came off as rude and petulant, befouling the decorum of the process. Thus, what might have been resolved as an unprovable he-said, she-said event suddenly was opened to the question of whether Kavanaugh had the right temperament to sit on the nation's highest court. Each senator would have to make a judgment call based on his or her standards, or the evidence or lack thereof.

For years the U.S. Senate had slid into a highly charged, partisan morass; it was not a comfortable dwelling place. This house was not a home; as in 1950 when Margaret Chase Smith addressed it, it was a house divided against itself. It was a place of rancor almost evenly divided between the two political parties. As the confirmation process moved from the hearing room to the floor of the Senate, the media reported on and contributed to the vitriolic atmosphere. It was at this juncture that Senator Susan Collins of Maine, a moderate Republican—and more importantly in this instance, a woman—came forward to explain her judgment call. Standing at her desk on the floor of the Senate, like Margaret Chase Smith, she began by recognizing the dialectical moment and then the fact that the Senate was no longer a proper dwelling place:

> Mr. President, the five previous times that I've come to the floor to explain my vote on the nomination of a justice to the United States Supreme Court, I have begun my floor remarks explaining my decision with a recognition of the solemn nature and the importance of the occasion. But today we have come to the conclusion of a confirmation process that has become so dysfunctional, it looks more like a caricature of a gutter-level political campaign than a solemn occasion. . . . Over-the-top rhetoric and distortions of his record and testimony at his first hearing produced short-lived headlines, which although debunked hours later, continued to live on and be spread through social media. Interest groups have also spent an unprecedented amount of dark money opposing this nomination. Our Supreme Court confirmation process has been in steady decline for more than 30 years. One can only hope that the Kavanaugh nomination is where the process has finally hit rock bottom.

Collins then reviewed the intent of the framers of the Constitution in an attempt to establish her record of objectivity and bipartisan support for presidential nominees to the Court, reminding her audience that she had voted for both so-called conservative *and* liberal nominees. She moved on to review Kavanaugh's judicial record and her conversations with him. He had assuaged any fears she had of him radically departing from precedent. On the issue of whether Kavanaugh might vote to protect President Trump should his case come before the Court, Collins concluded that like other nominees who faced the dilemma of ruling against the president who appointed them, Kavanaugh would be guided by his conscience.

Collins then turned to his record with regard to women, expanding on the dialectic between Kavanaugh and his accuser:

> Lisa Blatt, who has argued more cases before the Supreme Court than any other woman in history, testified, quote, "By any objective measure, Judge Kavanaugh is clearly qualified to serve on the Supreme Court. His opinions are invariably thoughtful and fair." Ms. Blatt, who clerked for and is an ardent admirer of Justice Ginsburg, and who is, in her own words, an unapologetic defender of a woman's right to choose, says that Judge Kavanaugh fits within the mainstream of legal thought. She also observed that Judge Kavanaugh is remarkably committed to promoting women in the legal profession.

By using the testimony of women and by invoking the name of Justice Ruth Bader Ginsburg, Collins directly confronted the opinion that Kavanaugh was unfit to serve on the Court.

Attempting to transcend the dialectic between Kavanaugh and his accuser, and the acrimonious divide in the Senate, Collins turned to Kavanaugh's accuser to move her audience toward the proper judgment call. Collins "found her testimony to be sincere, painful and compelling. I believe that she is a survivor of a sexual assault and that this trauma has upended her life. Nevertheless, the four witnesses she named could not corroborate any of the events of that evening gathering where she says the assault occurred." The "nevertheless" in the foregoing sentence is a turning point that leads Collins to her transcendent value: the "presumption of innocence," that one is innocent until proven guilty. That would eventually be the basis of her judgment call and the basis of her attempt to return civility to the Senate.

Some would condemn Collins for taking up a criminal standard instead of relying on the suitability standard to determine who should sit on the Court. That is, Collins could have claimed that Kavanaugh was temperamentally unsuited to the Court. However, she chose to use a standard that required a higher burden of proof.

But first, Collins turned to the issue of sexual harassment and condemned it, so that her vote could not be misconstrued as an endorsement of sexism but as one attempting to perfect the dwelling place she was building. She reinforced her position by again showing sympathy for Professor Ford. Collins then moved to her conclusion. Here she once again described the contentious moment, the breach into which she inserted herself. She described the causes of the divisive atmosphere and this time transcended the moment with an appeal to the Constitution and to the "perfect union" it tried to create. That is the home that Collins was making.

> Mr. President, the politically charged atmosphere surrounding this nomination has reached a fever pitch, even before these allegations were known, and it has been challenging even then to separate fact from fiction. We live in a time of such great disunity, as the bitter fight over this nomination both in the Senate and among the public clearly demonstrates. It is not merely a case of differing groups having different opinions. It is a case of people bearing extreme ill will toward those who disagree with them. In our intense focus on our differences, we have forgotten the common values that bind us together as Americans. When some of our best minds are seeking to develop even more sophisticated algorithms designed to link us to websites that only reinforce and cater to our views, we can only expect our differences to intensify. This would have alarmed the drafters of our Constitution, who were acutely aware that different values and interests could prevent Americans from becoming and remaining a single people. Indeed, of the six objectives they invoked in the preamble to the Constitution, the one that they put first was the formation of a more perfect union.

While one can argue with Collins's use of the "innocent until proven guilty" standard, one has to admire her desire to return a sense of civility to the Senate and the nation. In this case, the main audience was the Senate, with a second audience—the public—looking on. The Senate had no choice but to vote on the nomination in a highly charged arena. Thus, timing was not something a speaker could determine; the moment was thrust upon the speaker when she was recognized to speak. Her only choice was to speak or not speak; she could have simply passed and then voted when her name was called. Heroically, Collins seized the opportunity to perfect the Senate. For better or worse, Kavanaugh's nomination was approved by the Senate along almost straight partisan lines. However, by stepping into the political confrontation, Collins appeared to be the voice of reason that could move debate to a more comfortable and noble home. She hoped her colleagues would transcend their differences to return to civil discourse. She provides a telling example of Gorgias's "fitting timing" and Aristotle's forensic speech. She used a dialectical approach to reach her conclusion regarding justice.[11]

Senator Mitt Romney

Senator Collins failed in her effort to restore civility to the Senate, let alone the nation. By the fall of 2019, the House of Representatives was moving toward the impeachment of President Trump. While Trump could have been impeached on charges of obstruction of justice stemming from his reaction to the Mueller report regarding Russian interference in the election of 2016, he was instead indicted on two different counts: obstruction of Congress and abuse of power. Obstruction of Congress is not a normal legal category and abuse of power can cover a wide range of issues. This murkiness allowed the president and some senators to ridicule charges. The House had not issued subpoenas for White House witnesses, so how could they claim the president had obstructed their investigation? Congressman Adam Schiff, the leader of the impeachment effort, claimed that it was sufficient enough that the White House had turned down their requests for witnesses; they did not have to issue subpoenas. There were other rationales available to senators who wanted to let the president off the hook. By the time the articles reached the Senate, primaries had begun for the 2020 election. So why not just let the voters decide if Trump should be reelected? Others recalled that President Clinton had been impeached for lying to a grand jury; he had clearly committed perjury, for which he later apologized. Yet no Democrat had voted to remove him from office; instead they argued that his crime "did not rise to the level of an impeachable offense." That phrase fell from many of the Republican senators' lips in 2020.

At the core of the charges against the president was a call he made on July 25, 2019, to President Zelensky of the Ukraine. A coherent reading of the transcript of the call reveals that the president sought a quid pro quo: namely, that he would release $391 million in aid to the Ukraine in return for Zelensky ordering an investigation into Hunter Biden, who had a seat on the Ukrainian energy company Burisma. This was a clear violation of a 1974 Congressional Budget and Impoundment Control Act, which prohibited politicians from seeking foreign help in their election campaigns.

The debate over the impeachment charges was acrimonious in the House, which eventually voted to send the articles to the Senate. The president appeared to welcome the trial while dismissing the charges. Both sides then proceeded to present their cases to the Senate, which sat as the jury in the case. A finding of guilty would require a two-thirds vote of the Senate, a very unlikely scenario given that the Republicans held the majority in the Senate, and the fact that historically, no senator had ever voted to oust a president of his or her own party.[12]

On February 5, 2020, the same day as the Iowa caucuses, both sides rested their case and senators began to explain how they would vote. On February 6, adding to the political drama, President Trump came to the House Chamber to give his annual State of the Union Address. As he gave a copy of his speech to the Speaker of House, Nancy Pelosi extended her hand; but the president refused to shake it. His speech was filled with claims about the success of his administration. Sympathetic characters in the galleries were cheered. The right-leaning and often mendacious Rush Limbaugh was presented with the Presidential Medal of Freedom, the highest civilian honor available. It was a travesty. Limbaugh's attacks on "feminazis" were well known, including his charge that Hillary Clinton kept a "testicle lockbox." His attacks on "health Nazis" and global warming are well known. He had obviously been an inspiration of Trump's bar talk. An award that had gone to such citizens as Rosa Parks was now horribly sullied.

The acrimony of the evening was heightened when Nancy Pelosi publicly tore her copy of the president's speech into shreds after he finished speaking. One was reminded of the rending of garments in times of calamity. On February 5, just before their fateful vote, senators explained their votes on the articles of impeachment. One speech stood out: Senator Mitt Romney would become the only senator in history to vote to oust a president of his own party. Romney had been the Republican nominee for president in 2012. He had been the governor of the state of Massachusetts. He had brought order to the Olympic Games when put in charge. In short, the prior reputation of Romney gave him a great deal of credibility. And he did nothing to diminish it in his speech on the floor of the Senate.

The first words out of Romney's mouth—"The Constitution is at the foundation of our Republic's success"—set the tone for the speech. Like Senators Webster, Smith, and Collins, Romney was returning to the document that tried to establish "a more perfect union" as the proper dwelling place of the nation. One of the ways the Constitution tried to do that was by providing for "the vehicle of impeachment" when officials abused their power. Inside this proper dwelling place each senator should "respect each other's good faith." He reminded senators that he, like them, took an oath before God that was "enormously consequential" because Romney's faith was "at the heart of who" he was. At this point, Romney stopped to choke back his tears. He confessed that at the outset of the trial, he faced the most difficult decision of his career.

He then reviewed the charges against the president and the three defenses that had been issued by his lawyers. He began with the need for there to be a "statutory crime" in order to remove the president. He dismissed this defense in two ways. First, that it was not the Founders' intent. The president could commit many "egregious" acts that were legal but still an abuse of power. Second, the president clearly solicited an investigation of Hunter Biden because of his relation to Trump's possible opponent in the 2020 election. Romney acknowledged Biden's bad judgment but saw no evidence of crime on his part. However, the president's behavior was a violation of the law concerning foreign interference in American elections. Third, with regard to leaving the decision to the voters in November, Romney relied on the reasoning of Alexander Hamilton to argue that the "partisan sentiment" of the voters was inferior to the wisdom of the Senate. Romney then rendered his judgment: "The president asked a foreign government to investigate his political rival. The president withheld vital military funds from that government to press it to do so. The president delayed funds for an American ally at war with Russian invaders. The president's purpose was personal and political. Accordingly, the president is guilty of an appalling abuse of public trust. . . . [I]t was a flagrant assault on our electoral rights, our national security and our fundamental values." Romney then anticipated attacks that he was disloyal. He made clear that he had voted for the president's legislative agenda 80 percent of the time. But on this issue, he had decided to avoid exposing his "character to history's rebuke and the censure of my own conscience." In short, Romney's ethos was at stake if he did not heed the call of his conscience. He was particularly concerned about his "children and his children's children."

Like Jesus, Lincoln, and Smith, Romney not only failed to carry the day, he was subject to abuse and ridicule. On February 6, at a prayer breakfast no less, the president lashed out at Romney and Pelosi: "I don't like people who use their faith as justifications for doing what they know is wrong. Nor do I like people who say, 'I pray for you,' when you know that is not so." He called Pelosi a "horrible person." Then taking a victory lap from the White

House, the president apologized to his family "for having them have to go through a phony, rotten deal by some evil and sick people. . . . It was evil, it was corrupt, it was dirty cops, it was leakers and liars. . . . It was bullshit." And so, the president was back to name-calling and scatology.

Conclusion

While true eloquence stands the test of time, it often fails in the short run, perhaps because it is not robust enough for the present moment. To be more effective, as we have asserted, eloquence that seeks to perfect us must be adjusted to its situation and audience. That requires a sense of timing and appropriateness in terms of style. It requires an ethos that the audience accepts. It requires an appeal to the emotions that breaks through the barriers that the ignoble rhetoricians have put in place. It requires sealing the persuasion with evidence and arguments that have been sifted for their quality and relevance to the audience at hand. It requires a delivery that does not detract from the speech but holds the attention of the audience so that the true can become present. It requires revealing when sense has been made common and the audience is victim to manipulation and rhetorical choreography.

CHAPTER 7

Religious Calls and Sacred Eloquence

A s we have seen, because there is always a future before us and because there is always a contingent, uncertain world around us, we are constantly forced to ponder our situation and deal with it. That takes courage tempered with truth. But how do we find the truth? Plato shows us the dialectical path to the truth. Aristotle shows both logical and rhetorical means of coming to both true and probable judgments. And Buber and Jaspers show us that interpersonal eloquence in partnership with others can take us to transcendent truths. Over the centuries, religion, despite its many faults, has helped humans to find truths and cope with their contingent condition. At its best, the religious call displays eloquence that reveals truth. Thus, at this juncture we turn from the pragmatic eloquence outlined by Aristotle to the more transcendent eloquence of the sacred.

Earlier, we noted that God comes from nowhere and issues a call. Over time the theological understanding of God has evolved from Parmenides's perfect one to Plato's emanating good, to the Hebrews' God of power and wrath, to the Christian God of forgiveness and grace. God is omnipotent, omniscient, eternal—in short, perfect. It is that perfection that calls out of us so that we can perfect ourselves and others. God discloses itself, and to hear that call and understand that disclosure, we must be in a state of mind, a proper dwelling place to receive it. Religion provides one of those dwelling places. Once we have heard the call, we have a moral obligation to relay it to others using eloquence or some other form of art. As we pointed out in an earlier chapter, morality can be the completion of God's work. And our eloquence can call attention to the various presences that disclose God, the beauty of the waterfall, the sublime nature of Mont Blanc. These disclosures can perfect our understanding of the world beyond common sense. Thus, true eloquence is always revelatory and sometimes awe-inspiring.

We turn to three case studies of preachers who have heard the call, and how they relayed that call to others. They are the intermediaries between a perfect God and its imperfect creations. Each of them not only tends to their flock, but engages in disputation with others who would scatter their flock and/or misread God. We begin with St. Paul and then move on to St. Augustine and conclude with Jonathan Edwards. Why these three? Because each is eloquent, and their eloquence has stood the test of time. Each also uses different rhetorical forms. Paul issues his call in sermons and letters. Relying on Paul's theology, Augustine issues his call in teaching, books, and sermons. Edwards relies on the theology of Paul and Augustine to compose jeremiads, emotional calls to repent. Augustine relies on Paul for much of his theology, and Edwards relies on both of them for his. While each issues a religious call, they differ in the kinds of homemaking in which they engage. Paul employs ethos to great effect. Augustine is the great teacher. Edwards employs pathos to achieve his ends. Thus, each displays a different way by which we can make the call more robust even though their messages are very similar. Each of these preachers saw that the call-response is religious in nature as opposed to the question-answer, which is epistemological in nature.[1] And in making the call more robust, they are more effective at perfecting others through their translation of the divine logos. They believed that the call brought new knowledge to the one who was called. This new knowledge could be a new understanding of faith, or of God, or the world around them. This world is part of a spiritual world that imbues this world with significance. Our true end or ultimate dwelling place is in this spiritual universe. These preachers also knew that the call was transient; it could be repeated but could not be sustained for a very long time. However, with each recurrence a further development of faith or other forms of knowledge could be obtained.

While some who hear the divine call claim that it is ineffable, that is not the case with the preachers examined in this chapter.[2] St. Paul heard Jesus ask why Saul was persecuting him. St. Augustine believed that call in the form of divine illumination could be translated for his flock using rhetoric and other linguistic tools. Thus, he wanted all priests to be versed in language arts. Jonathan Edwards painted vivid pictures of heaven and hell to bring his followers to a proper dwelling place. Each of these preachers believed that one could respond to the call with prayers. Furthermore, oratory is a derivative of *oratio* and *horatio*, which are derivatives of *ora*, to pray.

St. Paul

After participating in the persecution of Christians, Saul of Tarsus, a Pharisee, was sent to Damascus for further rabbinical training. He was on the way to improving himself having heard the call of God. On the road, he was struck blind and heard a different call: "Saul, Saul, why dost thou persecute me?" After recovering his sight, Saul changed his name to Paul and his religion to Christian. He went on to become one of the most important figures in the propagation of the faith. His method of disclosing what he had witnessed was to call people to a state of grace using his eloquence. Paul's eloquence is retained in his Epistles, letters to various Christian settlements that advised them how to perfect themselves and how to maintain their church communities, their dwelling place for the reception of the word. These Epistles include Romans, First and Second Corinthians, First and Second Timothy, Galatians, Ephesians, Philippians, Colossians, First and Second

Thessalonians, Titus, and Philemon.[3] These letters relay the call that Paul hears. In Romans (4:17) God "calls into being what is not." In Ephesians (1:4), Paul tells his flock that they have the ability to listen because they are called, which extends and explains Paul's doctrine of election from Romans. Because I am called, I'm in a state of harkening attunement. I make a silence around me so that I can hear the call, the voice. In Latin that is *voco*, out of which vocation, our calling, evolves. Like many of the calls we have examined in this text, St. Paul's reverberates through the ages. For example, Kierkegaard relies on St. Paul's First Corinthians to reinforce his own belief that faith is more important than reason.[4] Most important, these letters would prove influential in uniting the early Christian churches under one catechism, which made it easier to fend off attackers and to condemn heretics. First Corinthians, for example, settled disputes in Corinth and reunited the Christians into one church. Paul's homemaking was successful.

These Epistles had a tremendous impact on thinkers that came after Paul. For example, the Enlightenment thinker John Locke wrote detailed commentaries on Paul's Epistles that helped reinforce their use as a foundation for Calvinist churches.[5] Locke goes so far as to claim that Paul had to be familiar with the *Rhetorica ad Herennium* and the rhetorical theories of Cicero.[6] After his study of Paul's letters, like Martin Luther, Locke was newly called to the doctrine of justification by faith instead of salvation by doing good works. Locke concluded that the call of revelation was superior to reason, clearly stepping away from his Enlightenment thinking in his *Essay on Human Understanding*.[7]

Paul's eloquence was a result of his Hellenistic and Jewish schooling in Tarsus. Born into the tribe of Benjamin, he became a Roman citizen who could write and speak in Greek, Latin, and the local tongue. At the Temple School in Jerusalem, he became a student of the famous Jewish seer Gamaliel, who had saved the Christians from persecution during their early years. It is Gamaliel who sends young Saul to Damascus to perfect him.

The Epistles are remarkable for their adaptation to their intended audiences. His homemaking included identification. Paul admitted as much:

And unto Jews, I became as a Jew, that I might gain the Jews; to them that are under the law, as under the law, that I might gain them that are under the law. To them that are without the law, as without the law … that I might gain them that are without the law. To the weak became I as weak, that I might gain the weak: I am all things to all men, that I might by all means save some.[8]

To meet their expectations, Paul relies on *ornatus*. He uses asyndeton, the removal of conjunctions: "Let no man despise thy youth; but be thou an example of the believers, in word, in conversation, in charity, in spirit, in faith, in purity."[9] There is adjunction (verb-subject reversal) combined with antithesis: "Rebuke not an elder, but entreat him as a father."[10] There are maxims with which the audience would feel comfortable: "For the love of money is the root of all evil."[11] However, more than any other of the tools of homemaking, Paul understood that ethos is powerful. Unless he could build a house of trust, he could not persuade Christians to unite and abide by his teachings, which he claims relay the teaching of Christ. Paul also had the burden of not having served Jesus personally as had those he called the "pillars" of Christianity, Peter, James the Greater, James the Lesser, and John the Divine. If he was to have a role in building this new church, he had to establish his credibility.

Earlier, we laid out the constituents of ethos, and they help us here to understand Paul's success in issuing the call to come to the home he is building. First, in terms of prior reputation, Paul had established it before writing his letters and then reminds his readers of it at the outset of almost every letter. For example, in the Epistle to the Galatians written in 51 CE, Paul claimed to be Christ's chosen officer because of his conversion experience. In Second Corinthians, he begins by enumerating his trials, sufferings, and tribulations. However, nothing burnishes Paul's prior reputation more than his conversion to Christianity by a blinding flash and the voice of God.

Once in Damascus, he did not go to the rabbinical schools; instead he sought out the Christians. After learning their faith, he retreated into the Arabian desert for three more years of becoming a Christian with deep understanding of Judeo-Christian theology. When Paul emerged to begin his cycles of preaching, he was often persecuted. Acts 1–3 tells the story of Paul and Barnabas entering a synagogue in Antioch. After a rabbi read from the scrolls, Paul preached and converted some of those present. Hearing what had happened, Gentiles attended his sermon on the next day and many were converted. Feeling threatened, the Jewish leadership expelled Paul and Barnabas from the region. When Paul moved on to preach in Iconium in Greece, more conversion occurred, but some Jews called for Paul to be stoned to death. Wounded, Paul escaped, but heroically, he would return to Iconium and Antioch to form Christian churches. He would recount his beatings, stonings, and imprisonments to enhance his reputation.[12]

As he continued to build a Christian home, in 47 CE, it became clear that Paul was narrowing his audience to Gentiles.[13] When he came to Corinth in 52, he again tried and failed with the Jews but was successful with the Gentiles. The pattern was the same whether in Philippi, in Macedonia, or in Rome. He often had to invoke his Roman citizenship to get imperial court protection from Jewish leaders who were hostile to his Christian homemaking. Still, he often had to endure imprisonment, especially in Caesarea and Rome, from which he wrote many of his epistles. In the end, Paul's letters are given additional credibility because he was martyred in 67 CE as part of Nero's scapegoating of the Christians for the fire that destroyed a large part of Rome.

In terms of wisdom and ethos, we can begin with the pragmatic fact that Paul had been an envoy from the Jews to the Romans. His travels around the eastern Mediterranean familiarized him with the peoples and languages of the area. Having studied to be a Pharisee, Paul, like Jesus, was steeped in the Mishnah and other Jewish theology; thus, he could speak to the Jews with authority. Like Jesus, Paul worked miracles. Like Jesus, Paul considered himself a teacher who comes to disclose the truth. Teachers are necessary, claimed Paul, because divine revelation comes to us as "through a glass darkly."[14] It is obscure and must be translated for the lay audience. Here

Paul not only established his sagacity, but identified himself with Jesus: "the truth of Christ is in me."[15] He was the intermediary of Christ's perfection.

With great clarity, Paul realized that Jesus evoked a "new eon" in the world;[16] the time for the old eon with its tangle of Pharisaic laws had passed. That revelation was a crucial part of Jesus's reform, and Paul's deciphering of it, is part of his claim to have divine wisdom. Paul says he saw "the light of knowledge of the glory of God in the face of Christ."[17] Furthermore, the sacrifice of Jesus allows God to shed its grace on the faithful gathered under Paul's roof.[18] For Paul, the revelation comes not by sight, but by faith.[19] Thus, Paul's morphology of perfection moves from the wisdom of the senses (*nous*) to the wisdom of the soul (*Sophia*). This is how he arrived at harkening attunement to the call: "And he that searcheth the hearts knoweth what is the mind of Spirit."[20] In First Corinthians, echoing Isaiah, Paul tells his readers that "Eye hath not seen, nor ear heard . . . the things which God hath prepared for them that love him. But God hath revealed them unto us by Spirit; for the Spirit searcheth all things, yea, the deep things of God."[21] For Paul, this is the call that lies at the heart of human existence.

To propagate his message, Paul called Christians into his house with displays of goodwill. You couldn't come much closer to Aristotle's definition of goodwill than Paul's call does. Everything he yearned for is for the good of his flock and he expected nothing in return. He led them to faith, which discloses God and promises perfecting salvation. As he wrote in Ephesians 3:1, "I Paul [am] the prisoner of Jesus for you Gentiles." He also gave his followers a new sense of liberty by reforming the rule-bound ways of the Jewish leadership.[22] At Romans 4:13, he is very clear: "For the promise, that he should be the heir of the world, was to Abraham, or to his seed, not through the law, but through the righteousness of faith." Paul provides another, even more dramatic freedom for "his children" at Romans 8:2: "For the law of the Spirit of life in Christ Jesus hath made me free from the law of sin and death." Eternal life frees Christians from the fear of death. This was important because as Nero's persecution continued, many Christians were heroically martyred. It was said that every drop of blood that fell to the floor of the arena created a new Christian.

All of those who became Christian received yet another gift from Paul. In First Corinthians 12:12–30 he reconstitutes his followers into the mystical body of Christ's church. In Galatians 3, Paul argues that his followers are not to be known by their ethnicity but by their oneness in Christ. And it is their taking of the communion, the body and blood of Christ, that solidifies this oneness with one another and with Christ. It is a perfect example of substantial identification leading to consubstantial identification.

Paul's ability to identify with an audience and convert it was nowhere more successful than in Athens. Gathering on Mars Hill overlooking the Areopagus, where Socrates had been accused of impiety, Paul opened by identifying the audience itself, "Ye men of Athens." Among them stood a diverse group of Epicureans, Stoics, and other pagans. To further unify them with his aim, he engaged in substantial identification by recognizing their altar to an unknown god. Praying to an unknown god is the height of ignorance; praying to a god that is superior to all of the other gods is much wiser—a direct appeal to the philosophers witnessing his sermon. And so Paul substitutes his perfect God for the unknown god. Paul claimed that "we live and move and have our being" in our one God.[23] This line paraphrases the Greek poet Epinenides, revealing the lengths to which Paul would go to identify with his audience. Later he quotes the poet Aratus and makes reference to the leading Stoic of the time, Cleanthes. Only when the identification has been strengthened does Paul move to his Christian message. Paul's God is the perfect father of us all and the creator of the universe. When you have faith in that God, He gives you grace. He sent his son to redeem mankind. All humans will be raised from the dead on Judgment Day. Paul did not win over a majority of his audience with his sermon; but some of its prominent members did convert, including Damaris, a female aristocrat, and Dionysus, a prominent judge who went on to become a bishop in the new church.

As we follow St. Paul's journey through the Acts of the Apostles and the epistles he pens, we see a man who has achieved character, the last of

Aristotle's constituents of ethos. He was a humble servant of Christ and loyal and magnanimous to his followers. He reinforced this virtuous character by praising and blaming various actions that become a theology of ethics. In Galatians, he argues that the spirit and the flesh oppose one another. Flesh pulls us into material greed and lust; the spirit lifts us to "love, joy, peace, longsuffering, gentleness, goodness, faith, meekness, temperance."[24] The vices include adultery, fornication, uncleanliness, lasciviousness, idolatry, witchcraft, hatred, and wrath. St. Paul's ethics drive him to an ultimate virtue in First Corinthians 13:2–13: "And though I have the gift of prophecy, and understand all mysteries, and all knowledge; and though I have all faith, so that I could remove mountains, and have not charity, I am nothing. . . . And now abideth faith, hope, charity, these three; but the greatest of these is charity."[25] Having provided a life of goodwill himself, he now returns to it and elevates it among his values. This is how one lives a life of character, how one becomes one's true self. Paul was perceived to be authentic because he practiced what he preached. And when he gives his life for his calling, he cements himself in church history. He too becomes a pillar of the Christian dwelling place. For centuries at Christian services, Paul was quoted more than Jesus. Having received divine revelation, he issued a call that reverberates still.

St. Augustine

Almost four centuries after the martyrdom of St. Paul, a young man named Augustine sat in a garden. In the process of becoming a Christian rhetor, he had been trained as a sophist and a lawyer in Carthage. After briefly teaching in his hometown of Thagaste, he established his own school in Carthage. There he became disaffected from the surface polishing of sophistry and converted to Manicheanism. The prophet Mani had divided the world between light and dark, knowledge and ignorance in attempting to bring all religions under one roof.

Over the next decade, Augustine's fame as a teacher led him to the center of the Empire in Rome and then to a chair of rhetoric in Milan in 384, where he embraced Platonic thought in his quest for spiritual meaning. He was particularly taken with Plato's notion of an eternal soul that traveled between phenomenal (material) and noumenal (spiritual) worlds, two very different dwelling places. At its best the phenomenal was the world of becoming, the world of potentiality. The noumenal was the world of perfection, the world of actuality and permanence. St. Augustine, reflecting his Platonic roots, says that beautiful things call to us. Their beautiful form appeals to our senses.[26] Like Plato, Augustine came to believe that the truth must precede eloquence. One must master the truth before one speaks.

Plato's influence can also be seen in Augustine's belief that reason can be used internally to reach the truth—that is, the doctrine of recollection. However, Augustine also realizes that the truth can come from an external source, divine illumination. Moses does not reason to recall the Ten Commandments; instead, he places himself into a state of harkening attunement and receives the Ten Commandments from God, writ into two tablets.

In his quest for spiritual nourishment, Augustine came under the influence of Milan's bishop, who advised the emperor. Ambrose introduced Augustine to Christianity, setting the young teacher on yet another path in his perfecting of self. Augustine was particularly moved by the biography of St. Anthony of Egypt. It encouraged Augustine to avoid carnal pleasure and perfect his soul. The first link to St. Paul's call came for Augustine in the form of a story about the life of Marius Victorinus. He too was a North African sophist and only converted to Christianity late in his life. Victorinus's commentaries on the Epistles of St. Paul moved Augustine to study them. Soon after, as he sat in a garden, he had a crisis of faith; tears welled in his eyes. And then he heard a voice, a disruption. It called out, "Read, read." Augustine took up St. Paul's Epistle to the Romans and had a conversion experience; it was a disclosive and sublime moment. Augustine described it thus: "It was as though a light of utter confidence shone in all my heart, and all the darkness of uncertainty vanished away."[27]

When he wrote about the event in his *Confessions*, it is clear that Augustine is responding to God's call: "Here I am!" With this response, Augustine converted his personal regime of destitution into a more fitting dwelling place for welcoming One who is "being in a supreme degree."[28] There Augustine took up an even more serious attempt at mastering the word of God. Ambrose baptized Augustine into the church in 387. After further training in an Italian abbey, Augustine became a monk and returned to Thagaste in North Africa. Augustine had mastered sophistry by the time he became a teacher. Now, he had mastered the Christian substance so that he could achieve eloquence. In 391 he was ordained as a priest and regularly traveled to the city of Hippo to say the mass and preach. His sermons became so popular that the Christians of Hippo insisted that he become their priest. He was elevated to bishop in 395. Among his good works, he could often be seen purchasing and freeing slaves held by the Vandals. But like Paul, Augustine maintained that true salvation was an act of faith.

Clearly, Augustine believed in an awesome, divine revelation. To receive it, he argued, one must first come to know oneself, as Augustine had done in his long journey from sophistry to Christianity. Then one must put oneself in harkening attunement to God.[29] That requires creating a home for the soul that is achieved through prayer, meditation, the study of theology, and participation in the sacraments. Augustine also believed it was not only the duty of priests to get to a place where they could receive divine revelation, but that they had an obligation to bring it to their parishioners. They were God's intermediaries. To perform that task, priests would have to become eloquent. Augustine knew that eloquence gives the priest the tools to disclose what is revealed in the awesome moment of divine revelation. That is why he wrote his master opus *De Doctrina Christiana* (*On Christian Doctrine*). The last of the four-part volume concentrated on achieving the eloquence necessary to translate divine illumination into something parishioners could understand and experience, thereby strengthening their faith, not to mention their sense of belonging in the church. Augustine put it this way: "In order that what we are thinking may reach the mind of the listener through the ears, that which we have in our mind is expressed in words and is called speech. But our thought is not transformed into sounds; it remains entire in itself and assumes the form of words . . . without any deterioration in itself. In the same way the Word of God was made flesh."[30]

That flesh was Jesus, who of course had a major influence on Augustine. Jesus was the Way and the Destination of Augustine. However, Jesus was also eloquent. He spoke to the crowds in parables; he refuted the Sadducees and Pharisees with argumentation; and he delivered the truth to his apostles in plain language. Augustine wrote that sacred orators must speak as if they were the living Christ, and that meant mastering oratory. But Augustine also learned from Jesus to use intentional obscurity to distract his audiences from this world and have them search for the sublime. Augustine claimed that obscurantism interrupts an audience's attendance to the material world and turns them toward the sublime.

What was also revolutionary about Augustine's *On Christian Doctrine* was that it retrieved the theories of Plato, Aristotle, and Cicero, who were considered pagans by other church fathers and were therefore forbidden in the schools of the Christian church. Augustine overcame this difficulty by arguing that had the ancients been exposed to Jesus and his teachings, they would have become Christians. But since they did not have that opportunity, it was unfair not to seek their council. As Charles Sears Baldwin makes clear, "the fourth book of his *De Doctrina* . . . out of all proportion to its size . . . begins rhetoric anew."[31] Augustine saw that Cicero's notion of expectation was key to adjusting an audience's ability to receive the word of God, the call to faith. For Augustine, God's existence is visible to the human soul in a retrieving moment of ascent.[32] Augustine was trying to build a home for the whole world, a catholic church, though he would die of fever while his home was under siege by Vandals in 430.

So what was it that so attracted Augustine to the ancients, particularly Cicero? Augustine knew that rhetoric could encourage and rationalize sin. Still, owing to the influence that Cicero's philosophy of rhetoric had on his thinking, Augustine acknowledged there was also a saving grace to the orator's art. Cicero's "exhortation to study philosophy," wrote Augustine, helped to change his life: "It gave me different values and priorities. Suddenly every vain hope became empty to me, and I longed for the immortality of wisdom with an incredible ardor in my heart."[33] Cicero's praise of philosophy as an invaluable source of truth for the orator's art directed Augustine toward its most metaphysical limits: God.

However, Cicero also insisted that "we are not born for ourselves alone," that "our country claims a share of our being," and that if we intend "to contribute to the general good," we must not disparage and retreat from the politics of public life but instead use "our skill, our industry, and our talents to cement human society more closely together, man to man."[34] The obligation stated here speaks to the importance of rhetoric in his civic healing role. Philosophy is essential for the education of the orator, but it is the "art of eloquence" (*oratio*) practiced by this advocate of the *vita activa* that instructs one on how to equip (*ornare*) knowledge of a subject in such a way that it can assume a publicly accessible form and thus function effectively in the social and political arena. For the good of the community, philosophy and rhetoric must work together. Cicero—who admitted "that whatever ability I possess as an orator comes, not from the workshops of the rhetoricians, but from the spacious grounds of the Academy"—would have it no other way:[35] "To be drawn by study away from active life is contrary to moral duty."[36] While Cicero saw rhetoric in the service of philosophy to heal the state, Augustine saw rhetoric in the service of theology to heal human beings. Cicero was devoted to Rome; Augustine was devoted to a catholic church with its City of God, the title of his book explaining how the sack of Rome in 410 disclosed the temporality of this world and issued a calling to the spiritual world. He sought to provide for the "eternal welfare" of humans.[37] Relying on Paul's Epistle to the Romans, Augustine reasoned that God gives the chosen the gift of faith, which releases them from the will's propensity to sin.[38]

Being much less concerned with the social and political workings of the state than he was with the heavenly kingdom of God, Augustine stressed that he did not read Cicero "for a sharpening of [his] literary expression." Rather, he "was impressed" by the author's "content." Rhetoric as eloquence serves the truth, which for Augustine ultimately requires that we "leave earthly things and fly back to [God]."[39] Eloquence, however, is not to be forsaken, for it serves a valuable purpose in helping to establish a way for others to come to terms with the Almighty. Augustine puts it this way:

> Since infants are not taught to speak except by learning the expressions of speakers, why can men not be made eloquent, not by teaching them the rules of eloquence, but by having them read and hear the expressions of the eloquent and imitate them in so far as they are able to follow them? Have we not seen examples of this being done? For we know many men ignorant of the rules of eloquence who are more eloquent than many who have learned them; but we know of no one who is eloquent without having read or heard the disputations and sayings of the eloquent.[40]

In the same work, we also find Augustine converting Cicero's uses of the three levels of style to inform his own sense of eloquence: "It is necessary, therefore, that the sacred orator, when urging something be done, should not only teach in order to instruct, and please in order to hold, but also move in order to win."[41] To achieve this winning conviction, eloquence must be suitable and fitting.[42] The sacred orators must subordinate their reputation to the glory of God's call. Achieving conviction in faith in your flock is more important than pleasing it.

Augustine was not only using eloquence to translate the word of God for his flock, he was using it to marshal arguments against those opposed to Christianity. In chapter 7 of Book 8 of *City of God*, he condemned the sense-bound Epicureans and Stoics, the very philosophers St. Paul attempted to convert on Mars Hill in Athens. They came down on the side of the city of Babylon (imperfection, materialism), and Augustine advanced the cause of the city of Jerusalem (perfection, spiritualism). He also condemned the Sophists, who lived for applause, putting their egos before God's call. The call is more important than the speaker. He also made clear that eloquence must be used in the defense of truth:

> For since by means of the art of rhetoric both truth and falsehood are urged, who would dare to say that truth should stand in the person of its defenders unarmed against lying, so that they who wish to urge falsehoods may know how to make their listeners benevolent, or attentive, or docile in the presentation, while the defenders of truth are ignorant of that art? Should they speak briefly, clearly, and plausibly while the defenders of truth speak so that they tire their listeners, make themselves difficult to understand and what they have to say dubious? Should they oppose the truth with fallacious arguments and assert falsehoods, while the defenders of truth have no ability either to defend the truth or to oppose the false? Should they, urging the minds of their listeners into error, ardently exhort them, moving them by speech so that they terrify, sadden, and exhilarate them, while the defenders of truth are sluggish, cold, and somnolent? Who is so foolish as to think this to be wisdom?[43]

St. Augustine sets out the way for priests to relate what they learn from divine revelation to their flocks gathered in dwelling places, whether churches or open fields. The task of priests was to make present the perfecting illumination received in the call from God. Augustine believed that moral preaching was the completion of God's work. Because not everything or everyone is moral, God's work and his work was not complete. And neither is our own.

Jonathan Edwards

Jonathan Edwards (1703–1758) understood this and took up Paul's and Augustine's torch to enlighten his own flock. In 1741 at Enfield, Connecticut, Edwards rose to give a sermon entitled "Sinners in the Hands of Angry God."

It brought together his knowledge of rhetoric and his study of theology. His books, *The End for Which God Created the World* and *Religious Affections*, were widely read in Protestant circles in the colonies and in Great Britain. His narrative about conversions that occurred in Northampton in 1737 was also studied by the "New Light" preachers, who changed the morphology of conversion from appeals to the intellect to appeals to the emotions to move the soul of the listener.

Edwards was only twelve when he entered Yale College. John Locke became his favorite philosopher, and like Locke he became fascinated with scientific observation. His thesis on spiders was widely read on college campuses for years. Spiders' threads and webs can be found in many of his sermons. At Yale, Edwards had a conversion experience when he realized that nature's perfection reveals God, and that God imparts a divine illumination to the human soul that allows it to receive saving grace. That became Edwards's version of the call. After graduation, he studied theology for two years in order to become a minister so he could become an intermediary for God.

Edwards's reputation was enhanced by the fact that he had inherited his grandfather Solomon Stoddard's pulpit in Northampton, Massachusetts, in 1729, after serving as his acolyte starting in 1727. Stoddard, known as the "Yankee Pope," had started the "New Light" sermons, and with them came the "First Great Awakening," an evangelical movement that swept the colonies. Edwards's sermon was delivered in the midst of the third of a string of revivals dating from 1734. He often traveled Massachusetts and Connecticut to stir these revivals with his jeremiads, named for the prophet Jeremiah who warned the Jews of impending doom.

During the revivals of 1740, Edwards met a preacher who had a direct impact on his emotionalism. George Whitefield was an English Methodist strongly committed to outdoor, highly emotional revivals. He regularly traveled to the colonies and was immensely successful. Unlike Edwards, Whitefield believed all humans could be saved, not just the "chosen ones." When Whitefield delivered a sermon in Edwards's church in Northampton, everyone including Edwards was reduced to tears. Whitefield's more democratic take on salvation induced Edwards to broaden his appeal.

In 1741, Edwards, then the most famous preacher in America, sought to move his audiences from one dwelling place to another. In their lethargy and newfound security, they had wandered from God. Saving experiences and conversion had fallen off. Church membership was eroded by dissent among parishioners. The "saints" of the church often fell into dispute over who had been saved and who had not. The parishioners were bored with sermons that had become overly intellectualized. The "Old Lights" of the Puritan church believed that souls could be moved to accept God's grace only through appeals to the mind. Edwards was one of the "New Lights" who believed appeals to the emotions would make the call of God more robust. To evoke emotion, he relied heavily on the theories of Aristotle and Cicero. The appeal needed to be phrased in such a way that it put the audience in the right state of mind, one that would encourage a harkening attunement to God's word, the perfecting logos. To achieve that goal, stylistic devices and descriptions would have to bring the causes of emotions close to the audience in time and space. Edwards knew how to do that. To bring his parishioners home, Edwards invoked the emotions of fear, pity, hopelessness, and joy. Contemporaneous accounts detail his effectiveness: "women fainted, and men cried out and wept."[44] A wave of hysteria swept the region. In short, Edwards reconstituted his audience from a wandering and indifferent flock into a unified, cohesive sect returning to their home to seek salvation.

Edwards was open with his audience about his intentions. In the beginning, he said that he sought to turn the attention of his audience away from "the good state of your bodily constitution, your care of your own life, and the means you use for your own preservation."[45] His condemnation continued: "The use of this awful subject may be for awakening unconverted persons in this congregation. This that you have heard is the case of every one of you that are out of Christ."[46] Using identification, Edwards linked his audience to the "wicked and unbelieving Israelites who were exposed to destruction" as opposed to good and faithful Israelites who were God's chosen people. He then named more members of his audience, opening a big tent to contain them: "Whether you be young or old! . . . It may be [that you] are now at ease, and hear all these things without much disturbance, and are now flattering [yourselves] that [you] shall escape."[47]

Like Aristotle, Edwards knew that imagination was a powerful force. Thus, using imagery was crucial to his task. One of the most sublime images is the Old Testament God's "wrath," which is portrayed as "everlasting fierceness," "black clouds," and "infinite." He then brought vivid images close to his audience in order to invoke their fear of God. He told them they were nothing more than "chaff before the whirlwind . . . stubble before devouring flames," and "heavy as lead" hanging by a "single thread" over the pit of hell. God holds the thread, and should He snap His fingers, you will sink to the devil in hell below, which provides another sublime image: "The old serpent is gaping for them; hell opens its wide mouth." When they fall, the unrepentant in Edwards's audience will hear the echo of his words in hell. The frightful images are reinforced by the fear of falling and then the pain of burning.

To intensify the fear of God, Edwards again relies on Aristotle's advice to create a "picture of some destructive or painful evil in the future."[48] Retrieving the image of the winepress, Edwards tells his audience that this fearful and angry God will "crush out your blood and make it fly."[49] By bringing God close to his listeners, he intensifies their fear. "O Sinner! Consider the fearful danger you are in. 'Tis a great furnace of wrath, a wide and bottomless pit, full of the fire of wrath, that you are held over in the hand of that God whose wrath is provoked and incensed as much against you as against many of the damned in hell."[50]

The feeling of fear was further intensified by descriptions of the hopeless state of his listeners: "Unconverted men walk over the pit of hell on a rotten covering, and there are innumerable places in this covering so weak they will not support your weight. . . . The arrows of death fly unseen." The hopelessness was reinforced by the fact that there is "nothing to lay hold of to save yourself, nothing to keep off the flames of wrath, nothing that you have ever done, nothing that we can do, to induce God to spare you one moment."[51] Edwards continues to intensify the fear by using substantial identification. The Old Testament God conceives of sinners as "some loathsome insect over the fire. [H]e abhors you, and is dreadfully provoked. . . . You are ten thousand times more abominable in his eyes than the most hateful venomous serpent."[52] Worse yet, God is under no obligation to save humankind because in a community that allowed sinners in their midst, even those innocent of sin had committed a wrong in God's eyes. Here is the heart of Edwards's call for a unified dwelling place. We must all be saved, or we are all condemned.

With a distraught and unified audience, Edwards could now point the way to a new dwelling place. He could change the state of mind of his audience members, moving them from fear to hope to the joy of salvation. He asks them to fly into Heaven instead of falling into Hell. In this way, he releases them from fear and calls them to the New Testament of God's mercy and the joy of salvation. The emotion of joy is intensified with proxemics: "Many are daily coming from the east, west, north and south; many that were very lately in the same miserable condition that you are in, are now in a happy state, with their hearts filled with love to him who has loved them, and washed them from their sins in his own blood, and rejoicing in hope of the glory of God." At this juncture, the audience was forced to decide between the fierce wrath of a powerful God or the gift of a dispensation from a merciful God: "Old men and women, or middle aged, or young people, or little children" are summoned to become part of the "elect" and "fly out of Sodom."[53] Edwards reminds us of how powerful emotional appeals can be when properly reinforced by bringing their causes close in space and time. His images invoke awe in his audience; they chase all other thoughts away and overwhelm. He moves his audience from helplessness to self-determination. It is their choice to make in the end. They can become faithful again and receive the grace of God. They can perfect their community and bring it under one roof.

Edwards took his preaching to Native Americans, where he achieved some success. To be closer to them, he moved to Stockbridge, Massachusetts, in 1751. A few years later, he was so famous that he was chosen to be president of the College of New Jersey (now Princeton); however, his tenure was cut short by smallpox, which caused his death in 1758.[54]

Conclusion

In this chapter, we have examined instances of religious eloquence that translated a call from God into a call to the preacher's flock. The process involves several steps: placing the speaker in harkening attunement to receive the word of God; divine illumination, that is, hearing the call; translating the call into eloquence; disclosing the truth to an audience that has been gathered in a welcoming place. In each case, the repeated call was put into the right words, at the right time, in the right way. St. Paul relied on his ethos to make his call more robust. St. Augustine relied on theories of Plato and Cicero and the example of Jesus to make his call more robust. Jonathan Edwards relied on pathos, identification, and style in language to make his call more robust. Their successes are different but certainly undeniable. In trying to unite and preserve a religious movement, each of them left their mark on history. St. Paul, who claimed to be a "slave of Christ," helped perfect a catechism that is still alive today. St. Augustine, who bought Christians out of slavery, reinforced St. Paul's work by training sacred orators to receive divine illumination, defend the faith, and convert the heathen. In the process, he also revived classical rhetoric. Jonathan Edwards, who became an early abolitionist, was part of the Great Awakening that is credited with instilling a sense of individual initiative in a population that would go on to fight for national independence.[55] A perfect God inspires perfecting.

CHAPTER 8

Art and the Call of the Self/Other

O ur focus now shifts to how the call of the other can be healing and inspirational. That inspiration can lead to the creation of art that calls to others we may not ever meet. That is to say, art has a discursive function, and that is part of what we examine here. At the outset of this book, we made a reference to Van Gogh's painting *Starry Night* and how it calls to us. In this chapter our main concern is the dialogic relationship between artists. We will return to Van Gogh to examine how his relationship with Gauguin inspired some of his other works.

We also began this book by talking about the roles various calls play in our lives. We concluded that the most important was the call that lies at the heart of human existence. Eloquence serves to build a home where people can hear that call. And eloquence then serves to relay the call to others. This truly authentic function of eloquence perfects and heals us. But it is not easy to achieve; even when one is versed in the tools of homemaking, failure can occur. Thus, before we examine the transcendent eloquence of artists, we briefly examine three films to explore that genre's discursive nature: one that cheats and two that do not. One that damages and two that heal. As we shall see, each uses narrative argument and identification to achieve its ends.

Art That Calls

We know that our country is far from perfect and that our human condition is also lacking. One reason is that sometimes on a subliminal level our worst prejudices are endorsed. The eloquence of films, their power to overwhelm, is well known. Narrative is a powerful weapon. They are effective and affective because they can use all of the categories of identification to overcome traditional binaries and create attractive and original characters that seduce audiences from the silver screen. The gender of the body, the gender of the psyche, and the projected persona can be complex. The scriptwriter in Hollywood can use these combinations to create characters that draw their audiences into their films in the comfortable home of a darkened movie theater. Once we identify, we are open to disclosures and to subliminal persuasion that can change our opinions, attitudes, and behaviors for good or ill. One of the powers of films is that they are present to us in a place that shuts out all distractions. We are taken to another reality, and often are so entranced by it that we have no idea that we are being subliminally persuaded by a healing ideology.

In 1939 Metro-Goldwyn-Mayer released the film *Gone with the Wind*. It has many characters with which audience members can identify, and that may explain why the film has remained popular to this day. The characters created by the scriptwriter cover the waterfront. Melanie Wilkes has a feminine psyche in a female body with an anaclitic persona; that is, she needs to be taken care of. Her husband, Ashley, has a feminine psyche in a male body with an anaclitic persona; representing Freud's second kind of anaclitic type, he seeks to take care of others. Rhett Butler has a masculine psyche in a male body with a narcissistic persona; he's a survivor seeking to save the present. Scarlett O'Hara has a masculine psyche in a female body with a narcissistic persona; she's a survivor seeking a better future.[1]

Along with these characters, the audience is drawn in by a compelling Civil War narrative, and by concrete and localized substantial identifications such as with the plantation Tara or the burning of Atlanta. In its totality, *Gone with the Wind* is a powerful place of multilevel identification that becomes a substantial and consubstantial dwelling place for its audience. And that makes it dangerous, because instead of disclosing the truth, the film rationalizes slavery and the lost cause of the South. While many find comfort in this home, it is an inauthentic place to be because it breeds hatred and racism instead of unity and accord. At the same time, we are surrounded with perfecting calls from films. They can reveal the consequences of unjust or impolitic military action, as was done in a raft of well-made films about the Vietnam War. They show us the evils of racism and prejudice against others, as in *In the Heat of the Night* or *To Kill a Mockingbird*. They can reveal the dangers of drug use, child neglect, homelessness, and spousal abuse. Suffice it to say, films can heal us.

One of the most beloved films of all time is *Casablanca*. It won the Academy Award and is on the top ten list of the American Film Institute. Released in 1942, the film went from a B movie to an A film when President Franklin Roosevelt and Prime Minister Winston Churchill met in the real Casablanca during World War II just after the film was released and the Allies had won their first victory in North Africa. The message of a world united to fight fascism was badly needed. After World War I, the United States Senate failed to ratify the treaty negotiated in Versailles on the ground that its provision to create a League of Nations took too much sovereignty from the United States. After a separate treaty was ratified, the United States went down the path of isolationism, alienated from Europe and its horrific war to end all wars. Tariffs went up, which led to a depression. Charles Lindbergh, the hero who flew across the Atlantic in 1927, accepted the Order of the German Eagle from Herman Göring in 1938. He returned home to lead the America First

Movement, which pledged to keep the United States out of European affairs. It took the catastrophic disruption of the Japanese bombing of Pearl Harbor to break through Lindbergh's "common sense" and bring the United States into the Second World War at the end of 1941.

Using dialectical tension and attractive characters created by the screenwriters, *Casablanca* advances an interventionist ideology by creating a dwelling place in which audience members could feel not only comfortable but proud. The title sequence begins the process of substantial identification. It looks like a newsreel because it begins with a map of the world and then narrows its focus to Casablanca. The voice of a newsreel-type narrative sets the scene. Immediately the audience is subjected to another instance of substantial identification: Rick's Café Américain, the locus of much of the action of the film.

Once the audience has been drawn in, the film advances its ideological agenda to cure the world of one of its worst evils. It demonizes the Nazis and praises the underground movement trying to overthrow them. It is based on a play by Joan Allison and Murray Burnett, who witnessed Nazi rule in the south of France under the Vichy regime, which collaborated with Nazis starting in 1940. The film score underscores the dramatic dialectic, but also at times entrances the audience, particularly the song "As Time Goes By" as sung by Dooley Wilson. However, the pinnacle of musical dialectical tension occurs when in the bar Nazi soldiers start to sing "Wacht Am Rhein" and the French émigrés sing them down with "The Marseillaise." The scene symbolizes the need to act courageously and to unify against evil.

While the settings and the music are important, it is the characters that create consubstantial identification. Each of the major characters appeals to different audience segments, pulling them together in the courageous fight and setting up the dialectic that drives the power narrative. The Norwegian Ilsa, played by Ingrid Bergman at the height of her career, is a romantic who is possessed of a feminine psyche and a female body. She is weak-willed and lets the men do her thinking for her. At one point she says she just wants to escape to America. Rick Blaine, played by Humphrey Bogart, is a cynical narcissist who morphs into a patriotic caregiver.[2] We first see him playing chess in his bar; the game represents the dialectic between the Nazi and Allied Forces. The Czechoslovakian Victor Lazlo, played by Paul Henreid, is an ideological saint of a narcissist who stands up to the Nazis. At one point he reinforces the dialectical tension of the film: "Each of us has a destiny, for good or evil." We know he is a hero because he escaped from a concentration camp and publishes underground propaganda against the Nazis. Other characters represent the darker side of life and provide more dialectical tension. Peter Lorre plays Guillermo Ugarte, a man on the run who is shot early in the film. The moment foreshadows many more that emphasize the temporality of our nature and bring our being unto death before us.

The lesser characters include Conrad Veidt, who plays the chief villain, Colonel Strasser, the head of the Nazis. He is in league with Louis Renault, played by Claude Raines, the head of the local police, who "blows with the wind." Renault is one of many ambiguous characters that call us in. We are curious to see how they will turn out. When Rick says he won't stick his neck out for anyone, Louis responds, "A wise foreign policy," thereby nailing the isolationists. A little later, Louis foreshadows Rick's change of heart: "I suspect that under that cynical shell you're at heart a sentimentalist." He thereby makes Rick ambiguous, which again draws the audience in. These characters provide a kind of double identification. We eventually lose ourselves to the filmic characters, but at the outset we identify them as movie stars we have seen before. All of those I've listed had made several successful films before *Casablanca*; they were box-office draws.

Another important point the characters make is that the world is made of many nationalities, breaking through the common-sense world of Caucasian superiority or Adolf Hitler's world of an Aryan master race. Along with the nationalities mentioned above, there are Russians, Arabs, Hispanics, and Dooley Wilson as the African American piano player, Sam. In fact, Sam and Rick form one of the many anaclitic relationships in the film. In the Paris flashback, it is Sam who pulls Rick onto the train to escape the Nazis when Ilsa fails to show up. At the end of the film, it is Renault and Rick who start a "beautiful friendship." Almost all of these characters have an aura of mystery about them that also attracts the audience. For example, in the flashback to Paris, where Rick and Ilsa have an affair, he turns her into an ambiguous character when he asks, "Who are you really? And what were you before?" We learn very little about Rick's gunrunning during the Italian invasion of Ethiopia, and his fighting in the Spanish Civil War on the side of the Loyalists against Franco's fascists. We do know that the loss of Ilsa, and the loss of the Ethiopian and Spanish causes have made Rick into a cynic.

As we have seen, the dialectical tensions of the plot draw us into the drama and reinforce the message of uniting the nations of the world to fight evil. The isolationist versus interventionist tension is obvious. Rick goes from one side of the equation to the other during the film. Early on he says, "I don't like disturbances in my place. Either lay off politics or get out." But later, he condemns the head-in-the-sand isolationists: "I'll bet they're asleep in New York. I'll bet they're asleep all over America." There is the contrast between the go-along-to-get-along Vichy French, led by Renault, and the French patriots committed to Liberty, Equality, and Fraternity, led by Lazlo. Underneath this surface, the cynicism versus idealism tension pervades the film. There are repeated references to the New World of America representing hope and freedom (the future utopia), and the Old World of Europe representing corruption and authoritarianism (the current dystopia). And of course, there is the tension of the love triangle among Ilsa, Rick, and Victor, which is not relieved until the very end of the film. There, Rick kills Strasser and then tells Ilsa that idealism is more important than love: "Look, I'm no good at being noble, but it doesn't take much to see that the problems of three little people don't amount to a hill of beans in this crazy world. Someday you'll understand that." Teary-eyed, Ilsa then flies off with Victor. Rick and Renault walk off into the fog on the tarmac, starting their "beautiful friendship."

Casablanca demonstrates that films can provide a place for the disclosure of truth. Settings can make us feel at home. A plot can draw us in with its twists, tensions, and characters. If we identify with them, we are much more likely to accept the message of the film. A United Nations Organization would be a good thing. Good people must be tolerant of all races. Good people must take care of one another. Good people must band together to fend off the evil forces of the world. And so they did. After the war, the United States led the fight to create a United Nations. In 1949, led by Eleanor Roosevelt, it composed and published its Declaration of Human Rights. *Casablanca* thus provides an example of how an art form can provide a healing eloquence.

We turn to another film that was awesome to its audiences in a different way. While *Casablanca* advanced a deliberative agenda at the expense of personal relationships, *Bonnie and Clyde* advanced an existential agenda about becoming an authentic person. After a somewhat tumultuous time at the hands of reviewers, the film was nominated for ten Academy Awards, including Best Picture. Burnett Guffey won the Oscar for his cinematography, which captured the look of the lower Midwest during the Depression. Estelle Parsons, in a breakthrough role, won Best Supporting Actress as the daughter of a preacher who arcs into a gang member. Gene Hackman, as Clyde's older brother Buck, was nominated for his portrayal and soon was seen as a major star. Warren Beatty as Clyde and Faye Dunaway as Bonnie became megastars after their nominations for the Oscar. After receiving bad reviews because of its portrayal of violence, the film caught fire on college campuses, evidently catching the spirit of rebellion brewing there in the late '60s. Then, Joe Morgenstern, who had written the first review for *Newsweek*, saw the film again, and decided to write a second review that praised the film and retracted his earlier comments. His friend Pauline Kael followed suit in the October issue of the *New Yorker*. By December the film was on the cover of *Time* and ready for a second run. Faye Dunaway's costumes led to a fashion revolution including the beret. Talk about identification.

Roger Ebert, a young critic newly on the scene, had proven the exception to the rule among the film's early critics. He believed the film was a masterpiece, a "milestone" of filmmaking. Ebert continues to be vindicated by such writers as Jake Horsley, who in his *Blood Poets* calls *Bonnie and Clyde* an "all but perfect piece of violent entertainment. . . . the first Hollywood movie to give the audience what it had been unconsciously waiting for:

a head-on encounter with sex and death." Talk about living unto death.[3] Horsley sees the eloquence of the film when he uncovers the unconscious implications in the appeal of the film. Nicole Rafter agrees: "The key factor in the movie's success was the way viewers empathized with Bonnie and Clyde. That audiences were able to identify with what were, after all, two long-dead punks arose from the scriptwriters' skillful downplaying of the characters' negative traits and emphasis on their virtues."[4] Rafter is right; like the films we reviewed above, this one relies heavily on identification to achieve its existential goal. *Bonnie and Clyde* projects various Freudian personae with which audience members can identify.

Clyde Barrow is the narcissist who is in love with his present self. From the beginning of the narrative, we see a cocky gangster confident of his talents. However, his psyche was not wedded to his body. For example, we learn that he maimed himself to get released from prison. While bullets cause him pain, they do not disable his spirit. It takes a hail of bullets to kill his body because he has become so spiritual. What made Clyde particularly attractive to college audiences was his vulnerability. Clyde appears to be impotent, or at least to have what we now call intimacy issues. In perhaps the most innovative scene of the film, Bonnie arouses and then attempts to consummate sex with Clyde. The moment surprises and scares him and he terminates the encounter. This may have been on the mark with insecure young men in the audience. Women might have been offended, feeling spurned, or they might have seen what Bonnie saw: the need to be loyal and to wait for the right moment to help Clyde overcome his shyness. When Clyde does overcome his sexual shyness, he arcs into a caretaker of Bonnie, thereby having more members of the audience identify with him.

Bonnie Parker's persona is complex. We first see her alone and bored in her bedroom putting on lipstick and admiring herself in the mirror. She bangs on the bars of her brass bed as if she were in prison. (Thus, in the opening minutes both Bonnie and Clyde are associated with prisons and the outlaw side of life.) She too appears to be a narcissist in love with her present self. But early on she arcs into a frustrated caregiver. "Your idea of love making," she says, "is no love making at all." When the two give that famous last glance to one another at the end of the film, we know that the trip has been worth it. Dreamers and romantics identify with Bonnie's creative side. She writes poetry, which actually gets published. She dreams of a new life, utopian in its dimensions.

Blanche Barrow is the voice of a superego. She is prim and proper, and rule-bound. But it is not long before Blanche wants her cut of the take after she survives the gang's first bank robbery. Suddenly she dresses in a black leather jacket and pants. Her unease with the unkempt C.W. Moss turns to friendship. It is clear too that she cares for her husband Buck and chooses him over her father's values. Big Brother Buck Barrow is the voice of conscience, but his loyalty to his younger brother and his desire to lead a meaningful life arc him into a caregiver. Avoiding Clyde's path, Buck has been trying to go straight. His marriage to Blanche symbolizes his desire to adhere to the establishment's common-sense life. However, Clyde's narcissistic masculinity overrides the call of social norms, as does the circumstance of the gang being trapped by the police. Despite Blanche's attempt to direct the police to Clyde and Bonnie's cabin, Buck overrules her and runs to help his brother escape. Blanche has little choice but to follow along. However, once she is blinded and hears the voice of a father figure, the Texas Ranger pursuing the gang, she arcs back into a crying little girl, who helps the forces of common sense succeed.

C.W. Moss is the quirkiest and perhaps the most rebellious of all the characters. He not only leaves his father behind, something with which college kids could certainly identify, but he steals all the money from the till in the process. Moss is the nerd of the group. He can fix anything. And thus, he picks up another segment of the audience. However, like Blanche, Moss is a key to the betrayal of the gang.

From the outset, the film pits Bonnie and Clyde against the corrupt establishment. After their first robbery, Clyde gives Bonnie a lesson on how to shoot a gun. They are out in the country behind a deserted house. A white farmer and his African American worker approach and reveal that this was their farm but that they lost it to the bank. Clyde hands the gun to the farmer, who shoots holes in the repossession sign. The farmer then gives the gun to his worker, who also shoots the sign. While the scene alienates the audience from the banks, it also demonstrates how Clyde can empower others, and that in this outlaw's world there would be no racism.

The existential ideology moves forward once the early identification is achieved. The film is arguing that you can't find real love until you know who you are. And you can't know who you are unless you take chances—certainly a counterpoint to common sense. As the gang goes through one crisis after another, those who have identified with them become even closer to them. They are bonded by the threat of death. So, they are imbued with the subliminal ideology unknowingly. After seeing the film, many college students must have felt more rebellious, more empowered, and more in need of exciting and dramatic moments in their lives. This may explain in part the rapid escalation of violence on campuses immediately after the film's release in 1967.

It also explains why the end of the film is not as excessively violent as some critics claimed. The machine-gun riddling of the bodies of Bonnie and Clyde by a group led by the Texas Ranger is meant to show that Bonnie and Clyde are so full of life that it takes not only someone Bonnie has kissed and someone who betrays the gang to kill them, it takes a lot of time and bullets to do it. This scene is in marked contrast to the quick killings of other characters. Bonnie and Clyde have become superhuman by the end of the film; they are content with themselves and with each other, as their last glance into each other's eyes reveals. Thus, Bonnie and Clyde evoke archetypes that produce an effect on the audience. In this case, the effect is identification that leads the audience into the outlaw's world of values that run contrary to common sense. Bonnie and Clyde are reconstructed images of the other, images that evoke the lost cathexis of Freud and the archetypes of Jung.

Art and the Call of the Self/Other

The power of art to speak to and perhaps inspire awe in its witnesses is a catalyst for reflection, inspiration, and a private conversation between the self who has heard the call and whose reflexive critical ability serves as an interlocutor conducting a reality check of the true meaning and significance that is being granted to the call. The basic question before the self is this: "Do I have it right?" In the name of truth, the give-and-take of the conversation, its dialectical and dialogical nature, should be ongoing for as long as it takes to come to a satisfactory answer, at least for the time being. And in the name of truth, the call that lies at the heart of existence calls for something more: an acknowledgment of others who serve as another reality check for the self's specific judgment of the awe-inspiring experience. When it comes to answering the call, respect for the truth and respect for the judgment of others go hand in hand.

Emmanuel Levinas makes much of the ethical nature of this relationship in his phenomenological analysis of the call of conscience, and maintains that his overall project constitutes a "philosophy of dialogue."[5] Dialogue is an activity of reciprocity whereby, as Levinas puts it, "'Thanks to God,' I am another for the others."[6] The self deserves from others what others deserve from the self. Involved in a dialogical struggle for the truth, we exist not merely as a self or other but rather as a self/other. The self as other calls for acknowledgment, as does the other as self. We also noted that what is missing in Levinas's philosophy is any concrete and detailed analysis of the rhetorical workings of the dialogical transaction involved here and the eloquence that facilities its progression. All of the case studies offered so far address this omission. These studies focus on selves seeking a dialogical relationship with a mass audience, the public. There is, of course, a much smaller audience that can be on hand as a reality check for the self: one other person who is willing and able to listen and respond to the self who seeks and welcomes critique, guidance, and further inspiration. At its best, this relationship, as it develops, becomes the collaborative deliberation of trusted friends engaged in the struggle for truth. The eloquence at work here not only involves using the right words, at the right time, and in the right way, but also displaying the appropriate interpersonal behavior that facilitates the bonding of friendship such that the individuals feel at home with each other as they struggle to disclose the truth of the presence of things in an awe-inspiring way.

To exemplify this kind of homemaking, we turn to real-world cases of creativity and transcendence being achieved because of harkening attunement to the calls of the self/other.[7] The process begins with acknowledgment of, and being open to, one's associate-become-friend. For example, George Sand (Amantine Dupin) and Frederick Chopin engaged in a dialogic relationship while living together in the French countryside and on the island of Majorca. The result was enormous productivity in terms of Chopin's music and Sand's prose. Chopin then left for a concert tour of Europe to raise funds for the Polish independence movement. He died of tuberculosis shortly thereafter.

William Wordsworth wrote "Tintern Abbey" in 1798 on the banks of the Wye River and claimed to be inspired by his sister Dorothy, who had helped him recover from a nervous breakdown. After she had joined him at Racedown, he began a great period of poetic creation. He entered into a similar relationship with Samuel Taylor Coleridge. After hiking in the mountains of Germany and witnessing the *Sturm und Drang* movement morph into Romanticism, the two brought the movement home to England. They became environmentalists in an effort to save Great Britain from the Industrial Revolution.[8] They were quintessential Romantic poets, advancing such themes as finding beauty in nature through careful observation, developing the self to its full potential, and creating sublime instances of transcendence, which they called "Romantic moments."[9] Perhaps Wordsworth's most famous one occurred when he looked out from the top of Mount Snowden, the highest peak in Great Britain. Above the moon-illuminated clouds, he realized that nature vastly expanded his mind and brought it into contact with nature's soul. He had heard a call that lies at the heart of human existence.

There are many other examples of creative dialogic relationships worthy of study, including the Germans Hannah Arendt and Martin Heidegger, and their French equivalents Simone de Beauvoir and Jean-Paul Sartre. To illustrate how dialogic communication can lead to authentic relationships and enhance artistic creativity, we turn to the case of Paul Gauguin and Vincent Van Gogh. Their letters allow us a glimpse of what must have been discussed when they lived together. The letters evince remarkable spontaneity, candor, acknowledgment, empathy, and risk. These exchanges are so rich that they have become scripts for public readings and have been studied as artworks in and of themselves.

Even before he met Gauguin, Van Gogh had experienced a transcendent moment of truth. The road to harkening attunement for Van Gogh began when he heard a sermon by Eliza Laurillard that claimed that Jesus was in nature. Laurillard was echoing a theme that often surfaced in the works of the Romantics: Observation of nature was the way to know God. Van Gogh concluded that his religion would be that authentic art imitates the soul of nature.[10] In Amsterdam he wrote, "Happy the one who is taught by truth, not by fleeting words but by *it*-self, showing *it*-self as *it* is."[11] Van Gogh's *Das is het* was a revelation of being that took his art to the next level. Heidegger, who admired Van Gogh's ability to reveal being in his paintings, explained this "it" moment phenomenologically. Heidegger emphasized that phenomenological inquiry seeks to disclose with "demonstrative precision" the appearance or "presencing" of some phenomenon, "to let that which shows itself [*phainesthai*] be seen from itself in the very way in which it shows itself from itself."[12] However, to further develop his ability to disclose being, Van Gogh needed authentic dialogue, and yet he, like Gauguin, withdrew not only from the public but from family, artistic circles, and salons.[13] Gauguin felt ostracized and "oppressed" by society. His wife had returned to her native Denmark, leaving Gauguin with only one of his six children. Gauguin put the boy in a boarding school and then left for Brittany. At the same time, his art moved from Impressionism to Symbolism and simplicity. Still, very few of his paintings sold. That's when he left for Martinique.

Having met the rebellious Gauguin in Paris, Van Gogh invited him to come to Arles, where Van Gogh had retreated after a miserable life of failure. Van Gogh wrote, "I wanted you to know that I have just rented a four-room house."[14] Van Gogh had repainted the house yellow, to brighten it up. He hoped to create a "fraternal marriage . . . a community [where] harmony reigned. . . . I should so much like to imbue you with a large share of my faith that we shall succeed in starting something that will endure."[15] In short, he was literally involved in homemaking. He wrote that he wanted to play Boccaccio to Gauguin's Petrarch, the famed Tuscan poets of the Renaissance. Like the retreat of the poets, the Yellow House had a garden nearby where Van Gogh envisioned the artists painting side by side. He also referred to many other relationships in the artistic community: Rembrandt and Hals, Corot and Daumier, Millet and Diaz, Flaubert and Maupassant. Van Gogh's brother Theo agreed to fund the venture. Gauguin was forty and Van Gogh was thirty-five. He had been rejected by the art studios and the salons of Paris. He had broken with everyone except his brother Theo.

Gauguin arrived in Arles in October 1888 after achieving some notoriety with his paintings of primitive subjects in Martinique. In Arles, Gauguin at times protected Van Gogh, and at other times enraged him. Van Gogh wrote to Theo that the relationship had become brotherly. Van Gogh did all the shopping; Gauguin did all the cooking.

Would their creativity have been significantly different had they not lived together? The answer is affirmative for several reasons. First, they would not have produced their incredible compendium of incandescent letters. We are quick to note that their letters to others have neither the intensity nor the creative power of their letters to one another. Second, each readily acknowledged the influence of the other on their art. When they lived together from October to the end of December 1888 and in April 1889, both created more artwork than in any other equivalent period of their lives. Gauguin later wrote, "Unbeknownst to the public, two men accomplished in the time a colossal amount of work, useful to both of them."[16] Later, Gauguin wrote this about their time together:

> When the two of us were together in Arles, both of us insane, and constantly at war over beautiful colors, I adored red; where could I find a perfect vermillion? . . . He loved yellow, did good Vincent, the painter from Holland. Gleams of sunlight warming his soul, which detested fog. A craving for warmth. . . . Taking his yellowish brush, [he] wrote on the sudden purple wall:
>
> > Je suis sain d'esprit
> >
> > Je suis Saint-Esprit
> >
> > [I am sane with spirit; I am the Holy Ghost.] We worked hard. . . . But
>
> between two human beings, he and myself, the one like a volcano and the other boiling . . . there was a battle in store.[17]

In their time together, Gauguin produced at least seventeen works; Van Gogh produced twenty-five, and the seeds for many later works were planted. Gauguin wrote to his wife, "Our days are taken up with work and ever more work; in the evening we are shattered and go to the café, followed by an early night."[18] The self-disclosive exchanges of their letters provide a clue to the furious creativity that eventually led first Gauguin and then posthumously Van Gogh to prominence. The role of identification in their relationship is evident in the letters. Once in desperation Van Gogh wrote: "Tell Gauguin to write to me, and that I am always thinking about him."[19] Van Gogh claimed that Gauguin "strongly encourages me to work often from pure imagination."[20] "Gauguin gives me the courage to imagine things," he wrote on another occasion.[21] Van Gogh believed Gauguin to be "something like a genius" who had inspired Van Gogh to exercise "free rein with abstraction."[22] Van Gogh imitated Gauguin's brushstroke method; Gauguin adopted Van Gogh's use of tarnished bronze. It was in Arles that Gauguin told Van Gogh his art was more like sculpting than painting. That is why to this day, prints of Van Gogh's works do not do them justice; one has to see the paintings for themselves to experience the thickness of being in them. For example, Van Gogh often did not paint the roots of trees; he squeezed them right out of the tube onto the canvas.

One can imagine that, like their letters, the dialogic communication between the recluses had its own style of eloquence: direct, tense, acknowledging, spontaneous, and stimulating. They created a space in which each man could express his love, his acknowledgment of the other and his art. Heidegger noticed this and spends several pages writing on how Van Gogh was able to represent the transcendence of being in his paintings. Heidegger concluded, "The artwork opens up in its own way the Being of beings."[23]

The relationship between Van Gogh and Gauguin was also dialogic in extended ways. An early drawing of a young girl by Van Gogh inspired three later paintings by Gauguin that contained the same figure. Even when apart, the two painters carried on their relationship not only in letters but in their very personal artwork. For example, Van Gogh sent a self-portrait to Gauguin along with his invitation to join Van Gogh in Arles. Gauguin responded with a self-portrait; in the corner of the painting was "a rendition of the self-portrait of Van Gogh as if it had been hung on Gauguin's wall in Brittany."[24] Many more self-portraits followed, as if the two were exchanging love letters.

Two things drove the pair apart. First, Van Gogh suffered bouts of physical illness, depression, and paranoia. On Christmas Eve, when Gauguin decided to go for a walk, Van Gogh mistook the event to mean that Gaugin was deserting their Yellow House for good. Van Gogh cut off his ear, wandered out into the streets of Arles seeking Gaugin, and finally handed his wrapped ear to an attendant outside of a bar with the request that she find Gauguin and give it to him, hoping to forestall his departure. Second, Theo Van Gogh had by this time become an art broker of some note in Paris. Monet was one of his clients. Theo had seen the virtue in Gauguin's work, and soon it was selling very well. Gauguin needed to return to Paris for the sake of his exhibitions. While Gauguin packed his bags in the Yellow House, Van Gogh was interned in restraints in a local hotel in Arles; sometimes he was tied to his bed or locked in his room after attendants removed all sharp objects. A local doctor checked in on him, as did a priest who reported his condition to Theo. Theo came at once, and spent a few hours with his brother often lying next to him in his bed. Then, Theo and Gauguin retreated to Paris. Van Gogh would see neither of them again. Theo arranged for the doctor and a priest to care for his deranged brother, who the doctor diagnosed with mental epilepsy.

After several recoveries and being allowed to return to the Yellow House, new bouts of depression and paranoia ensued. Van Gogh agreed to be committed to St. Paul Asylum in Saint-Rémy, where he began to paint again. One of his most famous paintings of his last few months was *Starry Night*. In May 1890, he was released from the asylum, which certified that he was mentally stable. He relocated to Auvers-sur-Oise, where he befriended some of the locals but was ridiculed by others. After he painted *Crows in a Field*, which depicts a crossroads in a wheat field and a sky studded with crows, he either shot himself or was accosted by hooligans. On July 29, 1890, he died of his wounds. When he heard the news, Gauguin wrote in his journal:

> The last letter I had from him ... told me that he hoped to recover enough to come and join me in Brittany, but that now he was obliged to recognize the impossibility of a cure: "Dear Master," (the only time he used the word), "after having known you and caused you pain, it is better to die in a good state of mind than in a degraded one." He sent a revolver shot into his stomach [Gauguin bought the local report which has now come into question], and it was only a few hours later that he died, lying in bed and smoking his pipe, having complete possession of his mind, full of love of his art, and without hatred for others. In *Les Monstres* Jean Dolent writes, "When Gauguin says 'Vincent' his voice is gentle." Without knowing it, but having guessed it, Jean Dolent is right.[25]

Gauguin died in French Polynesia in 1903 pursuing Rousseau's romantic return to nature. Gauguin and Van Gogh had encouraged each other to go places neither would have gone to without having an authentic relationship with the other. They had self-actualized their own souls. They then engaged each other in an I–Thou relationship that helped them see the transcendent in the short time together in the Yellow House.

Conclusion

Imagistic art can be discursive. We opened this chapter by showing that films can employ narrative argument and identification with powerful effects for good or ill. A film like *Gone with the Wind* can rationalize racism. *Casablanca* can call us to fight fascism. *Bonnie and Clyde* can force a deep introspection. And once we know and love ourselves, we can know and love others. It is hard to underestimate how powerful identification is in this type of cinematic eloquence. Audiences identify with scenes on the substantial level and with characters on the consubstantial level. Audiences are awed by the cinematography and lose themselves in plots. They are thrilled by the dialogical tension that drives the narrative and then is released in the dénouement of the story. All the while, they are being subjected to one degree or another to subliminal ideological messages, the call of the film.

We learn from the case study of Van Gogh and Gauguin that creative collaboration can be an added advantage of dialogic communication. Artists who engage in calling to one another seem to be more productive than those who do not. As Buber, Jaspers, and Heidegger tell us, it can inspire art that displays beauty, the sublime, and truth, and that thus may qualify as inciting the experience of awe.[26] All that is called for by the call that lies at the heart of human existence enables people to have and be educated by this experience.

Conclusion

We are beings on call: to be open to and in touch with otherness; to acknowledge the truth of its presence; to discover and use the right words in the right way and at the right time to communicate this truth to others; to gain skill in the rhetorical art of eloquence so to evoke in others an appreciation of the relevance of what we are saying about the truth in question; to work together with others in constructing dwelling places where we and they can feel at home with ourselves and with each other. The call's perfective impulse informs all of these activities. Its presence facilitates progress as it fuels our ability to act in the face of the challenge that comes with the call's objective uncertainty: Do you have it right in what you have to say about the truth, goodness, and justice? Are you sure? Questions are interruptions. The call that lies at the heart of human existence functions this way. We are beings on call. We are an interruption, a being always having to contend with the fact of being completely incomplete, perfectly imperfect, and wondering why this is so. The call that lies at the heart of human existence calls for this wonder—well-known for giving rise to and nourishing the callings of religion, science, philosophy, and the arts. A foundational claim of each of these callings is this: The more intense the wonder, the more we can be awed by what we find. Awe enhances our ability to be in touch and to stay in touch with the presence and truth of objects of consciousness.

The educational value of this claim is undeniable. Indeed, writes Rabbi Abraham Joshua Heschel, "There is . . . only one way to wisdom: awe. Forfeit your sense of awe, let your conceit diminish your ability to revere, and the universe becomes a marketplace for you. The loss of awe is the great block to wisdom."[1] Albert Einstein makes the point somewhat differently: "The most beautiful thing we can experience is the mysterious. It is the source of all true art and science. He to whom this emotion is a stranger, who can no longer pause to wonder and stand rapt in awe, is as good as dead: his eyes are closed."[2] Heschel's and Einstein's declarations imply a commitment on our part: We have an ethical obligation to cultivate our capacity to experience awe for the benefit of ourselves and others. And it all begins with the call that lies at the heart of human existence.

In this final chapter we offer a discussion that elaborates on the relationship between the call and the emotion of awe. Our discussion is structured to associate awe with the other happenings that, as noted above, are called for by the call. Awe lends itself to this arrangement and thereby enables us to provide what we hope is a fitting conclusion to and summary of our response to the call that we ourselves are. Selected writings of the Pulitzer Prize–winning author, nature writer, and narrative essayist Annie Dillard provide material for assessing the experience of being awed by the presence of whatever calls for attention. Dillard is a fitting choice for our purposes in that she is committed to the belief that human beings "were made and set here to give voice to . . . [their] own astonishment" (Greek: *ekplexis*, also translated as awe).[3] Moreover, Dillard holds fast to the belief that we have a responsibility to communicate to others what we have learned from our astonishment with the hope that they, too, may share in our awe-inspiring experience. With this responsibility comes a call for eloquence. We first offer some general observations on the scope and function of awe drawn from our case studies, most notably that of Donald Trump and what we termed his propensity to generate the "darkness of awe." Dillard's writings present a far more hopeful appreciation of the emotion.

The Call for Awe

All it takes is some degree of self-reflection to realize that the experience of awe is itself an awe-inspiring experience. We are awed by awe, by our wondrous ability to perceive and be moved in remarkable ways by experiences that qualify as being sublime. Awe is incited by the sublime: the remarkable and reverential nature of entities, environments, circumstances, and creative accomplishments. In its relationship with the sublime, awe is both an affect and an effect that legitimates the claim that some object of consciousness is sublime. No sublime, no awe. No awe, no sublime. Whether the experience of awe results in cheerful or distressing outcomes, the emotion warrants acknowledgment for its unequaled capacity to reveal "something more," an otherness, about the reality of our everyday existence that previously was concealed by our habitual ways of characterizing and understanding given objects of consciousness. All that we know, think we know, and seek to know is based on the workings of consciousness. Awe is an extraordinary consciousness-raising experience that situates us as witnesses to a momentous revelation of some intended object's truth—what it is.[4] For example, consider once again Vincent van Gogh's *Starry Night*. Created at the end of the nineteenth century, the painting became one of the twentieth century's most remarkable and celebrated paintings. Van Gogh was awed by various features of nature. Of all the majestic aspects of the painting's composition, the depiction of the sky's turbulence in the upper left side of the painting is the most awe-inspiring, at least for scientists who discovered that there is a precise mathematical correlation between van Gogh's creation and turbulence as measured in natural phenomena. This truth-revealing experience of awe becomes even more incredible when considering the following admission from the famed scientist Weiner Heisenberg: "When I meet God,

I am going to ask him two questions: why relativity? And why turbulence? I really believe he will have an answer for the first." The second is yet to come. What does that say about artistic genius, philosophy, science, God?

The experience of awe need not be as reverential as art, philosophy, science, and religion insist. For example, have you ever witnessed a three-year-old child receive her first piled-high triple-scoop ice cream cone? Her euphoric facial expression is a clear sign of awe. That is why the child was given the cone in the first place. The joy is overwhelming—a beautiful thing to behold. Yes, the whole experience is childish, but the awe is as real as can be. Also, let us not forget that awe need not be a joyful occasion. The experience of awe is commonly associated with states of fear, dread, and anxiety. A case in point is Edvard Munch's world-famous painting *The Scream*.

We encourage readers to search for the painting online. You will see that the painting discloses in a facial expression an experience of anxiety and terrifying awe that arose as the artist was forced to come to terms with certain horrors of existence: the gut-wrenching, painful cries of animals being butchered in a slaughterhouse, his fear of his neuroses, and the anxiety that can overwhelm human beings when they are forced to confront the uncertainty of existence. According to Munch scholar Sue Prideaux, "Munch renders [the experience] in a style which if pushed to extremes can destroy human integrity."[5] As we have shown, Donald Trump is a case in point.

Munch was awed by life and death, and if the depiction of the experience speaks to you, the awe will continue and perhaps intensify the more you reflect on *The Scream* and identify with what it says. Immanuel Kant makes brief mention of this intensification when he tells us: "Two things fill the mind with ever new and increasing admiration and awe, the oftener and more steadily we reflect on them: the starry heavens above and the moral law within."[6] Kant's awe of the identified objects is intensified ("ever new and increasing admiration") the more he wonders about their presence ("steadily reflect[s] on them"). That's what Aristotle terms "excessive wonderment," which can become more excessive as one continues to wonder about the awe-inspiring objects. There is awe, and then there is awe, and perhaps more awe after that. The experience of awe can vary in intensity. Subjectivity plays a significant role here.

Standing at the north rim of the Grand Canyon and witnessing its depth and breadth, one gains a sense of vastness and beauty that give a new expansive, sublime, and awe-inspiring meaning and significance to these phenomena. From the vantage point of astronauts journeying into space and walking on the moon, the vastness and the beauty of the Grand Canyon becomes invisible, lost in a pale blue dot. Vastness and beauty take on a whole new meaning and significance, as they did with astronaut John Glenn as he orbited the earth: "To look out at this kind of creation and not believe in God is to me impossible. . . . It just strengthens my faith."[7] The Apollo 14 astronaut Edgar D. Mitchell had this to say about the awe he experienced as the vast beauty and smallness of the earth's presence disclosed itself to him during his lunar moon walk: "You develop an instant global consciousness, a people orientation, an intense dissatisfaction with the state of the world, and a compulsion to do something about it. From out there on the moon, international politics looks so petty. You want to grab a politician by the scruff of the neck and drag him a quarter of a million miles out and say, 'Look at that, you son of a bitch.'"[8] Depending on a witness's lived experience and state of mind at the time, awe can vary in relevance and intensity and can foster a wide range of responses in witnesses and in those who are told by the witnesses about their experiences. In showing us that there is something more, an otherness, to the reality at hand, awe teaches us that truth-claims are debatable. When truth is on the line, the debate can be intense. Awe sanctions this form of communication.

In his ancient classic text *On the Sublime*, the rhetorical and literary critic Cassius Longinus emphasizes that cultivating our ability to experience awe "is the true end of man's being"—the "true end" being as much as possible a "perfect" understanding of the world.[9] Dillard finds the market-minded, instrumental, and common-sense ways and means that structure our every-day existence as the main factors conditioning people to develop a trained incapacity for being receptive to and awed by the truth. Dillard laments:

It is difficult to undo our own damage, and to recall to our presence that which we have asked to leave. It is hard to desecrate a grove and change our mind. The very holy mountains are keeping mum. We doused the burning bush and cannot rekindle it; we are lighting matches in vain under every green tree. Did the wind use to cry, and the hills shout forth praise? Now speech has perished from among the lifeless things of earth, and living things say very little to very few.[10]

For Dillard, the world "speaks" and its "words" call for a caring response of acknowledgment. Dillard is committed to offering this response by being as "wholly attentive" as possible to matters of concern, and by displaying the necessary rhetorical competence, an eloquent way with words, to move people to an understanding and appreciation of the awe-inspiring truth of some object of consciousness. Commenting on this second feature of the caring response, Dillard emphasizes that "the impulse to keep to yourself what you have learned is not only shameful, it is destructive. Anything you do not give freely and abundantly becomes lost to you. You open your safe and find ashes."[11] Displaying the necessary rhetorical competence needed to evoke an appreciation of some awe-inspiring truth helps to maintain and enhance the moral ecology of communal life—an ecology that is threatened by today's "post-truth" tendencies of people like Donald Trump to condone the obfuscation of facts and the practice of outright lying. Laboratory-based research by psychologists on how the experience of awe affects people's thinking and conduct supports this claim. Awe encourages people to enact altruistic and community-oriented behaviors, including diminishing selfish tendencies, being willing to help others, reducing persuasion by weak arguments, adopting more prosocial values, decreasing entitlement, and promoting patience and gratitude.[12] Awe is a catalyst for constructing dwelling places that help one feel at home.

Dillard's witnessing and narrative skills have led critics to place her in the company of such luminaries as Ralph Waldo Emerson, Henry David Thoreau, and Emily Dickinson. Recall what Emerson emphasizes about the heroism of the orator: This individual's rhetorical competence is made possible not only by "his power to connect his thought with its proper symbol, and so to utter it," but also, and primarily, by "his love of truth and . . . [the] desire to communicate it without loss."[13] Dillard is committed to this process.[14] Experiencing awe is incommensurate with being self-centered. Rather, it is otherness that has priority: the showing and saying of the sublime and the responsibility to share with others what one has learned from the experience. Awe, writes psychologist Paul Pearsall, "comes with an intensification of the need to connect not only with what inspired awe but to make a commitment to more loving, caring, protective relationships with others and the world in general."[15] Being the social creatures that we are, we have a responsibility to acquire wisdom and to communicate this wisdom as best as we can to others so to enhance the moral ecology of our communities. Dillard makes the point in a claim noted above. Human beings "were made and set here to give voice to . . . [their] own astonishment." This claim speaks of a fundamental purpose of human existence that entails a specific ability. Dillard maintains that we can turn to the science of evolutionary biology for an explanation of how we developed this purpose and ability. With this ability we enhance the chances and quality of our survival as a species the more we know the truth about the nature and workings of our environments and adapt accordingly. Dillard also maintains, however, that evolution is a result of God's creation. Wondering about the past, present, and future of this process, Dillard asks her Maker, "are you tired? finished?"

These are strange questions to put to One who is well known to have it all together, to be complete, perfect. The Ultimate Sublime! The questions, however, are rhetorically significant: they interrupt a taken-for-granted conception of God: God's ambiguous reply to Moses on Mount Sinai when asked Its Name: "*Ehyeh-Asher-Ehyeh*." "I am that I am" and "I shall be what I shall be." The ambiguity is interruptive, calling into question the truth of the matter. Dillard follows God's lead: "are you tired? finished?"

Commenting on her "adventures" of witnessing the "intricacies of nature" that have so far resulted from the evolution of God's becoming, Dillard hopes that what these adventures disclose of the truth of matters of concern may give some indication of God's truth. Dillard concludes that God "is apt to create anything." God will "stop at nothing."[16] For those who believe that God will reward them for assuming the responsibility of carefully attending to these intricacies, Dillard is not reassuring. Her religious orientation is deistic: As she puts it: "God does not, I regret to report, give a hoot." In directing the creation process "God needs nothing, asks for nothing, and demands nothing, like the stars."[17] God granted us a gift. The rest is up to us. We are beings on call.

Of course, such claims about God are at best conjecture, and Dillard knows it. She admits, "I don't know beans about God."[18] Martin Heidegger's way of dealing with the question of God would appeal to Dillard in that it affirms her hope that attending to the intricacies of nature may disclose truths that attest to whatever God may be. Heidegger's term for this revelatory phenomenon is "the truth of Being." He writes:

> Only from the truth of Being can the essence of the holy be thought. Only from the essence of the holy is the essence of divinity to be thought. Only in the light of the essence of divinity can it be thought or said what the word 'God' is to signify. . . . How can man at the present stage of world history ask at all seriously and rigorously whether the god nears or withdraws, when he has above all neglected to think into the dimension in which alone that question can be asked?[19]

One does not have to believe in God to realize that we are creatures who possess the ability to be awed by the ways the world speaks its truths. This ability and the truth of Being that it attends to are facts of life, givens, empirical phenomena that offer themselves for understanding as we turn the ability back on itself, its truth of Being, thereby making it an object of consciousness warranting careful analysis. Our study speaks to this task: the ability that calls to us to be and remain open to the scope and function of the call that lies at the heart of human existence. Being as open as possible to the truth of Being is essential to experience awe.

Exploring the marvels of nature near a creek in Virginia's Blue Ridge Mountains, Dillard speaks of her passion for discovering the truth showing itself in the environment at hand: "What I aim to do is not so much learn the names of the shreds of creation that flourish in this valley, but to keep myself open to their meanings, which is to try to impress myself at all times with the fullest possible force of their very reality. I want to have things as multiply and intricately as possible present and visible in my mind."[20] Dillard seeks to assume the function of a phenomenon that is essential to life: being an opening. Without openings we would have no places to be—nowhere, for example, to sit or stand, open the pages of this book, read the opening sentences of its introduction, and talk to others about what we read. "Our lives are so place-oriented and place-saturated," writes the philosopher Edward Casey, "that we cannot begin to comprehend, much less face up to, what sheer placelessness would be like."[21] Given what you are doing right now, you presently occupy a place where an opening act has happened (through an act of writing), is happening (through an act of reading), and may continue to do so as patience and interest persist. There are no beginnings, middles, and ends, no pasts, presents, and futures, without openings. And, of course, they are a biological necessity: placed all over our bodies, they enable us to see, hear, feel, communicate, breathe, procreate, take in nourishment, and get rid of waste. An encumbered or closed opening can be rather discomforting. Openings are to human beings what water is to fish. A fish out of water will die; so, too, a human being without openings.

Openings, to be sure, are remarkable. Imagine what being with others would be like if we were incapable of being open-minded and open-hearted toward them. And an equally significant fact of life regarding openings is this: The spatial and temporal fabric of human existence is itself an opening: that specific place in all of the cosmos that needs to be present in order for anything to call for attention, disclose its presence, and be appreciated in a meaningful way. We are what the call that lies at the heart of our existence calls us to be: a dwelling place where the truth of Being can happen and where we can feel at home as perfectly as possible with what it has to say and show. Dillard emphasizes the importance of our being ready and willing to witness this original disclosure: "If we were not here, material events like the passage of seasons would lack even the meager meanings we are able to muster for them. The show would play [not to a home but] to an empty house, as do all those falling stars which fall in the daytime."[22]

Hearing the silence happening here enhances one's ability to be attuned to the truth disclosed in a primordial event of communication. Dillard admits as much:

> At a certain point you say to the woods, to the sea, to the mountains, the world, Now I am ready. Now I will stop and be wholly attentive. You empty yourself and wait, listening. After a time you hear it: there is nothing there. There is nothing but those things only, those created objects, discrete, growing or holding, or swaying, being rained on or raining, held, flooding, or ebbing, standing, or spread. You feel the world's word as a tension, a hum, a single chorused note everywhere the same. This is it: this hum is silence. Nature does utter a peep—just this one.[23]

The experience of awe requires such devoted attunement, what might be termed a state of eloquent listening, which is what it takes to be the "perfect witness" that Dillard wants to be and what the philosophy of phenomenology identifies as "the proper dignity of human beings": demonstrating a receptive response to the call that lies at the heart of existence and all that it calls for. The effort," Dillard admits, "is really a discipline requiring a lifetime of dedicated struggle."[24] The call is ever present as the world speaks its truths. And to repeat an earlier noted claim of Dillard's, we "were made and set here to give voice to . . . [our] own astonishment," to our own experience of awe. She makes the point employing a metaphor intended to interrupt a simple, well-known saying ("What you see is what you get") and, in so doing, enhance the evocative and sublime potential of the saying, which she now associates with the well-being and quality of life of human beings: "It is dire poverty indeed when a man is so malnourished and fatigued that he won't stoop to pick up a penny. But if you cultivate a healthy poverty and simplicity, so that finding a penny will literally make your day, then, since the world is in fact planted in pennies, you have with your poverty bought a lifetime of days. It is that simple. What you see is what you get."[25] There is eloquence displayed here with the evocative use of metaphor.

The openness of human existence, forever present in its objective uncertainty, interrupts. Dillard follows suit. The interruptive nature of her discourse functions rhetorically to evoke a heightened state of consciousness of a "mundane" fact. Rhetoric is at work whenever language is employed to open people to ideas, positions, and circumstances that, if rightly understood, stand a better than even chance of getting people to think and act wisely. Orators are forever attempting to create these openings, for this is how they maximize the chance that the members of some audience will take an interest in and identify with what is being said and thus become more involved in judging the truthfulness of the orator's discourse. Neither persuasion nor collaborative deliberation can take place without the formation of this joint interest. Interests take form only to the extent that we develop emotional attachments to things happening in our environments. As we showed earlier, Aristotle offers the first detailed analysis of this fact of life in book 2 of his *Rhetoric*. The rhetorical practice of moving ideas to people and people to ideas is dependent on the ability of orators to attune their discourse to the emotional character of those being addressed.

We feel the world's word as we turn our witnessing ability back on itself and experience the openness that we are and that makes possible this ability. The primordial act of communication that takes place here calls us to assume the ethical responsibility of being an open-minded and devoted witness to the ways the world silently speaks its truths. Practice in responding to this call has as its one goal becoming what Dillard struggles to be: a "perfect witness" to the showing and saying of objects of consciousness. The perfective impulse embedded in the call is hard at work in Dillard's writings. The status of witnessing involved in being a perfect witness evolves as a process of noticing, acknowledgment, and awe:

Dillard is in the woods, sitting next to a creek, and noticing fish ("shiners") "flashing" back and forth and "feeding over the muddy sand in skittery schools." That lasted for a few moments and "Then I noticed white specks, some sort of pale petals, small, floating from under my feet on the creek's surface, very slow and steady." What follows is a description of her moving from noticing to an advanced form of witnessing: "So I blurred my eyes and gazed towards the brim of my hat and saw a new world. I saw the pale white circles roll up, roll up, like the world's turning, mute and perfect, and I saw the linear flashes, gleaming silver, like stars being born at random down a rolling scroll of time."[26] The new world that Dillard saw was the same world that she first noticed but that now was being attended to in a more open-minded and receptive way. An act of noticing had become an act of acknowledging, and an object of consciousness was becoming sublime.

We learn of the experience as Dillard continues her story. As her acknowledgment of the creek, petals, fish, and muddy sand intensified, "Something broke and something opened. I filled up like a new wineskin. I breathed an air like light; I saw a light like water. I was the lip of a fountain the creek filled forever; I was either, the leaf in the zephyr; I was flesh-flake, feather, bone. When I see this way, I see truly."[27]

Dillard's words are attuned to a primordial act of communication that, with its epideictic discourse, calls her to perfect her ability to be awed by the truth of some object of consciousness. Dillard tells us that when she assumes the ethical responsibility of responding to this call, her state of mind is that of "letting go" of everyday habits and routines of seeing the world and she becomes "transfixed and emptied." Dillard differentiates these two ways of seeing by comparing them to walking with and without a camera: "When I walk with a camera, I walk from shot to shot, reading the light on a calibrated meter. When I walk without a camera, my own shutter opens, and the moment's light prints on my own silver gut."[28] Seeing truly is the goal of a perfect witness. And employing the analogy that she does, Dillard displays the skill of eloquence.

At the moment that something broke, Dillard's witnessing of her environment advanced once again. A consciousness-raising experience was at hand. Something opened, and something became sublime. Acknowledgment turned into awe. Awe stretches our openness toward its limits, resulting in our being more receptive to what we are witnessing and what it has to say and show about the truth of some object of consciousness. Notice, too, that as she experiences this emotion, the rhetorical style of her discourse changes, taking on a sublime character. Metaphors flow as they are mixed and matched to convey the radically different way that awe situates her in an environment that she has been witnessing. Dillard's ethos (character), pathos (emotional disposition), and logos (the logical structure of her way with words) are transformed by the experience of awe.

The perfect witness is on the lookout for the sublime, the catalyst for awe, which Dillard maintains provokes an "unself-conscious state at any moment of pure devotion to any object. It is at once a receptiveness and total concentration." Dillard tells us, for example, that "If you wish to tell me that the city offers galleries, I'll pour you a drink and enjoy your company while it lasts; but I'll bear with me to my grave those pure moments at the Tate . . . where I stood planted, open-mouthed, born, before that one particular canvas, that river, up to my neck, gasping, lost, receding into watercolor depth and depth to the vanishing point, buoyant, awed, and had to be literally hauled away."[29] Dillard witnesses a picture that speaks a truth to her, and she, in turn, communicates to others what she experienced. This communication—with its spirited treatment of the passions, its employment of metaphor, and its elevation of composition structure—assumes a sublime and eloquent character meant to awe others and thus, perhaps, open them like never before to the sublime subject being discussed. Longinus emphasizes the importance of sublime discourse when he notes that it "is proper on all occasions to call on art as an ally to nature. By the combined resources of these two we may hope to achieve perfection."

Of course, what counts as sublime is in the eye of the beholder, and Dillard's rhetorical way with words may fail to evoke a favorable and rewarding response from others. As noted above, however, Dillard is dedicated to her calling: "The impulse to keep to yourself what you have learned is not only shameful, it is destructive. Anything you do not give freely and abundantly becomes lost to you. You open your safe and find ashes."[30] Dillard admits in her book *The Writing Life* that the effort involved can be a deathlike experience:

> I do not so much write a book as sit up with it, as with a dying friend. During visiting hours, I enter its room with dread and sympathy for its many disorders. I hold its hand and hope it will get better. This tender relationship can change in a twinkling. If you skip a visit or two, a work in progress can turn on you. A work in progress quickly becomes feral. It reverts to a wild state overnight.[31]

Later in her book she instructs the reader in a more personal and death-defying way: "Write as if you were dying. At the same time, assume you write for an audience consisting solely of terminal patients. That is, after all, the case. What would you begin writing if you knew you would die soon? What could you say to a dying person that would not enrage by its triviality?"[32]

From a phenomenological point of view, "being-towards-death" is unsurpassed in its overwhelming with terrifying awe our openness to the way the world speaks its truths. Death interrupts and ends the interruption that we are. As far as we know, death is a state of "nothingness," denying any possibility of feeling at home with ourselves, others, and our frequented environments. Recall that this dwelling place of comfort and security is so essential to our well-being that it holds a special status in the vernacular of religion and its promise that homelessness need not be our fate. "There is life after death. When you die, you can go home to your Maker."

This way of relating death, home, and God is warranted by how we exist as beings who, given their openness to the uncertainty of their future and the anxiety that is well known to arise from this fact of life, have developed a passionate longing for some degree of meaning, order, and completeness or perfection in their lives such that we can feel at home with ourselves and others. The loss of the feeling makes us homesick. People suffering this sickness are known to admit that they "feel like dying." Moreover, the sickness can develop to the point that it leads to one's demise. With its specific use of language, religion takes the lead in being a homemaker as it provides a dwelling place for people who are "sick to death" because of their homelessness.

The notion of home associated with God is, of course, ideal: it's a dwelling place offering security, convenience, cordiality, relaxation, happiness, and love; a place that encourages the development of personal relationships and strong family ties; a place of genuine care and comfort. Given this idealized conception of a much-cherished dwelling place, it makes sense to say that "There is no place like home," and that "Home is where the heart is." Dillard agrees, but she cautions against a possible consequence of making people feel too at home in their environments. This consequence manifests itself as the prescribed habits and routines of a given dwelling place to encourage a herd-like tendency to abide by a mindless conformism that disables people's ability to be open-minded in witnessing, being awed by, and expressing the ways the world speaks its truths. Dillard stays with the example of religion to illustrate the problem. She tells us, "On the whole, I do not find Christians [which Dillard is] outside the catacombs, sufficiently sensible of conditions" that present themselves in nature as the world speaks its truths.[33] Elsewhere she reports, "Many times in Christian churches I have heard the pastor say to God, 'All your actions show your wisdom and love.' Each time, I reach in vain for the courage to rise and shout, 'That's a lie!'—just to put things on a solid footing": those conditions of nature where the showing and saying of objects of consciousness disclose their truths.[34] Speaking of the mindless conformism displayed in the people in the pews, she displays her talent for eloquence as she makes her point with the story of an insect:

> I like insects for their stupidity. A paper wasp—Polistes—is fumbling at the
> stained-glass window on my right. I saw the same sight in the same spot last

Sunday. Psst! Idiot! Sweetheart! Go around by the door! I hope we seem as endearingly stupid to God—bumbling down into lamps, running half-wit across the floor, banging for days at the hinge of an opened door. I hope so. It does not seem likely.[35]

Indeed, recall that, for Dillard, God doesn't "give a hoot." Dillard, on the other hand, does. Of the ways of mindless conformism noted here, the most important one for our purposes is associated with the open door: the wasp is incapable of recognizing how this openness enables it to once again inhabit nature's larger landscape. More to the point, even God needs the openness of human being to be considered a topic worthy of thought, let alone a source of awe.

One suspects that God-fearing people will not think highly of Dillard's ethos, pathos, and logos—her character and emotion-driven way of using words to make her point. There is no identification going on here between Dillard and people in the pews. Dillard is an interruption directed at a world of common sense that, at its worst, is sense made common so that everything is comfortably cheapened by its touch. One also suspects, however, that members of her hoped-for supportive audience find the interruption liberating. An author devoted to being a perfect witness skilled in the rhetorical art of eloquence certainly hopes for such an outcome. It may be said that Dillard and her supporters find their counterparts to be so blinded and brainwashed by religious dogma that they have become rotten with perfection. The counterparts, of course, have a rebuttal. Dillard and her supporters, to be sure, are rotten with imperfection. Parties from either side are loath to identify with the other's arguments. Constructing a dwelling place by way of collaborative deliberation that accommodates and encourages respect for these differences seems to be out of the question. Indeed, interruptions are forbidden. The wasp will continue bumping at the door without remedy. An openness to otherness and acknowledgment of its presence have become needless activities. The call that lies at the heart of existence never goes away, but it offers no guarantee that it will be heard and obeyed. True believers display what they consider to be the highest form of eloquence when they utter the word "God." Dillard gives the impression that this word is really a perfect cheat of eloquence, or what the Nobel Prize–winning physicist and atheist Steven Weinberg describes as "a form of protective coloration" used as a rhetorical tool for ornamenting and thus beautifying discourse.

Dillard is critical of religion because it doesn't help the wasp find the open door that leads to the wonder of nature and the awe that it inspires. She employs the rhetorical art of eloquence to make the point:

> I am no scientist. I explore the neighborhood. An infant who has just learned to hold up his head has a frank and forthright way of gazing about him in bewilderment. He hasn't the faintest clue where he is, and he aims to find out. In a couple of years, what he will have learned instead is how to fake it: he'll have the cocksure air of a squatter who has come to feel he owns the place. Some unwonted, taught pride diverts us from our original intent, which is to explore the neighborhood, view the landscape, to discover at least where it is that we have been so startlingly set down, if we can't learn why.[36]

What Dillard is saying here about the infant is reminiscent of what Jesus Christ has to say to his followers about the importance of "becoming again a child" so to clear your mind of reified thought and close-minded tendencies that hinder your "God-given" ability to be awed by the truth of God's presence here on earth and beyond (Matthew 18:3). Dillard doesn't throw all of religion aside, only its blinders, which weakens its "wakefulness" and which Dillard maintains is a prerequisite for good health and the truth-disclosing experience of awe. She returns to the significance of the child to once again make the point:

> We teach our children one thing only, as we were taught: to wake up. We teach our children to look alive there, to join by words and activities the life of human culture on the planet's crust. As adults we are almost all adept at waking up. We have so mastered the transition we have forgotten we ever

learned it. Yet it is a transition we make a hundred times a day, as, like so many will-less dolphins, we plunge and surface, lapse and emerge. We live half our waking lives and all of our sleeping lives in some private, useless, and insensible waters we never mention or recall. Useless, I say. Valueless, I might add, until someone hauls their wealth up to the surface and into the wide-awake city, in a form that people can use.[37]

Dillard is committed to achieving this goal. The call that lies at the heart of human existence calls for the wealth of wakefulness, the ability to listen eloquently to all that is happening in the "neighborhood" of nature. With this ability comes the undivided attention of consciousness and the openings it makes possible by way of the strength and discipline of its attunement. The more one is attuned to whatever calls for attention, the more the experience of awe becomes a possibility. Dillard's story about her witnessing, being awed by, and engaging in the rhetorical endeavor of coming to terms with the cosmological event of an eclipse provides a lucid illustration of this possibility become real.

The story begins with a recall: "It had been like dying, that sliding down the mountain pass. It had been like the death of someone, irrational, that sliding down the mountain pass and into the region of dread. It was like slipping into fever or falling down that hole in sleep from which you wake yourself whimpering."[38] We are given an indication of what is to come: the loss of not feeling at home; a being-unto-death.

Dillard and her husband traveled from their home to a location high on a hill in central Washington to witness a total eclipse. Many other onlookers would be there, too. "It began with no ado. It was odd that such a well-advertised public event should have no starting gun, no overture, no introductory speaker. I should have known right then that I was out of my depth." Dillard admits that she once witnessed a partial eclipse, but it "bears almost no relation to a total eclipse. Seeing a partial eclipse bears the same relation to seeing a total eclipse as kissing a man does to marrying him, or as flying in an airplane does to falling out of an airplane." Continuing to prepare the reader for what is to come, Dillard tells us that "Usually it is a bit of a trick to keep your knowledge from blinding you. But during an eclipse it is easy. What you see is much more convincing than any wild-eyed theory you may know."39 A partial eclipse was becoming a total eclipse, a sublime event. The opening paragraph of Dillard's essay now continues:

> The sun was going, and the world was wrong. The grasses were wrong. . . . From all the hills came screams. A piece of sky beside the crescent sun was detaching. . . . It was an abrupt black body out of nowhere. . . . There was no sound. The eyes dried, the arteries drained, the lungs hushed. There was no world. . . . Seeing this black body was like seeing a mushroom cloud. The heart screeched. The meaning of the sight overwhelmed its fascination. It obliterated meaning itself.40

Continuing with her description and reaction to this instance of the sublime, she tells us that as the sun disappeared, "we saw a wall of dark shadow come speeding toward us. . . . It slammed our hill and knocked us out." It was like feeling "a slug of anesthetic shoot up your arm. . . . You can feel the deadness run up your arm; you can feel the appalling, inhuman speed of your own blood." The eclipse spoke of the "universe about which we have read so much and never before felt. . . . It was as though an enormous, loping god in the sky had reached down and slapped the earth's face."41 The intensity of Dillard's rhetoric is, itself, overwhelming, sublime. She is listening and speaking eloquently.

Dillard reports that when the sublime event concluded, "an odd thing happened . . . we all hurried away. We were born and bored at a stroke." Yes, an extended moment of awe was a terrifying, yet must-see event, but "enough is enough. One turns at last even from glory itself with a sigh of relief. From the depths of mystery, and even from the heights of splendor, we bounce back and hurry for the latitudes of home" with its habits, routines, and mindless conformism that grant much needed and welcomed stability and comfort to the chaos of life.[42]

Dillard and her husband were seated at a restaurant, listening to the repetitions of witnesses asking, "Did you see . . . ? Did you see . . . ?" Dillard's descriptions of the eclipse and its effects were intended to display a more carefully crafted and sublime acknowledgment of the awe-inspiring eclipse than what her fellow witnesses were saying about it. She admits her efforts were wanting at times: "In the black sky was a ring of light. It was a thin ring, an old, thin silver wedding band, an old worn ring. It was an old wedding band in the sky, or a morsel of bone."[43] But then a member of the crowd, a college student, addressed her with a question regarding a metaphor "which knocked [her] for a loop": "Did you see that little white ring? It looked like a Life Saver, it looked like a Life Saver up in the sky." "And so it did," admits Dillard. "The boy spoke well. He was a walking alarm clock. I myself had at that time no access to such a word. He could write a sentence, and I could not. . . . All those things for which we have no words are lost."[44] An awe-inspiring event showed itself as a Life Saver causing a "deadness" in a witness. The contradiction does what an eclipse does: interrupts the normalcy of daily life. The interruption evokes a higher state of consciousness of what is being disclosed. The contradiction helps reveal something of the truth of an eclipse and enhances the sublime character of Dillard's discourse. Experiencing awe challenges us with the ethical obligation of discovering and using the right words, at the right time, and in the right way so that we can share our experience effectively with others. Achieving this goal is sacred for Dillard:

> In the deeps of a total eclipse are the violence and terror of which psychology has warned us. But if you ride these monsters deeper down, if you drop with them farther over the world's rim, you find what our sciences cannot locate or name, the substrate, the ocean or matrix or ether which buoys the rest, which gives goodness its power for good, and evil its power for evil, the unified field: our complex and inexplicable caring for each other, and for our life together here. This is given. It is not learned.[45]

What the total eclipse shows and says about itself is far more sublime than the common, well-worn words in a dictionary's definition of the event. Indeed, it is "monsters" forcing you "farther over the world's rim."

Dillard witnesses, acknowledges, and is awed by the way the world, in moments of dread, speaks and shows what for her is a truth that makes possible all that our openness enables us to perceive, including openness itself: God. Dillard writes in the name of One who is most vividly thought to be in experiences of awe and who doesn't give a hoot about how this experience, or any other one for that matter, affects our thinking and behavior. Dillard maintains that we do not need to cultivate our ability to experience awe "unless [we] want to know God." Prayers, for example, can help. Dillard agrees, but she emphasizes that such noble activities "work on [us], not on" God.[46] Dillard needs the work. That is why she writes about her being awed by the ways the world speaks its truths.

This primordial act of communication manifests itself in a "given," what Dillard describes in the above quotation as "our complex and inexplicable caring for each other, and for our life together here" on earth, our home in the universe. Dillard is committed to enhancing the educational nature and value of this communal phenomenon. She does not want to open her safe and find ashes. For Dillard, an ethical responsibility calls her to be true to her openness, to witness and be awed by the way the world speaks its truths, and to have a way with words that can communicate to others as effectively as possible the truth in question. Perhaps, then, they too may be awed by the object of consciousness that directs the author's attention such that their understanding of the significance of the object's truth is enhanced. The call for responsible action is constant. The struggle goes on. Now, as they say, failure is not an option. Dillard tells a story that speaks to these concerns.

Shortly after becoming the youngest American woman to win the Pulitzer Prize for her *Pilgrim at Tinker Creek* (1974), the twenty-nine-year-old Dillard was camping alone in the Blue Ridge Mountains of Virginia, struggling to deal with various existential crises associated with her "empty dedicated life" and at a loss for words that might be used in her next, as yet unplanned project. Such an existential situation defines for a writer a state of homelessness that, if prolonged, becomes a form of being-towards-death whereby the writer's ethical responsibility of being awed by the truth of some object of consciousness and responding accordingly remains inoperative. For Dillard, God doesn't care. No acknowledgment here. She is on her own, alone with her openness, and listening for some epideictic discourse that can direct her attention such that she is awed by its truth. Then something happened: a display of evolution, a part of God's plan, at least for Dillard. The happening took place as Dillard was "convincing" herself "by [her] own rhetoric: commit yourself to a useless art! In art alone is meaning! In sacrifice alone is meaning! These . . . were issues for me at the time: dedication, purity, sacrifice." As Dillard's story unfolds, the earlier cited words of Longinus ring true: it "is proper on all occasions to call on art as an ally to nature. By the combined resources of these two we may hope to achieve perfection."

At night Dillard would read by candlelight. Moths kept flying into her candle. Dillard doesn't report that the reason moths fly into flames and other sources of light is evolutionary: they need to maintain a constant angle relative to a nearby point source of light to maintain the stability of their flight. This maneuver keeps them moving closer and closer to the flame while adjusting their relative position. Ultimately the moves end up at the light itself. The moths' fate is inevitable and easily taken for granted.

One night, Dillard noticed a moth fly into the candle: it "was caught, burnt dry, and held." A witnessing of nature, of God's creation, began. Dillard heeded the call of her openness. Noticing grew into an intense acknowledgment headed toward awe. Her discourse reflects the intensity: "A golden female moth, a biggish one with a two-inch wingspan . . . dropped her abdomen into the wet wax, stuck, flamed, frazzled and fried in a second." The moth's "moving wings ignited like tissue paper" enlarging the light coming from the candle and allowing Dillard to see more of her environment that until now was hidden in darkness. "At once the light contracted again and the moth's wings vanished in a fine, foul smoke. At the same time, her six legs clawed, curled, blackened, and ceased, disappearing utterly. And her head reared in spasms, making a spattering noise; her antennae crisped and burned away and her heaving mouth parts cracked like a pistol fire."[47]

Dillard wondered: Had the moth "been new, or old? Had she mated and laid her eggs, had she done her work? All that was left was the glowing horn shell of her abdomen and thorax—a fraying, partially collapsed gold tube jammed upright in the candle's round pool." And then awe happened: "this moth-essence, this spectacular skeleton, began to act as a wick. She kept burning. The wax rose in the moth's body from her soaking abdomen to her thorax to the jagged hole where her head should be and widened into flame." The candle now had two wicks. "The moth's head was fire. . . . She burned for two hours without changing, without bending or leaning—only glowing within, like a building fire glimpsed through silhouetted walls, like a hollow saint, like a flame-faced virgin gone to God, while I read by her light."[48]

Dillard ends the story by noting that she shared it with students in one of her poetry classes and asked them "which of you want to give your lives and be writers?" She wonders whether any of the students understood what the story shows about the truth of its topic. And then Dillard "tried to tell them what the choice must mean: you can't be anything else. You must go at your life with a broadax."[49] We are called to experience awe. Not by One who supposedly doesn't care at all, but most certainly by the fundamental structure and workings of our own existence. Dillard would have us think about the matter in this self-effacing way:

> How can people think that artists seek a name? A name, like a face, is something you have when you're not alone. There is no such thing as an artist: there is only the world, lit or unlit as light allows. When the candle is burning, who looks at the wick? When the candle is out, who needs it? But the world without light is wasteland and chaos, and a life without sacrifice is abomination. What can any artist set on fire but his world?[50]

This last question brings to mind an earlier noted question that Dillard raises for herself, her students, and all would-be devoted writers: "What would you begin writing if you knew you would die soon?" We are certain that Dillard would want readers of her story to read in the "light" that she praises as she is awed by the moth becoming a wick and increasing the light of the candle. The literary critic Linda Smith did so and rightly heard the call: "Sacrifice is not an incidental result of the artist's mission; it is an intrinsic part of the mission. It comes with the territory." The growing intensity of Dillard's sublime rhetoric as she moves from noticing to acknowledgment to experiencing awe speaks of this sacrificial way of being. The moth becoming a flaming wick that provides additional light to the situation at hand speaks to the possible worth of isolation, sacrifice, and a being unto death: The writer can live on after her death, having produced works that are valued for the awe they inspire with the truths they disclose. (We must admit, however, that we know no writer who wants to die the way the moth did. Sometimes eloquence can be quite alarming, like staring at Munch's *The Scream* and feeling sick to death.)

We do not know if Dillard would agree, but she certainly would remind us that feeling at home with the truth is a worthwhile goal—a "Life Saver," if you will. Dillard devotes her calling to educating her readers about this goal. We have an ethical responsibility to keep the openness of human being as wide open as possible so we can be awed by the saying and showing of truth and, with the necessary rhetorical competence, communicate it as effectively as possible to others. To repeat Dillard's foundational claim: "we are here to give voice to our own astonishment." Let the truth be told! The proper dignity of humankind is on the line—always. So, too, "our complex and inexplicable caring for each other, and for our life together here." As we showed in the previous chapter, Van Gogh, Jaspers, and Buber would agree. Being for others is a beautiful way to be.

Elaine Scarry's provocative and insightful assessment of beauty stresses this very point. Something deemed beautiful, argues Scarry, creates "the aspiration for enduring certitude [perfection]." It "calls" for the "perceptual acuity" (acknowledgment) that enables us to appreciate as perfectly as possible some object's or subject's disclosure, its truth, and thereby appropriate and cultivate the knowledge and wisdom made possible by this revelation. Scarry offers a wonderful example for the teacher and rhetorician:

> There is no way to be in a high state of alert toward injustices—to subjects that, because they entail injuries, will bring distress—without simultaneously demanding of oneself precisely the level of perceptual acuity that will forever be opening one to the arrival of beautiful sights and sounds. How will one even notice, let alone become concerned about, the inclusion in a political assembly of only one economic point of view unless one has also attended, with full acuity, to a debate that is itself a beautiful object, full of arguments, counterarguments, wit, spirit, ripostes, ironies, testing, contesting; and how in turn will one hear the nuances of even this debate unless one also makes oneself available to the songs of birds or poets?[51]

Listening eloquently and then speaking eloquently are needed if we intend to treat other people and other things with heartfelt concern and respect. The call that lies at the heart of human existence says as much. Being for others is a beautiful way to be and a beautiful thing to do. Heroism displays this way of being and doing. The call of human existence calls for heroes: people who have been educated and inspired by awe and whose endeavors are now awe-inspiring. These are the kind of people we had in mind when we first spoke of the heroism of the orator in our introduction when citing Ralph Waldo Emerson: people who have the power to connect their thoughts with the proper symbols so to disclose the truth of the presence of things and circumstances and communicate it without loss. Dillard is committed to this process.[52] Being on call for the awe of it all.

We have now come full circle, both in this chapter and in our study of the call, an essential event of communication. The event is ongoing in the fundamental spatial and temporal structure of our existence—a structure that we did not create but that nevertheless calls us with its perfective impulse to be open to otherness; to acknowledge the truth of its presence; to discover and use the right words in the right way and at the right time to communicate this truth to others; to gain skill in the rhetorical art of eloquence so to evoke in others an appreciation of the relevance of what we are saying about the truth in question; to work together with others in constructing dwelling places where we and they can feel at home with ourselves and with each other. The call speaks of the possibility of progress as it challenges us to act in the face of its objective uncertainty, which questions and thus interrupts the supposed truthfulness of our current thoughts and actions. The call never stops asking, "Are you sure?" and thereby reminds us of our being completely incomplete, perfectly imperfect. The reminder arises from something that is not a human creation, which more often than not goes by the name "God": "I am that I am." It's not that simple. Are you sure? The name speaks for itself: And don't forget "I shall be what I shall be." What is named God is a process of becoming whatever it is. Perfectibility and progress in the making. One need not look any farther than the call that lies at the heart of human existence to witness this process in action. We find that awe-inspiring. And we hope that what we have said about this essential communication event has been informative and eloquent enough to evoke an awareness of our topic that holds some degree of awe for readers.

Notes

PREFACE

1. Jean-Louis Chrétien, *The Call and the Response*, trans. Anne A. Davenport (New York: Fordham University, 2004), 1.

2. Harry G. Frankfurt, *On Truth* (New York: Alfred A. Knopf, 2017), 24.

3. Ralph Waldo Emerson, *The Journals and Miscellaneous Notebooks of Ralph Waldo Emerson*, vol. 13, trans. Ralph H. Orth and Alfred R. Ferguson (Cambridge, MA: Harvard University Press, 1977), 106.

4. Senator Howard Baker, quoted by Pulitzer Prize–winning author Jon Meacham, "A Conversation with Jon Meacham about the Legacy of Senator Howard Baker and Lessons Our Nation Can Learn from Him Today," McCallie School, January 20, 2020, https://www.mccallie.org/podcast.

5. Robert Coles, *The Call of Stories: Teaching and the Moral Imagination* (Boston: Houghton Mifflin, 1989), xix.

6. Quoted in James Conlon, Lyrics for Re-Creation: Language for the Music of the Universe (New York: Continuum, 1997), 44.

7. Martin Heidegger, *Existence and Being*, trans. Douglas Scott, R. F. C. Hull, and Alan Crick (South Bend, IN: Henry Regnery, 1949), 275.

8. Emmanuel Levinas, *Totality and Infinity*, trans. Alphonso Lingis (Pittsburgh, PA: Duquesne University Press, 1969), 261.

9. Emmanuel Levinas, *Outside the Subject*, trans. Michael B. Smith (Stanford, CA: Stanford University Press, 1994), 138–139.

10. For essays dealing specifically with Heidegger, see, for example, Michael J. Hyde and Craig R. Smith, "Hermeneutics and Rhetoric: A Seen but Unobserved Relationship," *Quarterly Journal of Speech* 65 (1979): 347–363; Craig R. Smith, "Heidegger's Theory of Authentic Discourse," *Analecta Husserliana*, vol. 15, ed. Calvin Schrag (World Institute for Advanced Phenomenological Research; Dordrecht, Holland: D. Reidel Publishing Co., 1983), 209–217; Michael J. Hyde, "Heidegger on Rhetoric," *Analecta Husserliana*, vol. 15, ed. Calvin Schrag (World Institute for Advanced Phenomenological Research; Dordrecht, Holland: D. Reidel Publishing Co., 1983), 65–72; Craig R. Smith, "Martin Heidegger and the Dialogue with Being," *Communication Studies* 36 (1985): 256–269; Craig R. Smith and Michael J. Hyde, "Rethinking 'The Public': The Role of Emotion in Being-with-Others," *Quarterly Journal of Speech* 77 (1991): 446–466; Craig R. Smith, "Existential Responsibility and Roman Decorum: A New Praxis," *Western Journal of Communication* 56 (1992): 68–89; Michael J. Hyde and Craig R. Smith, "Aristotle and Heidegger on Emotion and Rhetoric: Questions of Time and Space," in *The Critical Turn: Rhetoric and Philosophy in Contemporary Discourse*, ed. Ian Angus and Lenore Langsdorf (Carbondale, IL: Southern Illinois University Press, 1993), 68–99; Michael J. Hyde, "A Matter of the Heart: Epideictic Rhetoric and Heidegger," in *Heidegger and Rhetoric*, ed. Daniel M. Gross and Ansgar Kemmann (New York: State University of New York Press, 2005). For a series of works in communication ethics and rhetorical criticism that include critical assessments of both Heidegger and Levinas, see Michael J. Hyde, *The Call of Conscience: Heidegger and Levinas, Rhetoric and the Euthanasia Debate* (Columbia: University of South Carolina Press, 2001); Michael J. Hyde, *The Life-Giving Gift of Acknowledgment* (West Lafayette, IN: Purdue University Press, 2006); Michael J. Hyde, *Perfection: Coming to Terms*

with Being Human (Columbia: University of South Carolina Press, 2010); Michael J. Hyde, *Openings: Acknowledging Essential Moments in Human Communication* (Waco, TX: Baylor University Press, 2012); Michael J. Hyde, *The Interruption That We Are: The Health of the Lived Body, Narrative, and Public Moral Argument* (Columbia: University of South Carolina Press, 2018). For works emphasizing the history, philosophy, and the practice of rhetoric, see Craig R. Smith, *Romanticism, Rhetoric and the Search for the Sublime* (Newcastle upon Tyne, UK: Cambridge Scholars Publishing, 2018); Craig R. Smith, *Rhetoric and Human Consciousness: A History*, 5th ed. (Prospect Heights, IL: Waveland, 2017); Craig R. Smith, *The Quest for Charisma: Christianity and Persuasion* (Westport, CT: Praeger Press, 2000); and Craig R. Smith, *Confessions of a Presidential Speech Writer* (East Lansing: Michigan State University Press, 2014).

11. Chrétien, *The Call and the Response*, 83.

12. Joyce Kilmer, "Trees," *Poetry: A Magazine of Verse* (1913): 160.

13. Theodore Rousseau, *Selections from His Writings* (New York: Metropolitan Museum of Art, 1979), 61.

14. Roger de Piles, *Course on Painting by Principles*, tells us that pictorial beauty calls us: "A genuine painting is therefore one that calls us, so to speak, by taking us off guard." (Paris: Ed. J. Thuillier, 1989), 8. Commenting on Plato's *Symposium*, Jean-Louis Chrétien claims that "beauty calls by its very essence. . . . visible beauty calls for spoken beauty . . . amorous sight of a single beautiful body makes one 'generate beautiful speeches' (210A)." *The Call and the Response*, 11.

15. The call, in other words, displays an ontological status. Hyde began developing this point in his *The Call of Conscience*. Here, too, he demonstrated how the call exhibits a primordial rhetorical function in its "showing-forth" (epideictic) display of the truth of objects of consciousness. It may thus be said that the phenomenon of the call makes possible what James Crosswhite terms the "ontology of deep rhetoric," which defines the way "things give and receive being to and from each other communicatively, in the process of their becoming intelligible in

logos." See his *Deep Rhetoric: Philosophy, Reason, Violence, Justice, Wisdom* (Chicago: University of Chicago Press, 2013), 259. Crosswhite cites Hyde's *The Call of Conscience* as an example of a text that draws direction from Heidegger in effecting "a convergence of philosophy and rhetoric" (381 n. 2), which is the central goal of Crosswhite's praiseworthy study. But he offers no discussion of Hyde's extensive treatment of the ontological, existential, and rhetorical status and function of the call and its workings in the euthanasia debate (as well as in numerous case studies offered in his books on acknowledgment, perfection, and openings). The reality of deep rhetoric presupposes the workings of the call. No call, no callings. No call, no human beings. And without the workings of the call, there is no deep rhetoric to speak of. An additional point is called for: In his commendation on the back cover of Crosswhite's book, the rhetorical scholar and philosopher John Arthos writes: "This is not just a *study of* but a *call for* a reconfiguration of the disciplines." Indeed, Professor Crosswhite heard and responded to a call and in so doing produced a stunning and wide-ranging piece of scholarship that masterfully succeeds in effecting a convergence of philosophy and rhetoric.

16. Kenneth Burke, *Counter-Statement* (Berkeley: University of California Press, 1968), 167.

Chapter One. In the Beginning, and Before That, Too

1. Martin Rees, *Before the Beginning: Our Universe and Others* (Reading, MA: Perseus Books, 1997), 1.

2. Kenneth Burke, *Language as Symbolic Action: Essays in Life, Literature, and Method* (Berkeley: University of California Press, 1966), 16.

3. Charles Gusdorf, *Speaking (La Parole)*, trans. Paul T. Brockelman (Evanston, IL: Northwestern University Press, 1965), 127.

4. David A. Cooper, *God Is a Verb: Kabbalah and the Practice of Mystical Judaism* (New York: Riverhead Books, 1997), 67.

5. Lawrence Kushner, *The Book of Words: Talking Spiritual Life, Living Spiritual Talk* (Woodstock, VT: Jewish Lights, 1993), 28.

6. For an excellent discussion and analysis of Luria's life and teachings, see Lawrence Fine, *Physician of the Soul, Healer of the Cosmos: Isaac Luria and His Kabbalistic Fellowship* (Stanford, CA: Stanford University Press, 2003). Also see *The Zohar* (Pritzker Edition), trans. Daniel C. Matt, 3 vols. (Stanford, CA: Stanford University Press, 2004–2006).

7. Marc-Alain Ouaknin, *Mysteries of the Kabbalah*, trans. Josephine Bacon (New York: Abbeville Press, 2000), 200.

8. Abraham Joshua Heschel, *God in Search of Man: A Philosophy of Judaism* (New York: Noonday Press, 1955), 136.

9. Genesis 17:1–2.

10. Robert Nisbet, *History of the Idea of Progress* (New York: Basic Books, 1980), ix.

11. Gaston Bachelard, *The Poetics of Space*, trans. Maria Jolas (Boston: Beacon Press, 1969), 6–7.

12. William Earle, *Public Sorrows and Private Pleasures* (Bloomington: Indiana University Press, 1976), 157.

13. Leonard Susskind, *The Cosmic Landscape: String Theory and the Illusion of Intelligent Design* (New York: Little, Brown, 2006), 66, 255.

14. Steven Weinberg, *Facing Up: Science and Its Cultural Adversaries* (Cambridge, MA: Harvard University Press, 2001), 242.

15. Paul Davies, *God and the New Physics* (New York: Simon & Schuster, 1983), 70, 209. Also see Paul Davies, *The Fifth Miracle: The Search for the Origin and Meaning of Life* (New York: Simon & Schuster, 2000).

16. Charles H. Kahn, *The Art and Thought of Heraclitus: An Edition of the Fragments with Translation and Commentary* (New York: Cambridge University Press, 1979), 11. Kahn's discussion of Heraclitus is superb and was invaluable for our purposes.

17. Quoted in Kahn, *The Art and Thought of Heraclitus*, 16.

18. Kahn, *The Art and Thought of Heraclitus*, 9–23.

19. Quoted in Kathleen Freeman, *Ancilla to the Pre-Socratic Philosophers: A Complete Translation of the Fragments in Diels, Fragmente der Vorsokratiker* (Cambridge, MA: Harvard University Press, 1966), 22.

20. W. H. S. Jones, *Hippocrates: Law*, vol. 2 (London: William Heinemann, 1923), iv.

21. Vladimir Nabokov, "The Art of Literature and Common Sense," in *Lectures on Literature*, ed. Fredson Bowers (New York: Mariner Books, 2002), 372.

22. Quoted in Kahn, *The Art and Thought of Heraclitus*, Fragment 54: 170; Fragment 118: 267.

23. Quoted in Freeman, *Ancilla to the Pre-Socratic Philosophers*, 22.

24. Quoted in Kahn, *The Art and Thought of Heraclitus*, xxxvi.

25. Quoted in Kahn, *The Art and Thought of Heraclitus*, xxxvii.

26. Quoted in Kahn, *The Art and Thought of Heraclitus*, xxx.

27. Quoted in Kahn, *The Art and Thought of Heraclitus*, xxxii.

28. Quoted in Kahn, *The Art and Thought of Heraclitus*, xiv.

29. Quoted in Kahn, *The Art and Thought of Heraclitus*, iv.

30. Quoted in Kahn, *The Art and Thought of Heraclitus*, xvi.

31. Quoted in Kahn, *The Art and Thought of Heraclitus*, ii.

32. Quoted in Kahn, *The Art and Thought of Heraclitus*, lxxxii.

33. Quoted in Kahn, *The Art and Thought of Heraclitus*, x.

34. Quoted in Kahn, *The Art and Thought of Heraclitus*, lii.

35. Quoted in Kahn, *The Art and Thought of Heraclitus*, vii.

36. Kahn, *The Art and Thought of Heraclitus*, 107.

37. Thucydides, *History of the Peloponnesian War*, trans. Rex Warner (New York: Penguin Books, 1954), 2.43.

38. Raphael Demos, "On Persuasion," *Journal of Philosophy* 29 (1932): 229.

39. Longinus, *On the Sublime*, trans. Benjamin Jowett (New York: CreateSpace Independent Publishing Platform, 2014), viii, xxx, xxxv; Edmund Burke, *A Philosophical Enquiry into the Origin of Our Ideas of the Sublime and Beautiful* (New York: Oxford University Press, 1999), vii.

40. Harry G. Frankfurt, *On Truth* (New York: Alfred Knopf, 2017), 56–57.

41. Alan H. Guth, *The Inflationary Universe: The Quest for a New Theory of Cosmic Origins* (New York: Basic Books, 1998).

42. Francis S. Collins, *The Language of God: A Scientist Presents Evidence for Belief* (New York: Free Press, 2006), 1–3.

43. Henry R. Morris, *The Long War against God* (New York: Master Books, 2000), 15.

44. Collins, *The Language of God*, 3.

45. Collins, *The Language of God*, 107.

46. Collins, *The Language of God*, 123–124.

47. Collins, *The Language of God*, 233.

48. Sam Harris, *The Moral Landscape* (New York: Free Press, 2010), 160.

49. John Locke, *An Essay Concerning Human Understanding*, ed. Kenneth P. Winkler (New York: Hackett, 1996), 372.

50. See Richard Dawkins, Daniel C. Dennett, Sam Harris, and Christopher Hitchens, *The Four Horsemen: The Conversation That Sparked an Atheist Revolution* (New York: Centre for Inquiry, 2019).

CHAPTER TWO. THE ELEMENTS OF ELOQUENCE

1. Ralph Waldo Emerson, "Language," in *The Essential Writings of Ralph Waldo Emerson: Nature*, ed. Brooks Atkinson (New York: Modern Library, 2000), 15; "Heroism," *The Essential Writings: Essays*, 228.

2. Gorgias, *Encomium of Helen*, trans. D. M. MacDowell (London: Bristol Classical Press, 1991), 9.

3. Cicero, *De officiis*, trans. Walter Miller (Cambridge, MA: Harvard University Press, 1913), 1.7.22.

4. Cicero, *Orator*, trans. H. M. Hubbell (Cambridge, MA: Harvard University Press, 1962), 3.12.

5. Cicero, *De officiis*, 1.6.29.

6. Quintilian, *Institutes of Oratory*, trans. H. E. Butler (Cambridge, MA: Harvard University Press, 1980), 9.4.62.

7. *Copia* was updated by Erasmus in the Renaissance and included in Kenneth Burke's rhetorical toolbox.

8. Hugh Blair, *Lectures on Belles Lettres* (London: J. Cantwell, 1838), 362. Sara Ahmed, *The Promise of Happiness* (Durham, NC: Duke University Press, 2010) provides a contemporary counterpart in her affects theory (38). See also Brian Massumi, *Parables for the Virtual: Movement, Affect, Sensation*

(Durham, NC: Duke University Press, 2002); Gregory J. Seigworth and Melissa Gregg, *The Affect Theory Reader* (Durham, NC: Duke University Press, 2010); Martha C. Nussbaum, *Political Emotions: Why Love Matters for Justice* (Cambridge, MA: Harvard University Press, 2013).

9.   Hugh Blair, *Lectures*, 11.

10.   Longinus, "On the Sublime," in *The Great Critics*, ed. James Harry Smith and Ed Winfield Parks (New York: W.W. Norton, 1959), 71–79.

11.   Stephen Battaglio, "A Talk-Show Match Worth Fighting For," *Los Angeles Times*, February 17, 2020, E4.

12.   The line is from the Inaugural Address of John F. Kennedy in 1961.

13.   Blair, *Lectures*, 52.

14.   Aristotle, *On Rhetoric: A Theory of Civic Discourse*, trans. George A. Kennedy, 2nd ed. (New York: Oxford University Press, 2007). We use the universal numbering system in our notes so that any text of *The Rhetoric* can be used for reference.

15.   *Rhetoric*, 1355a12.

16.   *Rhetoric*, 1356a4–6.

17.   See 1356a4ff. In his commentary, Kennedy makes much of the fact that Aristotle claims in these lines that *ethos* is generated in the speech by the speaker. Rhys Roberts translates the lines this way: "Persuasion is achieved by the speaker's personal character when the speech is so spoken as to make us think him credible. We believe good men more fully and more readily than others."

18.   *Rhetoric*, 1418b25.

19.   *Rhetoric*, 1366a25.

20.   *Rhetoric*, 1378a5.

21.   *Rhetoric*, 1377b21.

22.   *Rhetoric*, 1366a4.

23.   *Ethics*, 1094a.

24.   *Ethics*, 1106b36–40.

25.   *Ethics*, 1095b20. Aristotle's comparing humans to the herd predates the same sentiment expressed by such existentialists as Soren Kierkegaard and

Martin Heidegger.

26. Later at 1177b27–1178a3, Aristotle argues that the "divine element" in humans allows them to rise above the material and to become proactively immortal. Again reflecting Plato, he writes, "for however much this element may lack in substance, by much more it surpasses everything in power and value."

27. *Ethics*, 1102a15.

28. *Ethics*, 1106b14.

29. *Ethics*, 1107a26–1107b22.

30. *Ethics*, 1105a25–1105b5.

31. *Ethics*, 1366b14–15.

32. Edward L. Pross, "Practical Implications of the Aristotelian Concept of Ethos," *Southern Speech Journal* 17 (1952): 259.

33. *Ethics*, 1139b14–1141b24.

34. *Ethics*, 1143a6–8, 1144a1–10.

35. *Ethics*, 1144a11–25.

36. *Rhetoric*, 1356a4.

37. *Rhetoric*, 1380b2.

38. *Rhetoric*, 1361b16.

39. *Rhetoric*, 1378a6.

40. Aristotle's holistic notion of *ethos* significantly influenced Roman rhetorical theory. In *The Arts of Poetry* Horace concurred, "if a speaker's words are out of gear with his fortunes, all Rome, horse and foot, will guffaw," in *Literary Criticism: Plato to Dryden*, ed. Allan H. Gilbert (Detroit: Wayne State University Press, 1962), 131.

41. *Rhetoric*, 1377b24.

42. *Rhetoric*, 1354a24–25.

43. His other pairings include anger-calm, friendship-enmity, shame-shamelessness, kindness-cruelty, pity-indignation, and envy-emulation.

44. 1378a22–28.

45. Craig R. Smith, *Rhetoric and Human Consciousness*, 5th ed. (Long Grove, IL: Waveland Press, 2017), 82–84.

46. Aristotle also discusses fallacies, which he calls "sham enthymemes." These include such tactics as "equivocating."

47. Sigmund Freud, *A General Selection from the Works of Sigmund Freud*, ed. John Rickman (New York: Doubleday, 1957), 185–189.

48. Kenneth Burke, *A Rhetoric of Motives* (Berkeley: University of California Press, 1966), xiv.

49. These first two are what Freud labeled "anaclitic." Sigmund Freud, *A General Introduction to Psychoanalysis* (New York: Pocket Books, 1952), 114.

50. Freud, *A General Introduction to Psychoanalysis*, 433–434.

51. A. D. Weisman, *The Existential Core of Psychoanalysis: Reality, Sense and Responsibility* (Boston: Little, Brown and Co., 1965), 183, 191. See also Alice Miller, *The Drama of the Gifted Child: The Search for Self*, trans. R. Ward (New York: Basic Books, 1981), 24, 25, 62.

52. Freud, *A General Selection*, 183.

53. Burke, *A Rhetoric of Motives*, 37.

54. Burke, *A Rhetoric of Motives*, 37.

55. Richard McKeon, "The Method of Rhetoric and Philosophy: Inventional Judgment," in *The Classical Tradition: Literary and Historical Studies in Honor of Harry Caplan*, ed. L. Wallach (Ithaca, NY: Cornell University Press, 1966), 1–15.

56. John Stewart, "Foundations of Dialogic Communication," *Quarterly Journal of Speech* 64 (1968): 183–201. Later he extended his theory to a full book, *Bridges Not Walls* (New York: Random House, 1986).

57. Roderick Hart and Dan Burkes, "Rhetorical Sensitivity and Social Interaction," *Speech Monographs* 39 (1972): 75–91; Ron Arnett, "Toward a Phenomenology of Dialogue," *Western Journal of Speech Communication* 42 (1981): 201–212.

58. Richard Johannesen, "The Emerging Concept of Communication as Dialogue," *Quarterly Journal of Speech* 57 (1971): 373–382.

59. Martin Heidegger, *Being and Time*, trans. J. Macquarrie and E. Robinson (New York: Harper and Row, 1962), 156–159, 317–348.

60. Karl Jaspers, *Philosophy*, trans. E. B. Ashton, vol. 2 (Chicago: University of

Chicago Press, 1970), 14.

61. Jaspers, *Philosophy*, 2:363.

62. Jaspers, *Philosophy*, 2:186.

63. Martin Buber, *Knowledge of Man* (New York: Harper and Row, 1965), 115.

64. Buber is clearly influenced here by Jean Paul Sartre's differentiation between essence and existence. Sartre argues that our authentic existence gets covered over by essences, by which he means history, categories of race, etc. Therefore, existence precedes essence. To be authentic, we must get back to—that is, uncover—our existence.

65. Martin Buber, *Pointing the Way* (London: Routledge and Kegan Paul, 1957), 83.

66. Martin Buber, *I and Thou* (New York: Charles Scribner and Sons, 1954), 27.

67. Buber, *I and Thou*, 65.

68. Jaspers, *Philosophy*, 2:70.

69. Jaspers, *Philosophy*, 2:70.

70. Johann Fichte anticipates Buber: "You and I are not separated. Your voice resonates within me and mine echoes it back within you." *Man's Destination*, trans. Janet Sennet (Paris: Molitor, 1965), 280.

71. Jaspers, *Philosophy*, 2:234.

72. Jaspers, *Philosophy*, 2:274.

73. Jaspers, *Philosophy*, 1:52–53.

74. Buber, *Between Man and Man* (New York: Macmillan, 1965), 175.

75. Buber, *Between Man and Man*, 25.

76. Heidegger, *Poetry, Language and Thought*, trans. A. Hofstadter (New York: Harper and Row, 1971), 58.

77. Heidegger, *Poetry, Language and Thought*, 71.

78. Heidegger, *Being and Time*, 73.

CHAPTER THREE. CHEATING ELOQUENCE

1. Tony Blair, *A Journey: My Political Life* (New York: Alfred A. Knopf, 2010), 431.

2. Craig R. Smith and Theodore Prosise, "The Supreme Court's Ruling in *Bush*

v. Gore: A Rhetoric of Inconsistency," *Rhetoric and Public Affairs* 4 (2001): 605–632.

3. David Frum, *The Right Man: The Surprise Presidency of George W. Bush* (New York: Random House, 2003).

4. Martin J. Medhurst has noted that Bush's "religion is a major source of his rhetorical invention," in "Introduction," *Rhetoric and Public Affairs* 7 (2004): 445.

5. Particularly relevant to this study is Martin J. Medhurst's examination of George W. Bush's use of religious rhetoric in the 2000 election campaign, which explains how Bush used this style to turn out self-identified Christian voters in large numbers. "Religious Rhetoric and the *Ethos* of Democracy: A Case Study of the 2000 Presidential Campaign," in *The Ethos of Rhetoric*, ed. Michael J. Hyde (Columbia: University of South Carolina Press, 2004), 114–135. Also relevant is Denise Bostdorff's study of Bush's use of civil religion following the tragedy of September 11th, 2001, tying it to the "saints" of World War II; "George W. Bush's Post–September 11 Rhetoric of Covenant Renewal: Upholding the Faith of the Greatest Generation," *Quarterly Journal of Speech* 89 (2003): 293–319. See also C. D. Riswold, "A Religious Response Veiled in a Presidential Address: A Theological Study of Bush's Speech on 20 September 2001," *Political Theology* 5 (2004): 39–46. Building on these studies, we argue that within this broad spectrum lies a narrower take on civil religion that is Manichaean in nature. Historian Dante Germino examines this style in Harry S. Truman's "supernation" rhetoric in his Inaugural; see *The Inaugural Addresses of American Presidents: The Public Philosophy and Rhetoric* (Lanham, MD: University Press of America, 1984), 15–20. Other subsets of civil religion include apocalyptic rhetoric and the political jeremiad. See, for example, Steven O'Leary and M. McFarland, "The Political Use of Mythic Discourse: Prophetic Interpretation in Pat Robertson's Presidential Campaign," *Quarterly Journal of Speech* 75 (1989): 433–452; Sacvan Bercovitch, *The American Jeremiad* (Madison: University of Wisconsin Press, 1978). In her book *Critiques of Contemporary Rhetoric* (Belmont, CA: Wadsworth

Publishing, 1972), Karlyn Kors Campbell attempts to examine "Manichean" rhetoric using Spiro Agnew as a case study (94–109); however, her use of the term refers to his vituperative and divisive attacks on the news media. Campbell does not link the term to civil religion.

6.   "Presidential Election of 2004, Electoral and Popular Vote Summary," Infoplease, https://www.infoplease.com/us/government/elections/presidential-election-of-2004-electoral-and-popular-vote-summary.

7.   At the request of George H. W. Bush, Craig R. Smith served as a third-party witness to the conversation between Bush and the minister from Midland. Bush's chief political advisor at this time was Lee Atwater; his protégé was Karl Rove.

8.   Frum, *The Right Man.*

9.   Stephen Buttery, "Candidates Focus on Christian Beliefs," *Des Moines Register*, December 15, 1999, A1.

10.   Rhetorical constructions of political images have been studied for many years. See, for example, Robert O. Anderson, "The Characterization Model for Rhetorical Criticism of Political Image Campaigns," *Western Speech* 37 (1973): 75–86; Robert Hariman, *Political Style: The Artistry of Power* (Chicago: University of Chicago Press, 1995); Kenneth L. Hacker, ed., *Candidate Images in Presidential Elections* (Westport, CT: Praeger, 1995). Regarding presidential image making and leadership see Leroy G. Dorsey, ed., *The President and Rhetorical Leadership* (College Station: Texas A&M University Press, 2002).

11.   See, for example, Tim LaHaye, *The Coming Peace in the Middle East* (Grand Rapids, MI: Zondervan Publishing House, 1984); Tim LaHaye and Thomas Ice, *The End of Times Controversy* (Eugene, OR: Harvest House Publishers, 2003); Hal Lindsay, *Apocalypse Code* (Palos Verdes, CA: Western Front Ltd., 1997). Both Falwell quotations are as quoted in Craig R. Smith, *Herod from Hell* (Bloomington, IN: AuthorHouse, 2013), 368. The URLs to these sermons are no longer available. The sermons are Jerry Falwell, "Revelation Chapter 11: Hell on Earth!," January 23, 1998, and Jerry Falwell, "Revelation Chapter 17: The Great Whore and the Scarlet Beast," January 22, 1998.

12. The subgenre of a "Manichaean construct" can be found in George Marsden's research on evangelism in America. George Marsden, *Fundamentalism and American Culture: The Shaping of Twentieth-Century Evangelicalism, 1870–1925* (New York: Oxford University Press, 1980); Marsden, "The Collapse of American Evangelical Academia," in *Faith and Rationality*, ed. A. Plantinga and N. Wolterstorff (Notre Dame, IN: University of Notre Dame Press, 1984), reprinted in D. G. Hart, *Reckoning with the Past: Historical Essays on American Evangelicalism from the Institute for the Study of American Evangelicals* (Grand Rapids, MI: Baker Books, 1995), 221–266. His construct has been used by scholars in communication studies. See, for example, Tom D. Daniels, Richard J. Jensen, and Allen Lichtenstein, "Resolving the Paradox in Politicized Christian Fundamentalism," *Western Journal of Speech Communication* 49 (1985): 248–266. In that study, the Manichaean construct is used to examine the rhetoric of Pat Robertson and Jerry Falwell.

13. Robert Ivie, "Metaphor and the Rhetorical Invention of the Cold War 'Idealists,'" *Communication Monographs* 54 (1987): 165–182. Janet Lyon claims that "The manifesto declares a position; the manifesto refuses dialogue or discussion; the manifesto fosters antagonism and scorns conciliation," in *Manifestoes: Provocations of the Modern* (Ithaca, NY: Cornell University Press, 1999), 9. See also Mary Ann Caws, ed., *Manifesto: A Century of Isms* (Lincoln: University of Nebraska Press, 2001). Phillip Wander, "The Rhetoric of American Foreign Policy," *Quarterly Journal of Speech* 70 (1984): 344–357 (see particularly 344, 346, 357). Robert L. Ivie, "Presidential Motives for War," *Quarterly Journal of Speech* 60 (1974): 337–345.

14. In George W. Bush, "Remarks to Employees at the Pentagon and an Exchange with Reporters in Arlington, Virginia," September 17, 2001, Compilation of Presidential Documents, https://www.govinfo.gov/app/collection/cpd/.

15. John Murphy picks up on this approach when he analyzes Bush's use of the epideictic mode in "Our Mission and Our Moment: George W. Bush

and September 11," *Rhetoric and Public Affairs* 6 (2003): 607–632. Denise Bostdorff follows in this vein in "George W. Bush's Post-September 11 Rhetoric."

16.   Hariman, *Political Style*, 4.

17.   George W. Bush, "State of the Union Address, 2002," The White House: President George W. Bush, January 29, 2002, https://georgewbush-whitehouse.archives.gov/news/releases/2002/01/20020129-11.html. When the phrase drew criticism from the media and other sources, David Frum, the speechwriter responsible for the phrase, was asked to resign. Frum then wrote *The Right Man: The Surprise Presidency of George W. Bush*, in which he claimed that "An American overthrow of Saddam Hussein—and a replacement of the radical Baathist dictatorship with a new government more closely aligned with the United States—would put America more wholly in charge of the region than any power since the Ottomans, or maybe the Romans" (232–233). I cite this passage to demonstrate how deeply the Manichaean style penetrated the president's speechwriting staff. Michael Gerson, Bush's head speechwriter until he moved over to the political unit, was an evangelical Christian. Marc Thiessen, who succeeded him, was also an evangelical Christian from the staff of Senator Jesse Helms.

18.   George W. Bush, "State of the Union Address, 2003," The White House: President George W. Bush, January 28, 2003, https://georgewbush-whitehouse.archives.gov/stateoftheunion/chamberessay/.

19.   Mark West and Chris Carey, "(Re)Enacting Frontier Justice: The Bush Administration's Tactical Narration of the Old West Fantasy after September 11," *Quarterly Journal of Speech* 92 (2006): 379–412. George W. Bush, "Remarks to Employees at the Pentagon and an Exchange with Reporters in Arlington, Virginia," September 17, 2001, Compilation of Presidential Documents, https://www.govinfo.gov/app/collection/cpd/. See also George W. Bush, "Guard and Reserves 'Define Spirit of America': Remarks by the President to Employees at the Pentagon," September 17, 2001, Compilation of Presidential Documents, https://www.govinfo.gov/

app/collection/cpd/.

20. Karlyn K. Campbell and Kathleen Jamieson in *Deeds Done in Words: Presidential Rhetoric and Genres of Governance* (Chicago: University of Chicago Press, 1990) claim there are three "processes" that characterize this genre: "(1) public meditations on values, (2) assessments of information and issues, and (3) policy recommendations" (139). While these elements are present in Bush's State of the Union speech, they do not dominate them and certainly don't characterize them up until 2006.

21. George W. Bush, "Second Inaugural Address," www.vlib.us/amdocs/texts/bush012005.html.

22. And even that bill, which would have legalized stem-cell research, came forward because it was supported by a Republican senator, Bill Frist, a doctor.

23. Frederick A. O. Schwartz Jr. and Aziz Z. Huq, *Unchecked and Unbalanced: Presidential Power in a Time of Terror* (New York: New Press, 2007). The authors provide a review of relevant poll data showing the significant decline in Bush's approval ratings between the 2004 election and the 2006 State of the Union Address.

24. Shwartz and Huq, *Unchecked and Unbalanced.*

25. Marc Sandalow, "Bush Claims Mandate, Sets 2nd-Term Goals," SFGATE, November 5, 2004, https://www.sfgate.com/politics/article/Bush-claims-mandate-sets-2nd-term-goals-I-2637116.php.

26. "Bush Shifts Approach on Social Security Reform," *Financial Times*, April 28, 2005, A1.

27. See "Katrina Response a Failure of Leadership," at www.cnn.com/2006/POLITICS/02/13/katrina.congress/index.html, which reports on the condemnatory congressional findings with Republicans still in charge of the Congress. See also online "McCain Condemns Federal Response to Katrina," wsj.com/article/SB120907997453343265.html, which includes comments by Senator John McCain (R-AZ) criticizing the administration.

28. Spenser S. Hsu and Susan Glasser, "FEMA Director Singled Out by Response Critics," *Washington Post*, September 6, 2005, A1.

29. George W. Bush, "The President's News Conference," January 26, 2006, Compilation of Presidential Documents, https://www.govinfo.gov/app/collection/cpd/.

30. Craig R. Smith, "Moving Federal Court Appointments into the Public Sphere," *Controversia: The International Journal of Argumentation* 4 (2006): 15–50.

31. They were proved correct when in April 2007 Alito was the crucial vote in a five-to-four decision upholding a ban on "partial birth abortions."

32. Bob Deans, "'Lennon-McCartney' Creative Team; Speechwriters Find President a Tough Editor," *Atlanta Journal-Constitution*, January 29, 2006, 7B.

33. "In the State of the Union Address, presidents revive principles to which they committed their presidencies." Campbell and Jamieson, *Deeds Done in Words*, 73.

34. Deans, "'Lennon-McCartney' Creative Team," 7B.

35. George W. Bush, "Address before a Joint Session of the Congress on the State of the Union," January 31, 2006, Compilation of Presidential Documents, https://www.govinfo.gov/app/collection/cpd/.

36. Later, on August 10, 2006, Bush referred to terrorists as "Islamic fascists"; "Bush: U.S. at War with Islamic Fascists," www.cnn.com/2006/POLITICS/08/10/washington.terror.plot/index.html.

37. George Bush, "Address before a Joint Session of the Congress on the State of the Union," January 23, 2007, Compilation of Presidential Documents, https://www.govinfo.gov/app/collection/cpd/.

38. It is fascinating to note that the poll was not released until September 12, 2006. Was Baylor protecting the president? See Mark I. Pinsky, "Meet the New Evangelicals," *Los Angeles Times*, September 16, 2006, B15. The poll also shows that 94.8 percent of Americans believe in God; only 5.2 percent self-identified as atheists. Fifty-four percent "embraced" an involved God that has Manichaean features. Forty percent embraced a more distant God, "who really does not interact with the world" or is "a cosmic force which set the laws of nature in motion."

39. Gary Trudeau, "Doonesbury," *Los Angeles Times*, August 6, 2006, H5.

40. "Acceptance of the Democratic Presidential Nomination," June 27, 1936.

41. More than 1,600 people responded. The paper posted 29 responses, which supposedly offered a fair representation of the major reasons that were offered by the majority of respondents. See "Why I Voted for Trump," *Washington Post*, November 10, 2016.

42. John R. O'Donnell and James Rutherford, *Trumped! The Inside Story of the Real Donald Trump—His Cunning Rise and Spectacular Fall* (New York: Simon and Schuster, 1988), 127.

43. Ben Kamesar, "Trump: I Could Shoot People in Streets and Not Lose Support," *The Hill*, January 23, 2016.

44. Nick Corasaniti and Maggie Haberman, "Donald Trump Suggests 'Second Amendment People' Could Act against Hillary Clinton," *New York Times*, August 9, 2016.

45. Nick Corasaniti, Nicholas Confessore, and Michael Barbaro, "Donald Trump Says Hillary Clinton's Bodyguards Should Disarm to 'See What Happens to Her,'" *New York Times*, September 16, 2016.

46. Ashley Alman, "*New York Times* Dedicates 2 Page Spread to the People and Things Trump Insulted, *New York Times*, September 24, 2016.

47. Stephen M. Lepore, "A Guide to Everyone Who Loves Donald Trump, according to Donald Trump," *New York Daily News*, October 21, 2015.

48. Heather Dockray, "Trump Says He'll Be the Greatest Job Producer God Has Ever Created, and Twitter Is Skeptical," *Mashable*, January 11, 2017.

49. Jeremiah Johnson, "Prophesy: Donald Trump Shall Become the Trumpet," *Charisma Magazine*, July 28, 2015.

50. Delany and Edwards-Levy, "Donald Trump Is a Gift from God to His Supporters."

51. Paula Bolyard, "Trumpette Calls Trump 'God' and Says He Will Come Down to Help Us All," PJ Media, October 1, 2016, https://pjmedia.com/trending/2016/10/01/watch-trumpette-says-trump-is-a-god-thats-going-to-come-down-and-help-us-all/.

52. Kyle Mantyle, "Michael Brown on Trump's Election: 'God Raised Him

Up, No Question,'" *Right Wing Watch*, December 8, 2016, http://www.rightwingwatch.org/post/michael-brown-on-trumps-election-god-raised-him-up-no-question/.

53. Denna Zaru, "Michele Bachman: 'God Raised Up Trump to Be GOP Nominee,'" *CNN Politics*, August 31, 2016.

54. Jessie Hellmann, "Trump: 'I'm Not Perfect,'" *The Hill*, August 12, 2016; "Transcript: Donald Trump's Speech Responding to Assault Charges," *PBS News Hour*, October 13, 2016.

55. Mark Goulston, "Why Trump Is the Perfect Candidate," *Huffington Post*, August 2, 2016.

56. Political Staff, "Full Transcript: Mitt Romney Remarks on Donald Trump and the 2016 Race," *Politico*, March 3, 2016.

57. Soopermexican, "Trump's Awesome Answer to the Question: 'Who Is God to You?'" *The Rightscoop*, September 3, 2016, https://therightscoop.com/trumps-awesome-answer-to-the-question-who-is-god-to-you/.

58. Jack Shafer, "Donald Trump Talks Like a Third-Grader," *Politico Magazine*, August 13, 2006.

59. Longinus, *On the Sublime*, I. 3, in *The Great Critics*, ed. James Harry Smith and Ed Winfield Parks (New York: W.W. Norton, 1959).

60. Shafer, "Donald Trump Talks Like a Third-Grader."

61. Melanie Arter, "Pence: 'I Believe in Forgiveness,'" *CNSNEWS*, October 10, 2016, http://www.cnsnews.com/news/article/melanie-hunter/pence-i-believe-forgiveness.

62. Paul Pearsall, *Awe: The Delights and Dangers of Our Eleventh Emotion* (Deerfield Beach, FL: Health Communications, Inc., 2009), 196.

63. Erick Erickson, "Donald Trump Is God's Anointed," *The Resurgent*, November 3, 2016. *The Resurgent* was only available online at Resurgent.com. The URL is no longer available.

64. "Republican Messiah," rightforever.com, November 8, 2016 (quotation no longer contained on website). The Evangelist Franklin Graham added this two days after the election: "Hundreds of thousands of Christians from across the United States have been praying. This year they came out to

every state capitol to pray for this election and for the future of America. Prayer groups were started. Families prayed. Churches prayed. Then Christians went to the polls, and God showed up." Cited in Jennifer Harper, "Franklin Graham on the Presidential Election and Trump's Victory: 'God Showed Up,'" *Washington Times*, November 10, 2016.

65. Katherine Steward, "Eighty-One Percent of White Evangelicals Voted for Trump," *The Nation*, November 17, 2017.

66. Gershom Scholem, *Kabbalah* (New York: Meridian, 1974).

67. The literature on Trump's rhetoric is, to be sure, immense and growing. In the field of communication, exemplary assessments of the topic include Roderick P. Hart, *Trump and Us: What He Says and Why People Listen* (Cambridge: Cambridge University Press, 2020); and Jennifer R. Mercieca, *Demagogue for President: The Rhetorical Genius of Donald Trump* (College Station: Texas A&M University Press, 2020).

68. Trump repeated the charge on Fox News's "Media Buzz," July 5, 2015: "What can be simpler or more accurately stated? The Mexican Government is forcing their most unwanted people into the United States. They are, in many cases, criminals, drug dealers, rapists, etc.," http://insider.foxnews.com/2015/07/05/donald-trump-fires-back-media-buzz-his-critics-immigration-stance.

69. Michael Finnegan and Noah Bierman, "Conflict Fuels Rallies for Trump," *Los Angeles Times*, March 14, 2016, A1, 10.

70. As quoted in Dan P. McAdams, "The Mind of Donald Trump," *The Atlantic* (June 2016): 80. McAdams is a professor of psychology at Northwestern University.

71. McAdams, "The Mind of Donald Trump," 80.

72. Claire Cohen, "Donald Trump Sexism Tracker: Every Offensive Comment in One Place," *The Telegraph* (London), June 4, 2016.

73. Maggie Haberman, "Trump Says His Mocking of New York Times Reporter Was Misread," *New York Times*, November 11, 2015.

74. See his speech of July 23, 2015, at the border in Laredo, Texas. Nick Corasanti, "Donald Turmp at Mexican Border Claims Close Ties to

Hispanics," *New York Times*, July 23, 2015, https://www.nytimes.
com/2015/07/24/us/politics/donald-trump-at-mexican-border-claims-
close-ties-to-hispanics.html. For a collection of his remarks see Dana
Milbank, "Donald Trump Is a Bigot and a Racist," *Washington Post*,
December 1, 2015.

75. Jon Greenberg, "Trump's Pants on Fire Tweet That Blacks Killed 81% of
White Homicide Victims," Polifact.com, November 23, 2015, http://www.
politifact.com/truth-o-meter/statements/2015/nov/23/donald-trump/
trump-tweet-blacks-white-homicide-victims/.

76. Trump interview by John Dickerson on CBS *Face the Nation* on June 5,
2016, http://www.cbsnews.com/news/donald-trump-its-possible-muslim-
judge-would-treat-me-unfairly.

77. See also Cathleen Decker, "Republicans Sounding Alarm Bells," *Los Angeles
Times*, February 6, 2016, A10.

78. Chris Cilliza, "Pat Buchanan Says Donald Trump Is the Future of the
Republican Party," *Washington Post*, January 13, 2016. Governor Nikki
Haley, the child of Indian immigrants, dissented in her reply to the State
of the Union Address when she said we must resist "the siren call of the
angriest voices." Cathleen Decker, "GOP Divided on Haley's Speech," *Los
Angeles Times*, January 14, 2016, A9. Buchanan wrote *State of Emergency:
The Third World and the Conquest of America* (New York: St. Martin's Press,
2006), an anti-immigration screed.

79. CNN Super Tuesday coverage, March 1, 2016.

80. "I Called It," KTLA 5, http://ktla.com/2016/06/12/i-called-it-trump-says-
he-predicted-terrorist-attack-criticizes-obama-and-clinton/.

81. Lisa Mascaro, "Trump Takes a Swing at His 'Haters,'" *Los Angeles Times*, July
23, 2016, A5.

82. Politifact.com is a product of researchers at the *Tampa Bay Times*. The
project has won a Pulitzer Prize. These statistics were accessed at http://
www.politifact.com/personalities/donald-trump/.

83. Confirming numbers were also accessed at "Fox News Hits
Ratings Record," http://www.foxnews.com/politics/2015/08/07/

fox-news-makes-ratings-record-with-primetime-gop-debate.html.

84. Stephen Battaglio, "The Democrats Pull 7.85 Million," *Los Angeles Times*, December 22, 2015, E2; Stephen Battaglio, "GOP Debate Draws Fewer Viewers," *Los Angeles Times*, January 16, 2016, C6; Steven Herbert, "A Live Event Leads Again," *Los Angeles Times*, March 9, 2016, E8.

85. In Virginia, for example, the Republican vote of more than a million was 50 percent higher than the highest Republican primary turnout in the state ever. The same was true of Tennessee and Kansas. Records were achieved in every Super Tuesday Republican primary. Stephen Dinan, "Donald Trump Drives GOP's Record Turnout; Democrats Lack Enthusiasm," *Washington Times*, March 1, 2016, A1.

86. Stephen Battaglio, "GOP Confab a Cable News Hit," *Los Angeles Times*, July 20, 2016, C3; Stephen Battaglio, "35 Million TV Viewers Watch Trump's Speech," *Los Angeles Times*, July 23, 2016, C5. That was 5 million more than watched the Romney acceptance speech in 2012. Furthermore, as Battaglio points out, this number does not include those who streamed the speech over various devices not counted in the ratings.

87. Donald Trump, "Excerpts from the Acceptance Speech: 'Americanism . . . will be our credo,'" *Los Angeles Times*, July 22, 2016, A3.

88. Donald Trump, "Excerpts from the Acceptance Speech: 'Americanism . . . will be our credo,'" *Los Angeles Times*, July 22, 2016, A3.

89. Janet Hook, "Donald Trump Attacks Ben Carson," http://blogs.wsj.com/washwire/2015/11/13/donald-trump-attacks-ben-carson-on-personal-story-temper/?mod=videorelated.

90. Team Fix, "The Fox News GOP Debate Transcript Annotated," *Washington Post*, March 3, 2016.

91. Ryu Spaeth, "Donald Trump Has Come Up with His Clinton Nickname," *New Republic*, April 17, 2016.

92. As quoted in Chris Megerian, "At Davos, Trump Dismisses Climate Crisis," *Los Angeles Times*, January 22, 2020, A5.

93. "Spread of Propaganda by White Supremacists Soars," *Los Angeles Times*, February 13, 2020, A9.

94. See, for example, Craig R. Smith, "Does Trump's Fascist Rhetoric Foreshadow Fascist Action?," *Communication Currents*, June 18, 2019, https://www.natcom.org/communication-currents/does-trumps-fascist-rhetoric-foreshadow-fascist-action.

95. Thirty-seven prominent Republican lawmakers signed a letter refuting the argument of Trump's lawyers.

96. Incitement to riot is difficult to prove. The most important precedent on the subject is the Supreme Court's 1969 ruling in *Brandenburg v. Ohio*. The Court said that the incitement had to present a "true threat"—that is, it had to be imminent, capable of being accomplished, and directed at specific persons. In the context of his remarks in hailing distance of the Capitol on the day of the riot, Trump's remarks easily meet the first two criteria of a true threat. It is the final criterion, specificity, that may have been missing from the president's remarks.

97. On February 4, 2020, the Gallup Poll shows Trump's approval rating at 49 percent, the highest of his presidency, and this comes after an impeachment trial.

98. Robert N. Bellah, R. Madsen, W. M. Sullivan, A. Swidler, and S. M. Tipton, *Habits of the Heart: Individualism and Commitment in American Life* (New York: Harper and Row, 1985), 162, 251.

99. Margaret Sullivan, *Ghosting the News* (New York: Columbia Global Reports, 2020). This is a publication of Columbia University.

100. Since the Bloomberg incident, Facebook changed its rules to allow campaigns to use this tool only if they were authorized by Facebook to run political ads and disclose who paid for the sponsored posts. Facebook, which owns Instagram, is a private company that has been granted First Amendment rights under the *Citizens United* ruling of the Supreme Court.

101. Yuriy Gorodnichenko, Tho Pham, and Oleksandr Talavera, "Social Media, Sentiment and Public Opinion: Evidence from #brexit and #uselection," National Bureau of Economic Research, May 2018, https://www.nber.org/papers/w24631.

102. George Washington, "First Inaugural Address," in *Inaugural Addresses of*

the Presidents of the United States (Washington, DC: Government Printing Office, 1974), 1–4.

CHAPTER FOUR. EPIDEICTIC ELOQUENCE

1.   Barack Obama, "Inaugural Address" (Washington, DC, January 20, 2009), Compilation of Presidential Documents, https://www.govinfo.gov/app/collection/cpd/.

2.   Barack Obama, "A More Perfect Union" (Philadelphia, March 18, 2008). For a transcript of the speech, see https://www.npr.org/templates/story/story.php?storyId=88478467. For an insightful analysis of the speech that employs W. E. B. Du Bois's theory of "double consciousness" in interpreting Obama's rhetorical competence, see Robert E. Terrill, "Unity and Duality in Barack Obama's 'A More Perfect Union,'" *Quarterly Journal of Speech* 95 (2009): 363–386. My reading of the speech is aligned with Terrill's praise of Obama's rhetorical competence. Our treatments differ in that I seek to uncover and interpret the ontological significance of Obama's discourse as it creates an opening, a dwelling place, for deliberation.

3.   Mark L. McPhail and David A. Frank, "Slouching toward Coherence: Rhetoric, Religion, and the Broken Promissory Note of Racial Justice in the United States," *Southern Communication Journal* 74 (2009): 210.

4.   For a more in-depth discussion of this "media event," see Jodi Kantor, "A Candidate, His Minister and the Search for Faith," *New York Times*, April 30, 2007.

5.   Our use of the Latin for "conscience" revises Heidegger's and Levinas's use of the term.

6.   Walter Fisher, *Human Communication as Narration: Toward a Philosophy of Reason, Value, and Action* (Columbia: University of South Carolina Press, 1987); David Carr, *Time, Narrative, and History* (Bloomington: Indiana University Press, 1991).

7.   Michael J. Hyde, *The Life-Giving Gift of Acknowledgment* (West Lafayette, IN: Purdue University Press, 2006).

8.   Frans H. van Emeren, Rob Grootendorst, and Francisca Snoeck Henkemans, *Fundamentals of Argumentation Theory: A Handbook of*

Historical Backgrounds and Contemporary Developments (Mahwah, NJ: Lawrence Erlbaum Associates, 1996).

9. Robert Wade Kenny, "Truth as Metaphor: Imaginative Vision and the Ethos of Rhetoric," in *The Ethos of Rhetoric*, ed. Michael J. Hyde (Columbia: University of South Carolina Press, 2004), 40.

10. Many thanks to Elizabeth Mills and Ryan Thames for bringing this point to our attention. For an excellent essay on the interruptive nature of beauty, see John Poulakos, "Special Delivery: Rhetoric, Letter Writing, and the Question of Beauty," in *The Ethos of Rhetoric*, ed. Michael J. Hyde (Columbia: University of South Carolina Press, 2004), 89–97.

11. Loughner was at first ruled mentally incompetent. He was a paranoid schizophrenic. That holding was later reversed and he pled guilty to nineteen counts and was sentenced to life in prison.

12. Obama gave a number of eulogies during his administration in the face of gun violence. For an analysis of one of the most important, see Denise M. Bostdorff and Steven R. Goldzwig, "Barack Obama's Eulogy for the Reverend Clementa Pinckney, June 26, 2016: Grace as the Vehicle for Collective Salvation and Obama's Agency of Civil Rights," *Rhetoric and Public Affairs* 23 (2020): 107–152.

13. Karlyn Kohrs Campbell and Kathleen Jamieson, *Deeds Done in Words: Presidential Rhetoric and Genres of Governance* (Chicago: University of Chicago Press, 1990), 57, 102–103.

14. For other analyses of this eulogy, see the special issue of *Rhetoric and Public Affairs* 17 (2014) including Francis Marie Smith and Thomas A. Hollihan, "'Out of Chaos Breathes Creation': Human Agency, Mental Illness and Conservative Arguments Locating Responsibility for the Tucson Massacre"; and David A. Frank, "Facing Moloch: Barack Obama's National Eulogies and Gun Violence."

CHAPTER FIVE. DELIBERATIVE ELOQUENCE

1. Kenneth Branagh produced, directed, and starred in a 1989 film version of the play.

2. *Register of Debates*, 21st Congress, 1st Session, 43.

3. Free Soilers advocated free soil in the West for settlers. While most opposed slavery, that was not their essential concern.

4. Clay was being disingenuous. California had already declared itself a free state. His strategy undercut his credibility with his colleagues.

5. The full speech can be found in Daniel Webster, *The Papers of Daniel Webster: Speeches and Formal Writings*, ed. Charles Wiltse and Alan R. Berolzheimer (Hanover, NH: University Press of New England, 1987), 2:553–578.

6. Karlyn Kohrs Campbell and Kathleen Jamieson, *Deeds Done in Words: Presidential Rhetoric and Genres of Governance* (Chicago: University of Chicago Press, 1990), 53.

7. Campbell and Jamieson, *Deeds Done in Words*, 73.

8. In the interest of disclosure, allow us to point out that Craig Smith worked as a writer/researcher for CBS News in 1968, 1972, 1974, and specifically for Dan Rather at the 1984 Republican Convention and the 1985 Inaugural coverage. He was also the manager of a senate campaign for which Roger Ailes served as the media consultant in 1980. He had checked the narrative here with both parties in 1989. See Craig R. Smith, *Confessions of a Presidential Speechwriter* (East Lansing: Michigan State University Press, 2014), 256–258.

9. Rather's dislike for the Bushes would eventually result in his being terminated as anchor for CBS. In 2000, he ran a story claiming George W. Bush received favorable treatment while in the National Guard. The source for the story proved not to be credible. These events were made into the film *Trust*, starring Robert Redford as Dan Rather.

10. As the director of Senate Services for the Republican Conference of the U.S. Senate, Craig Smith attended a meeting in the Capitol in 1981 at which Reagan said that SDI was part of the defense spending for which he was calling to "spend the Russians into the ground." Smith, *Confessions*, 195–196.

11. Earlier in his administration, Reagan had brokered a budget agreement to hold down spending. For example, it included a provision under which

a member could put a new spending item in the budget or increase one without providing a reduction to balance it.

12. Later she would rephrase the line for Vice President Bush's acceptance speech in New Orleans at the Republican Convention. There, on the issue of volunteerism, he would call for "a thousand points of light." Noonan is a Catholic and therefore may have read, at some point in her life, *The Chronicles of Narnia* by C. S. Lewis (New York: HarperCollins Publishers, 1956). On page 61, Lewis writes, "One moment there had been nothing but darkness; next moment a thousand, thousand points of light leapt out."

13. Some of the arms we supplied in this case were funneled to Taliban fighters, who would take over the country and fund terrorism internationally.

CHAPTER SIX. FORENSIC ELOQUENCE

1. Mark 3:25.

2. Richard Hofstadter, *The Paranoid Style in American Politics and Other Essays* (New York: Random House, 1957), 36–37.

3. *Congressional Record*, Senate, 81st Cong., 2nd sess. (1 June 1950): 7894–7895.

4. Members of Congress cannot be sued for libel or slander if their words are spoken or written in the Congress, including its committees. They can only be censored by the bodies to which they belong. However, should they step out of the Congress and speak, such as at a town hall, they can be sued for libel or slander.

5. Robert A. Divine, *Since 1945: Politics and Diplomacy in Recent American History* (New York: John Wiley and Sons, 1975), 34.

6. This fact explains why the young Robert Kennedy became a committee staff member for Senator Joseph McCarthy.

7. Poyntz Tyler, *Immigration and the United States* (New York: H.W. Wilson Co., 1956). For President Truman's veto message, see Henry S. Commager, *Documents of American History*, 9th ed. (Englewood Cliffs, NJ: Prentice-Hall, 1973), 578–582. See also Nat Hentoff, *The First Freedom* (New York:

Delacorte Press, 1980), 137–138.

8. *New York Times*, July 10, 1952, A1. See also Herbert S. Parmet, *Eisenhower and the American Crusades* (New York: Macmillan Co., 1972), 95.

9. Emile de Antonia and Daniel Talbot, *Point of Order* (New York: Screenplay, 1964), 9.

10. Twenty million people watched the hearings on the ABC and Dumont networks.

11. Kavanaugh undoubtedly read Collins's defense of his nomination. It might have inspired him to listen more closely to his conscience. In one of his first rulings, he stopped the persecution of a black man, Curtis Flowers, who had endured six trials for the same crime, and at which the prosecutor had barred any African Americans from sitting on the jury.

12. Impeached but not found guilty, Andrew Johnson was a Democrat whom Lincoln put on the ticket in 1864 to try to unify the nation. No Democrat voted for his removal.

CHAPTER SEVEN. RELIGIOUS CALLS AND SACRED ELOQUENCE

1. Paul Ricoeur explores this difference in "Experience and Language in Religious Discourse," in *Phenomenology and Theology*, ed. Chrétien et al. (Paris: Criterion, 1992): 17–18. Heidegger also embraces the call-response structure for his analysis of language as the house of being. He goes on to develop from this structure a theory of how humans "correspond" to calls with their response. "Speech is the highest and everywhere comes first." *Poetry, Language, and Thought*, trans. A. Hofstadter (New York: Harper and Row, 1971), 216.

2. While Kierkegaard's leap of faith and discussion of God reinforces the ineffable side of the equation, his version of the call is explicit. It is Jesus's "Come hither!," which Kierkegaard examines at length in *Training in Christianity*, trans. Walter Lowrie (Princeton, NJ: Princeton University Press, 1967), 13ff. Kierkegaard claims that Jesus's authenticity and commitment are bound up in this call: "With the silent and veracious eloquence of deeds His life expresses, even if He had never given utterance

to these words, 'Come hither to me, all ye that labor and are heavy laden.' He is true to His word, He is what He says, and in this sense also He is the Word." This is true eloquence. Kierkegaard only heard the call after he cleared an obstacle in his way. He had fallen into a dissolute life, which caused a break with his father; Kierkegaard moved out of their home. When he was twenty-four, he reconciled with his father and moved back in. Soon after that, in May 1848, he found an "indescribable joy," something that must have been wonderful to a soul plagued by depression and depravity. At this juncture, Christianity became more important to him than philosophy. He claimed that religion was "more real" than philosophy and had more impact on existence, especially when one achieved faith. This revelation made him into a new man, one on the lonely path to God. He returned to the church. Then his father died, leaving Kierkegaard with a large house and a small fortune. He was free to pursue his theology—he completed a master's degree in the subject—and the task of bringing faith to the fore in Christianity, echoing St. Paul's call for justification by faith.

3. Some scholars suspect that First and Second Timothy and Titus may not be by Paul. See Calvin J. Roetzel, *The Letters of Paul: Conversations in Context* (Atlanta: John Knox Press, 1975), 80.

4. Kierkegaard's goal is to bring authentic Christianity back to Christendom, his term for the contemporary church of Denmark, which had lost its sense of humility, suffering, and faith.

5. Albert Schweitzer, *Paul and His Interpreters* (New York: Macmillan, 1951), v, vii, 2.

6. John Locke, *A Paraphrase and Notes on the Epistles of St. Paul* (Oxford: Clarendon Press, 1987). Watson E. Mills, *Mercer Dictionary of the Bible* (Macon, GA: Mercer Press, 1994), 661.

7. Locke, *Paraphrase*, 112–114.

8. 1st Corinthians 9:21–22.

9. 1st Timothy 4:12.

10. 1st Timothy 5:1.

11. 1st Timothy 6:10.

12. See, for example, 2nd Corinthians 11:24–33.
13. Paula Fredricksen, "Paul and Augustine: Conversion Narratives, Orthodox Tradition, and the Retrospective Self," *Journal of Theological Studies* 37 (1986): 3–34.
14. 1st Corinthians 13:11–13.
15. 2nd Corinthians 11:10.
16. Galatians 4:4.
17. 2nd Corinthians 4:6.
18. This message is what makes the Epistle to the Romans so powerful. See particularly Romans 5:6–10, 8:31–32.
19. 2nd Corinthians 5:7.
20. Romans 8:26.
21. 1st Corinthians 2:9–10.
22. Romans 9:1, 32; 10:21; Galatians 2:4.
23. The speech can be found in Acts 17.
24. Galatians 5:22–23.
25. Charity is sometimes translated as a form of love.
26. Augustine, *City of God*, trans. Henry Bettenson (New York: Penguin Classics, 1984), Book 11.27.2. Johann G. Fichte reflects Augustine's divine illumination when he writes, "[My responsibility] is immediately revealed to me by a voice that reaches me from the spiritual realm." *Man's Destination*, trans. Jane Sinnet (Paris: Molitar, 1965), 271.
27. Augustine, *Confessions*, trans. William Watts (Cambridge, MA: Harvard University Press, Loeb Classical Library, 1977), 8.12.29.
28. Augustine, *Confessions*, 1.6.10. Augustine's ideological arc runs from sophist to Platonist to Manichaean to Catholic.
29. According to Margaret R. Miles, Augustine "was the first Christian author to begin his thinking and writing with an analysis of human experience. In place of beginning, as the pre-Socratic philosophers did, with speculation about the physical world, or as Plato did with a cosmological scheme, or yet with Aristotle's question about behavior of people and things, Augustine began examining the human condition, in particular his own human

condition—the texture, the subjective color of the fabric of his life."
See her "The Body and Human Values in Augustine of Hippo," in *Grace,
Politics, and Desire: Essays on Augustine*, ed. Hugo A. Meynell (Calgary,
Canada: University of Calgary Press, 1990), 55.

30. Augustine, *On Christian Doctrine*, trans. J. F. Shaw (Chicago: Encyclopedia
    Britannica, 1952), 1.13.

31. Charles Sears Baldwin, *Medieval Rhetoric and Poetic* (Gloucester, MA: Peter
    Smith Press, 1959), 51.

32. Augustine, *De Genesis ad litteram*, in *The Works of St. Augustine*, trans.
    Edmund Hill, ed. John Rotelle (Brooklyn, NY: New City Press, 1991), 8.12.26.

33. Augustine, *Confessions*, 3.4.7.

34. Cicero, *De officiis*, trans. Walter Miller (Cambridge, MA: Harvard
    University Press, 1913), 1.7.22. Augustine's hunger for a meaningful
    philosophy was first spurred by Cicero's *Hortensius* when Augustine was
    nineteen.

35. Cicero, *Orator*, trans. H. M. Hubbell (Cambridge, MA: Harvard University
    Press, 1962), 3.12.

36. Cicero, *De officiis*, 1.6.29.

37. Augustine, *On Christian Doctrine*, 4.3.35.

38. Romans 5:12–21; 9. Augustine completed his commentaries on the Epistles
    of St. Paul in 396.

39. Augustine, *Confessions*, 3.4.7–8.

40. Augustine, *On Christian Doctrine*, 4.3.5.

41. Augustine, *On Christian Doctrine*, 4.21.29.

42. Augustine, *On Christian Doctrine*, 4.7.21.

43. Augustine, *On Christian Doctrine*, 4.2.3.

44. Bernard L. Brock, "Jonathan Edwards," in *American Orators before 1900*,
    ed. Bernard K. Duffy and Halford Ryan (Westport, CT: Greenwood Press,
    1987), 148.

45. Jonathan Edwards, "Sinners in the Hands of Angry God," in *Three Centuries
    of American Discourse*, ed. Ronald F. Reid (Prospect Heights, IL: Waveland
    Press, 1988), 70. All of the following quotations are from this source.

46. Edwards, "Sinners," 71.

47. Edwards, "Sinners," 75.

48. Aristotle, *Rhetoric*, Book 2, chapter 5.

49. Edwards may have been inspired by the Book of Revelation 14:20: "And the winepress was trodden without the city, and blood came out of the winepress, even unto the horse bridles."

50. Edwards, "Sinners," 72.

51. Edwards, "Sinners, 72.

52. Edwards, "Sinners," 71.

53. Edwards, "Sinners," 77.

54. Edwards was the grandfather of Aaron Burr, who became vice president of the United States under Thomas Jefferson in 1801. Burr attended the College of New Jersey, as did James Madison.

55. Heimert and, much more recently, Dickey support the thesis that the Great Awakening laid the foundations for the Revolution. Alan Heimert, *Religion and the American Mind* (Cambridge, MA: Harvard University Press, 1966); J. D. Dickey, *American Demagogues: The Great Awakening and the Rise and Fall of Populism* (New York: Pegasus, 2020). The year 1742, one year after Edwards's "Sinners," was marked by mob riots in Boston led by James Davenport, an evangelical preacher in the mold of Whitefield.

CHAPTER EIGHT. ART AND THE CALL OF THE SELF/OTHER

1. Most of these actors were nominated for Academy Awards, including Hattie McDaniel, who won the supporting actress award for her role as "Mammy." It is ironic that the first person of color to win an Academy Award came out of a racist film.

2. Having played a similar character in *The Maltese Falcon*, Bogart was perfect for the part.

3. Jake Horsley, *The Blood Poets: A Cinema of Savagery, 1958–1999*, vol. 1 (Lanham, MD: Scarecrow Press, 1999), 41.

4. Nicole Rafter, *Shots in the Mirror: Crime Films and Society* (New York: Oxford University Press, 2000), 156.

5.   Emmanuel Levinas, *Alterity and Transcendence*, trans. Michael B. Smith (New York: Columbia University Press, 1999), 97.

6.   Emmanuel Levinas, *Otherwise Than Being, or Beyond Essence*, trans. Alphonso Lingis (Boston: Klumer, 1991), 158.

7.   This section is a reworking of Craig R. Smith and Paul H. Arntson, "Identification in Interpersonal Relationships: One Foundation of Creativity," *Southern Communication Journal* 57 (1991): 61–72.

8.   For a complete discussion of the relationships between Dorothy Wordsworth and her brother, and Wordsworth and Coleridge, see Jonathan Bate, *Radical Wordsworth: The Poet Who Changed the World* (New Haven, CT: Yale University Press, 2020). Bate claims that the quality of Wordsworth's poetry declined markedly after he and Coleridge grew apart, partly because Wordsworth became more and more conservative. The Coleridge-Wordsworth dialogical relationship is also explored by Adam Nicolson in *The Making of Poetry: Coleridge and the Wordsworths, and Their Year of Marvels* (New York: Farrar, Straus and Giroux, 2020).

9.   For a full discussion of Romanticism, see Craig R. Smith, *Romanticism, Rhetoric and the Search for the Sublime* (Newcastle upon Tyne, UK: Cambridge Scholars Publishing, 2018).

10. Steven Naifeh and Gregory White Smith, *Van Gogh: A Life* (New York: Random House, 2012), 172.

11. Naifeh and Smith, *Van Gogh: A Life*, 175.

12. Martin Heidegger, *Being and Time*, trans. J. Macquarrie and E. Robinson (New York: Harper and Row, 1962), 58.

13. Naifeh and Smith, *Van Gogh: A Life*.

14. Naifeh and Smith, *Van Gogh: A Life*, 589.

15. Naifeh and Smith, *Van Gogh: A Life*, 591, 626.

16. Paul Gauguin, "In His Own Words," *Wilson Quarterly* 2 (1978): 171–172.

17. Paul Gauguin, "In His Own Words," *Wilson Quarterly* 2 (1978): 171–172.

18. Naifeh and Smith, *Van Gogh: A Life*, 672.

19. Paul Cabanne, *Van Gogh* (London: Thames and Hudson, 1974), 164.

20. Robert Goldwater, *Symbolism* (New York: Harper and Row, 1979), 134.

21. Naifeh and Smith, *Van Gogh: A Life*, 677.

22. Goldwater, *Symbolism*, 134.

23. Martin Heidegger, *Poetry, Language and Thought*, trans. A. Hofstadter (New York: Harper and Row, 1971), 37.

24. Goldwater, *Symbolism*, 87.

25. Paul Gauguin, *Intimate Journals*, trans. Van W. Brooks (New York: Liveright, 1921), 38.

26. In his *Philosophical Fragments*, Kierkegaard comes close to Heidegger's notion of creating beauty when he says that God's "love is creative" and that it is discovered autodidactically, which puts Kierkegaard in line with the Romantics of his day. Trans. David Swenson (Princeton, NJ: Princeton University Press, 1971), 38.

<h3 style="text-align:center">CONCLUSION</h3>

1. Abraham Joshua Heschel, *God in Search of Man: A Philosophy of Judaism* (New York: Noonday Press, 1955), 78.

2. Albert Einstein, *Living Philosophies* (New York: Simon and Schuster, 1931), 14.

3. Annie Dillard, *The Writing Life* (New York: HarperCollins, 1989), 68. Dillard was the youngest woman (age twenty-nine) at the time (1975) to be awarded the Pulitzer Prize for her *Pilgrim at Tinker Creek* (1974; New York: Harper Perennial, 2000).

4. See Kirk J. Schneider, *Awakening to Awe: Personal Stories of Profound Transformation* (New York: Jason Aronson, 2009); Paul Pearsall, *Awe: The Delights and Dangers of Our Eleventh Emotion* (Deerfield Beach, FL: Health Communications, Inc., 2009), 85.

5. Cited in "The Scream, 1893 by Edvard Munch," EdvardMunch.org, http://www.edvardmunch.org/the-scream.jsp.

6. Immanuel Kant, *Critique of Practical Reason*, trans. Thomas Kingsmill Abbott (New York: Barnes & Noble, 2004), 141.

7. Cited in Julie Zauzner, "In Space John Glenn Saw the Face of God," *Washington Post*, December 8, 2016.

8. *People* Staff, "Edgar Mitchell's Strange Voyage," *People* magazine, April 8, 1974.
9. Longinus, *On the Sublime*, xxxv.
10. Annie Dillard, *Teaching a Stone to Talk: Expeditions and Encounters* (New York: HarperCollins, 1988), 88.
11. Dillard, *The Writing Life*, 78–79.
12. See, for example, Michelle N. Shiota, Dacher Keltner, and Amanda Mossman, "The Nature of Awe: Elicitors, Appraisals, and Effects on Self-Concept," *Cognition and Emotion* 21 (2007): 944–963; Vladas Griskevicus, Michelle N. Shiota, and Samantha L. Neufeld, "Influence of Different Positive Emotions on Persuasion Processing: A Functional Evolutionary Approach," *Emotion* 10 (2010): 190–206; Melanie Rudd, Kathleen D. Vohs, and Jennifer Aaker, "Awe Expands People's Perception of Time, Alters Decision Making, and Enhances Well-Being," *Psychological Science* 23 (2012): 1130–1136; Paul K. Piff, Pia Dietze, Matthew Feinber, Daniel M. Stancato, and Dacher Keltner, "Awe, the Small Self, and Prosocial Behavior," *Journal of Personality and Social Psychology* 108 (2015): 883–899; and Kathleen E. Darbor, Heather C. Lench, William E. Davis, and Joshua A. Hicks, "Experiencing versus Contemplating: Language Use during Descriptions of Awe and Wonder," *Cognition and Emotion* 30 (2016): 1188–1196.
13. Ralph Waldo Emerson, "Language," 15, and "Heroism," 228; both in *The Essential Writings of Ralph Waldo Emerson: Essays*, ed. Brooks Atkinson (New York: Modern Library, 2000), 220–231.
14. Dillard tells stories about childhood experiences that first nourished her commitment. See her *American Childhood* (New York: Harper and Row, 1989). Also see Linda L. Smith, *Annie Dillard* (New York: Twayne, 1991) for more background on the life of her commitment.
15. Pearsall, *Awe*, 85.
16. Dillard, *Pilgrim at Tinker Creek*, 136.
17. Dillard, *Teaching a Stone to Talk*, 49.
18. Annie Dillard, *For the Time Being* (New York: Vintage, 1999), 169.

19. Martin Heidegger, "Letter on Humanism," trans. Frank A. Capuzzi, in *Basic Writings*, ed. David Farrell Krell (New York: Harper and Row, 1977), 230.

20. Dillard, *Pilgrim at Tinker Creek*, 139, italics added.

21. Edward S. Casey, *Getting Back into Place: Toward a Renewed Understanding of the Place-World* (Bloomington: Indiana University Press, 1993), ix. Also see his *The Fate of Place: A Philosophical History* (Berkeley: University of California Press, 1997).

22. Dillard, *Teaching a Stone to Talk*, 90–91.

23. Dillard, *Teaching a Stone to Talk*, 89–90.

24. Dillard, *Pilgrim at Tinker Creek*, 34–35.

25. Dillard, *Pilgrim at Tinker Creek*, 17.

26. Dillard, *Pilgrim at Tinker Creek*, 34.

27. Dillard, *Pilgrim at Tinker Creek*, 34.

28. Dillard, *Pilgrim at Tinker Creek*, 33–34.

29. Dillard, *Pilgrim at Tinker Creek*, 83.

30. Dillard, *The Writing Life*, 78–79.

31. Dillard, *The Writing Life*, 52.

32. Dillard, *The Writing Life*, 52.

33. Dillard, *Teaching a Stone to Talk*, 58.

34. Dillard, *For the Time Being*, 85.

35. Dillard, *Teaching a Stone to Talk*, 58–60.

36. Dillard, *Teaching a Stone to Talk*, 32.

37. Dillard, *Teaching a Stone to Talk*, 22–23.

38. Dillard, *Teaching a Stone to Talk*, 9.

39. Dillard, *Teaching a Stone to Talk*, 15.

40. Dillard, *Teaching a Stone to Talk*, 14–19.

41. Dillard, *Teaching a Stone to Talk*, 25–26.

42. Dillard, *Teaching a Stone to Talk*, 28.

43. Dillard, *Teaching a Stone to Talk*, 18.

44. Dillard, *Teaching a Stone to Talk*, 23–24.

45. Dillard, *Teaching a Stone to Talk*, 19–20.

46. Dillard, *Teaching a Stone to Talk*, 49.

47. Annie Dillard, *Holy the Firm* (New York: Perennial, 1977), 16.

48. Dillard, *Holy the Firm*, 16–17.

49. Dillard, *Holy the Firm*, 16–17.

50. Dillard, *Holy the Firm*, 71–72.

51. Elaine Scarry, *On Beauty and Being Just* (Princeton, NJ: Princeton University Press, 1999), 52–53, 60–61, 109.

52. See her *American Childhood*. Also see Linda L. Smith, *Annie Dillard*, for more background on the life of her commitment.

Bibliography

Ahmed, Sara. *The Promise of Happiness*. Durham, NC: Duke University Press, 2010.

Alman, Ashley. "*New York Times* Dedicates 2 Page Spread to the People and Things Trump Insulted." *New York Times*, September 24, 2016

Anderson, Robert O. "The Characterization Model for Rhetorical Criticism of Political Image Campaigns." *Western Speech* 37 (1973): 75–86.

Aristotle. *On Rhetoric: A Theory of Civic Discourse*. Translated by George A. Kennedy. 2nd ed. New York: Oxford University Press, 2007.

Arnett, Ron. "Toward a Phenomenology of Dialogue." *Western Journal of Speech Communication* 42 (1981): 201–212.

Arter, Melanie. "Pence: 'I Believe in Forgiveness.'" *CNSNEWS*, October 10, 2016.

Augustine. *City of God*. Translated by Henry Bettenson. New York: Penguin Classics, 1984.

———. *Confessions*. Translated by William Watts. Cambridge, MA: Loeb Classical Library, 1977.

———. "De Genesis ad litteram." In *The Works of St. Augustine*, translated by Edmund Hill, edited by John Rotelle. Brooklyn, NY: New City Press, 1991.

———. *On Christian Doctrine.* Translated by J. F. Shaw. Chicago: Encyclopedia Britannica, 1952.

Bachelard, Gaston. *The Poetics of Space.* Translated by Maria Jolas. Boston: Beacon Press, 1969.

Baldwin, Charles Sears. *Medieval Rhetoric and Poetic.* Gloucester, MA: Peter Smith Press, 1959.

Bate, Jonathan. *Radical Wordsworth: The Poet Who Changed the World.* New Haven, CT: Yale University Press, 2020.

Battaglio, Stephen. "35 Million TV Viewers Watch Trump's Speech." *Los Angeles Times,* July 23, 2016, C5.

———. "A Talk-Show Match Worth Fighting For." *Los Angeles Times,* February 17, 2020, E4.

———. "The Democrats Pull 7.85 Million." *Los Angeles Times,* December 22, 2015, E2.

———. "GOP Confab a Cable News Hit." *Los Angeles Times,* July 20, 2016, C3.

———. "GOP Debate Draws Fewer Viewers." *Los Angeles Times,* January 16, 2016, C6.

Bellah, Robert N., R. Madsen, W. M. Sullivan, A. Swidler, and S. M. Tipton. *Habits of the Heart: Individualism and Commitment in American Life.* New York: Harper and Row, 1985.

Bercovitch, Sacvan. *The American Jeremiad.* Madison: University of Wisconsin Press, 1978.

Blair, Hugh. *Lectures on Belles Lettres.* London: J. Cantwell, 1838.

Blair, Tony. *A Journey: My Political Life.* New York: Alfred A. Knopf, 2010.

Bolyard, Paula. "Trumpette Calls Trump 'God' and Says He Will Come Down to Help Us All." PJ Media, October 1, 2016. https://pjmedia.com.

Bostdorff, Denise. "George W. Bush's Post–September 11 Rhetoric of Covenant Renewal: Upholding the Faith of the Greatest Generation." *Quarterly Journal of Speech* 89 (2003): 293–319.

Bostdorff, Denise M., and Steven R. Goldzwig. "Barack Obama's Eulogy for the Reverend Clementa Pinckney, June 26, 2016: Grace as the Vehicle for Collective Salvation and Obama's Agency of Civil Rights." *Rhetoric and Public Affairs* 23 (2020): 107–152.

Brock, Bernard L. "Jonathan Edwards." In *American Orators before 1900,* edited by

Bernard K. Duffy and Halford Ryan. Westport, CT: Greenwood Press, 1987.

Brown, Michael. "Donald Trump: President by the Sovereign Intervention of God." *Christian Post*, November 9, 2016.

Buber, Martin. *Between Man and Man*. New York: Macmillan, 1965.

———. *I and Thou*. New York: Charles Scribner and Sons, 1954.

———. *Knowledge of Man*. New York: Harper and Row, 1965.

———. *Pointing the Way*. London: Routledge and Kegan Paul, 1957.

Buchanan, Patrick. *State of Emergency: The Third World and the Conquest of America*. New York: St. Martin's Press, 2006.

Burke, Edmund. *A Philosophical Enquiry into the Origins of Our Ideas of the Sublime and Beautiful*. New York: Oxford University Press, 1999.

Burke, Kenneth. *A Rhetoric of Motives*. Berkeley: University of California Press, 1966.

———. *Counter-Statement*. Berkeley: University of California Press, 1968.

———. *Language as Symbolic Action: Essays in Life, Literature, and Method*. Berkeley: University of California Press, 1966.

Bush, George W. "Address before a Joint Session of the Congress on the State of the Union." January 31, 2006. Compilation of Presidential Documents. https://www.govinfo.gov/app/collection/CPD/.

———. "Address before a Joint Session of the Congress on the State of the Union." January 23, 2007. Compilation of Presidential Documents. https://www.govinfo.gov/app/collection/CPD/.

———. "Guard and Reserves 'Define Spirit of America': Remarks by the President to Employees at the Pentagon." September 17, 2001. Compilation of Presidential Documents. https://www.govinfo.gov/app/collection/CPD/.

———. "The President's News Conference." January 26, 2006. Compilation of Presidential Documents. https://www.govinfo.gov/app/collection/CPD/.

———. "Remarks to Employees at the Pentagon and an Exchange with Reporters in Arlington, Virginia." September 17, 2001. Compilation of Presidential Documents. https://www.govinfo.gov/app/collection/CPD/.

"Bush Shifts Approach on Social Security Reform." *Financial Times*, April 28, 2005, A1.

Buttery, Stephen. "Candidates Focus on Christian Beliefs." *Des Moines Register*, December 15, 1999, A1.

Cabanne, Paul. *Van Gogh.* London: Thames and Hudson, 1974.

Campbell, Karlyn Kohrs. *Critiques of Contemporary Rhetoric.* Belmont, CA: Wadsworth Publishing, 1972.

Campbell, Karlyn Kohrs, and Kathleen Jamieson. *Deeds Done in Words: Presidential Rhetoric and Genres of Governance.* Chicago: University of Chicago Press, 1990.

Carr, David. *Time, Narrative, and History.* Bloomington: Indiana University Press, 1991.

Casey, Edward S. *The Fate of Place: A Philosophical History.* Berkeley: University of California Press, 1997.

———. *Getting Back into Place: Toward a Renewed Understanding of the Place-World.* Bloomington: Indiana University Press, 1993.

Caws, Mary Ann, ed. *Manifesto: A Century of Isms.* Lincoln: University of Nebraska Press, 2001.

Chrétien, Jean-Louis. *The Call and the Response.* Translated by Anne A. Davenport. New York: Fordham University Press, 2004.

Cicero, *De officiis.* Translated by Walter Miller. Cambridge, MA: Harvard University Press, 1913.

———. *Orator.* Translated by H. M. Hubbell. Cambridge, MA: Harvard University Press, 1962.

Cilliza, Chris. "Pat Buchanan Says Donald Trump Is the Future of the Republican Party." *Washington Post*, January 13, 2016.

Cohen, Claire. "Donald Trump Sexism Tracker: Every Offensive Comment in One Place." *The Telegraph* (London), June 4, 2016, A1.

Coles, Robert. *The Call of Stories: Teaching and the Moral Imagination.* Boston: Houghton Mifflin, 1989.

Collins, Francis S. *The Language of God: A Scientist Presents Evidence for Belief.* New York: Free Press, 2006.

Commager, Henry S. *Documents of American History.* 9th ed. Englewood Cliffs, NJ: Prentice-Hall, 1973.

Conlon, James. *Lyrics for Re-Creation: Language for the Music of the Universe.* New York: Continuum, 1997.

Cooper, David A. *God Is a Verb: Kabbalah and the Practice of Mystical Judaism.* New York: Riverhead Books, 1997.

Corasaniti, Nick, and Maggie Haberman. "Donald Trump Suggests 'Second Amendment People' Could Act against Hillary Clinton." *New York Times*, August 9, 2016.

Corasaniti, Nick, Nicholas Confessore, and Michael Barbaro. "Donald Trump Says Hillary Clinton's Bodyguards Should Disarm to 'See What Happens to Her.'" *New York Times*, September 16, 2016.

Crosswhite, James. *Deep Rhetoric: Philosophy, Reason, Violence, Justice, Wisdom.* Chicago: University of Chicago Press, 2013.

Dane, Billie. "Bakker Predicts 'Messiah' Trump Will Slay the 'Great Serpent.'" *Business Standard News*, September 6, 2016.

Daniels, Tom D., Richard J. Jensen, and Allen Lichtenstein. "Resolving the Paradox in Politicized Christian Fundamentalism." *Western Journal of Speech Communication* 49 (1985): 248–266.

Darbor, Kathleen E., Heather C. Lench, William E. Davis, and Joshua A. Hicks. "Experiencing versus Contemplating: Language Use during Descriptions of Awe and Wonder." *Cognition and Emotion* 30 (2016): 1188–1196.

Davies, Paul. *The Fifth Miracle: The Search for the Origin and Meaning of Life.* New York: Simon & Schuster, 2000.

———. *God and the New Physics.* New York: Simon & Schuster, 1983.

Dawkins, Richard, Daniel C. Dennett, Sam Harris, and Christopher Hitchens. *The Four Horsemen: The Conversation That Sparked an Atheist Revolution.* New York: Centre for Inquiry, 2019.

de Antonia, Emile, and Daniel Talbot. *Point of Order.* New York: Screenplay, 1964.

de Piles, Roger. *Course on Painting by Principles.* Paris: Gallimard, 1989.

Deans, Bob. "'Lennon-McCartney' Creative Team; Speechwriters Find President a Tough Editor." *Atlanta Journal-Constitution*, January 29, 2006, 7B.

Decker, Cathleen. "GOP Divided on Haley's Speech." *Los Angeles Times*, January 14, 2016, A9.

——. "Republicans Sounding Alarm Bells." *Los Angeles Times*, February 6, 2016, A10.

Delany, Arthur, and Ariel Edwards-Levy. "Donald Trump Is a Gift from God to His Supporters." *Huffington Post*, March 1, 2016.

Demos, Raphael. "On Persuasion." *Journal of Philosophy* 29 (1932): 229.

Dickerson, John. "Interview of Donald Trump." *CBS Face the Nation*, June 5, 2016. http://www.cbsnews.com/news/donald-trump-its-possible-muslim-judge-would-treat-me-unfairly.

Dickey, J. D. *American Demagogues: The Great Awakening and the Rise and Fall of Populism.* New York: Pegasus, 2020.

Dillard, Annie. *American Childhood.* New York: Harper and Row, 1989.

——. *For the Time Being.* New York: Vintage, 1999.

——. *Holy the Firm.* New York: Harper Perennial, 1977.

——. *Pilgrim at Tinker Creek.* New York: Harper Perennial, 2000.

——. *Teaching a Stone to Talk: Expeditions and Encounters.* New York: HarperCollins, 1988.

——. *The Writing Life.* New York: HarperCollins, 1989.

Dinan, Stephen. "Donald Trump Drives GOP's Record Turnout; Democrats Lack Enthusiasm." *Washington Times*, March 1, 2016, A1.

Divine, Robert A. *Since 1945: Politics and Diplomacy in Recent American History.* New York: John Wiley and Sons, 1975.

Dockray, Heather. "Trump Says He'll Be the Greatest Job Producer God Has Ever Created, and Twitter Is Skeptical." *Mashable*, January 11, 2017.

Dorsey, Leroy G., ed. *The President and Rhetorical Leadership.* College Station: Texas A&M University Press, 2002.

Earle, William. *Public Sorrows and Private Pleasures.* Bloomington: Indiana University Press, 1976.

Edwards, Jonathan. "Sinners in the Hands of Angry God." In *Three Centuries of American Discourse*, edited by Ronald F. Reid. Prospect Heights, IL: Waveland Press, 1988.

Einstein, Albert. *Living Philosophies.* New York: Simon and Schuster, 1931.

Emerson, Ralph Waldo. "Heroism." In *The Essential Writings of Ralph Waldo*

Emerson: Essays, edited by Brooks Atkinson, 220–231. New York: Modern
Library, 2000.

———. *The Journals and Miscellaneous Notebooks of Ralph Waldo Emerson*. Vol. 13.
Edited by Ralph H. Orth and Alfred R. Ferguson. Cambridge, MA: Harvard
University Press, 1977.

———. "Language." In *The Essential Writings of Ralph Waldo Emerson: Nature*,
edited by Brooks Atkinson, 11–21. New York: Modern Library, 2000.

Erickson, Erick. "Donald Trump Is God's Anointed." *The Resurgent*, November 3,
2016.

Fichte, Johann. *Man's Destination*. Translated by Jane Sinnet. Paris: Molitar, 1965.

Fine, Lawrence. *Physician of the Soul, Healer of the Cosmos: Isaac Luria and His
Kabbalistic Fellowship*. Stanford, CA: Stanford University Press, 2003.

Finnegan, Michael, and Noah Bierman. "Conflict Fuels Rallies for Trump." *Los
Angeles Times*, March 14, 2016, A1, 10.

Fisher, Walter. *Human Communication as Narration: Toward a Philosophy of
Reason, Value, and Action*. Columbia: University of South Carolina Press,
1987.

Frank, David A. "Facing Moloch: Barack Obama's National Eulogies and Gun
Violence." *Rhetoric and Public Affairs* 17 (2014): 585–618.

Frankfurt, Harry G. *On Truth*. New York: Alfred Knopf, 2017.

Fredricksen, Paula. "Paul and Augustine: Conversion Narratives, Orthodox
Tradition, and the Retrospective Self." *Journal of Theological Studies* 37
(1986): 3–34.

Freeman, Kathleen. *Ancilla to the Pre-Socratic Philosophers: A Complete Translation
of the Fragments in Diels, Fragmente der Vorsokratiker*. Cambridge, MA:
Harvard University Press, 1966.

Freud, Sigmund. *A General Selection from the Works of Sigmund Freud*. Edited by
John Rickman. New York: Doubleday, 1957.

———. *A General Introduction to Psychoanalysis*. New York: Pocket Books, 1952.

Frum, David. *The Right Man: The Surprise Presidency of George W. Bush*. New York:
Random House, 2003.

Gauguin, Paul. "In His Own Words." *Wilson Quarterly* 2 (1978): 171–172.

———. *Intimate Journals*. Translated by Van W. Brooks. New York: Liveright, 1921.

Germino, Dante. *The Inaugural Addresses of American Presidents: The Public Philosophy and Rhetoric*. Lanham, MD: University Press of America, 1984.

Goldwater, Robert. *Symbolism*. New York: Harper and Row, 1979.

Gorodnichenko, Yuriy, Tho Pham, and Oleksandr Talavera. "Social Media, Sentiment and Public Opinion: Evidence from #brexit and #uselection." *National Bureau of Economic Research* (May 2018): 1–5.

Goulston, Mark. "Why Trump Is the Perfect Candidate." *Huffington Post*, August 2, 2016.

Greenberg, Jon. "Trump's Pants on Fire Tweet That Blacks Killed 81% of White Homicide Victims." Politifact.com, November 23, 2015.

Griskevicus, Vladas, Michelle N. Shiota, and Samantha L. Neufeld. "Influence of Different Positive Emotions on Persuasion Processing: A Functional Evolutionary Approach." *Emotion* 10 (2010): 190–206.

Gusdorf, Charles. *Speaking (La Parole)*. Translated by Paul T. Brockelman. Evanston, IL: Northwestern University Press, 1965.

Guth, Alan H. *The Inflationary Universe: The Quest for a New Theory of Cosmic Origins*. New York: Basic Books, 1998.

Haberman, Maggie. "Trump Says His Mocking of New York Times Reporter Was Misread." *New York Times*, November 11, 2015, A1.

Hacker, Kenneth L., ed. *Candidate Images in Presidential Elections*. Westport, CT: Praeger, 1995.

Hariman, Robert. *Political Style: The Artistry of Power*. Chicago: University of Chicago Press, 1995.

Harper, Jennifer. "Franklin Graham on the Presidential Election and Trump's Victory: 'God Showed Up.'" *Washington Times*, November 10, 2016.

Harris, Sam. *The Moral Landscape*. New York: Free Press.

Hart, D. G. *Reckoning with the Past: Historical Essays on American Evangelicalism from the Institute for the Study of American Evangelicals*. Grand Rapids, MI: Baker Books, 1995.

———. *Trump and Us: What He Says and Why People Listen*. Cambridge: Cambridge University Press, 2020.

Hart, Roderick, and Dan Burkes. "Rhetorical Sensitivity and Social Interaction." *Speech Monographs* 39 (1972): 75–91.

Heidegger, Martin. *Being and Time.* Translated by J. Macquarrie and E. Robinson. New York: Harper and Row, 1962.

———. *Existence and Being.* Translated by Douglas Scott, R. F. C. Hull, and Alan Crick. South Bend, IN: Henry Regnery, 1949.

———. "Letter on Humanism." Translated by Frank A. Capuzzi in collaboration with J. Glenn Gray. In *Basic Writings*, edited by David Farrell Krell, 229–234. New York: Harper and Row, 1977.

———. *Poetry, Language and Thought.* Translated by A. Hofstadter. New York: Harper and Row, 1971.

Heimert, Alan. *Religion and the American Mind.* Cambridge, MA: Harvard University Press, 1966.

Hellmann, Jessie. "Trump: 'I'm Not Perfect.'" *The Hill*, August 12, 2016.

Hentoff, Nat. *The First Freedom.* New York: Delacorte Press, 1980.

Herbert, Steven. "A Live Event Leads Again." *Los Angeles Times*, March 9, 2016, E8.

Heschel, Abraham Joshua. *God in Search of Man: A Philosophy of Judaism.* New York: Noonday Press, 1955.

Hofstadter, Richard. *The Paranoid Style in American Politics and Other Essays.* New York: Random House, 1957.

Horace. "The Arts of Poetry." In *Literary Criticism: Plato to Dryden*, edited by Allan H. Gilbert. Detroit: Wayne State University Press, 1962.

Horsley, Jake. *The Blood Poets: A Cinema of Savagery, 1958–1999.* Vol. 1. Lanham, MD: Scarecrow Press, 1999.

Hsu, Spenser S., and Susan Glasser. "FEMA Director Singled Out by Response Critics." *Washington Post*, September 6, 2005, A1.

Hyde, Michael J. "A Matter of the Heart: Epideictic Rhetoric and Heidegger." In *Heidegger and Rhetoric*, edited by Daniel M. Gross and Ansgar Kemmann. New York: State University of New York Press, 2005.

———. *The Call of Conscience: Heidegger and Levinas, Rhetoric and the Euthanasia Debate.* Columbia: University of South Carolina Press, 2001.

———. "Heidegger on Rhetoric." In *Analecta Husserliana*, vol. 15, edited by Calvin

Schrag, 65–72. Dordrecht, Holland: D. Reidel Publishing Co., 1983.

———. *The Interruption That We Are: The Health of the Lived Body, Narrative, and Public Moral Argument.* Columbia: University of South Carolina Press, 2018.

———. *The Life-Giving Gift of Acknowledgment.* West Lafayette, IN: Purdue University Press, 2006.

———. *Openings: Acknowledging Essential Moments in Human Communication.* Waco, TX: Baylor University Press, 2012.

———. *Perfection: Coming to Terms with Being Human.* Columbia: University of South Carolina Press, 2010.

Hyde, Michael J., and Craig R. Smith. "Aristotle and Heidegger on Emotion and Rhetoric: Questions of Time and Space." In *The Critical Turn: Rhetoric and Philosophy in Contemporary Discourse,* edited by Ian Angus and Lenore Langsdorf, 68–99. Carbondale, IL: Southern Illinois University Press, 1993.

———. "Hermeneutics and Rhetoric: A Seen but Unobserved Relationship." *Quarterly Journal of Speech* 65 (1979): 347–363.

Ivie, Robert. "Metaphor and the Rhetorical Invention of the Cold War 'Idealists.'" *Communication Monographs* 54 (1987): 165–182.

———. "Presidential Motives for War." *Quarterly Journal of Speech* 60 (1974): 337–345.

Jaspers, Karl. *Philosophy.* Translated by E. B. Ashton. Vol. 2. Chicago: University of Chicago Press, 1970.

Johannesen, Richard. "The Emerging Concept of Communication as Dialogue." *Quarterly Journal of Speech* 57 (1971): 373–382.

Johnson, Jeremiah. "Prophesy: Donald Trump Shall Become the Trumpet." *Charisma Magazine,* July 28, 2015.

Jones, W. H. S. *Hippocrates: Law.* Vol. 2. London: William Heinemann, 1923.

Kahn, Charles H. *The Art and Thought of Heraclitus: An Edition of the Fragments with Translation and Commentary.* New York: Cambridge University Press, 1979.

Kamesar, Ben. "Trump: I Could Shoot People in Streets and Not Lose Support." *The Hill,* January 23, 2016.

Kant, Immanuel. *Critique of Practical Reason.* Translated by Thomas Kingsmill

Abbott. New York: Barnes & Noble, 2004.

Kantor, Jodi. "A Candidate, His Minister and the Search for Faith." *New York Times*, April 30, 2007, A30.

Kenny, Robert Wade. "Truth as Metaphor: Imaginative Vision and the Ethos of Rhetoric." In *The Ethos of Rhetoric*, edited by Michael J. Hyde. Columbia: University of South Carolina Press, 2004.

Kierkegaard, Soren. *Philosophical Fragments*. Translated by David Swenson. Princeton, NJ: Princeton University Press, 1971.

———. *Training in Christianity*. Translated by Walter Lowrie. Princeton, NJ: Princeton University Press, 1967.

Kilmer, Joyce. "Trees." *Poetry: A Magazine of Verse* (1913): 160.

Kushner, Lawrence. *The Book of Words: Talking Spiritual Life, Living Spiritual Talk*. Woodstock, VT: Jewish Lights, 1993.

LaHaye, Tim. *The Coming Peace in the Middle East*. Grand Rapids, MI: Zondervan Publishing House, 1984.

LaHaye, Tim, and Thomas Ice. *The End of Times Controversy*. Eugene, OR: Harvest House Publishers, 2003.

Lepore, Stephen M. "A Guide to Everyone Who Loves Donald Trump, according to Donald Trump." *New York Daily News*, October 21, 2015.

Levinas, Emmanuel. *Alterity and Transcendence*. Translated by Michael B. Smith. New York: Columbia University Press, 1999.

———. *Otherwise Than Being, or Beyond Essence*. Translated by Alphonso Lingis. Boston: Klumer, 1991.

———. *Outside the Subject*. Translated by Michael B. Smith. Stanford, CA: Stanford University Press, 1994.

———. *Totality and Infinity*. Translated by Alphonso Lingis. Pittsburg, PA: Duquesne University Press, 1969.

Lewis, C. S. *The Chronicles of Narnia*. New York: HarperCollins Publishers, 1956.

Lindsay, Hal. *Apocalypse Code*. Palos Verdes, CA: Western Front Ltd., 1997.

Locke, John. *An Essay Concerning Human Understanding*. Edited by Kenneth P. Winkler. New York: Hackett, 1996.

———. *A Paraphrase and Notes on the Epistles of St. Paul*. Oxford: Clarendon Press,

1987.

Longinus. "On the Sublime." In *The Great Critics*, edited by James Harry Smith and Ed Winfield Parks. New York: W.W. Norton, 1959.

———. *On the Sublime*. Translated by Benjamin Jowett. New York: CreateSpace Independent Publishing Platform, 2014.

Lyon, Janet. *Manifestoes: Provocations of the Modern*. Ithaca, NY: Cornell University Press, 1999.

Mantyle, Kyle. "Michael Brown on Trump's Election: 'God Raised Him Up, No Question." *Right Wing Watch*, December 8, 2016.

Marsden, George. "The Collapse of American Evangelical Academia." In *Faith and Rationality*, edited by A. Plantinga and N. Wolterstorff. Notre Dame, IN: University of Notre Dame Press, 1984.

———. *Fundamentalism and American Culture: The Shaping of Twentieth-Century Evangelicalism, 1870–1925*. New York: Oxford University Press, 1980.

Mascaro, Lisa. "Trump Takes a Swing at His 'Haters.'" *Los Angeles Times*, July 23, 2016, A5.

Massumi, Brian. *Parables for the Virtual: Movement, Affect, Sensation*. Durham, NC: Duke University Press, 2002.

McAdams, Dan P. "The Mind of Donald Trump." *The Atlantic* (June 2016): 78–84.

McCarthy, Joseph. "Address to GOP Convention." *New York Times*, July 10, 1952, A1.

McKeon, Richard. "The Method of Rhetoric and Philosophy: Inventional Judgment." In *The Classical Tradition: Literary and Historical Studies in Honor of Harry Caplan*, edited by L. Wallach. Ithaca, NY: Cornell University Press, 1966.

McPhail, Mark L., and David A. Frank. "Slouching toward Coherence: Rhetoric, Religion, and the Broken Promissory Note of Racial Justice in the United States." *Southern Communication Journal* 74 (2009): 210.

Meacham, Jon. "A Conversation with Jon Meacham about the Legacy of Senator Howard Baker and Lessons Our Nation Can Learn from Him Today." McCallie School, January 20, 2020. https://www.mccallie.org/podcast.

Medhurst, Martin J. "Introduction." *Rhetoric and Public Affairs* 7 (2004): 445–448.

———. "Religious Rhetoric and the *Ethos* of Democracy: A Case Study of the 2000

Presidential Campaign." In *The Ethos of Rhetoric*, edited by Michael J. Hyde, 114–135. Columbia: University of South Carolina Press, 2004.

Megerian, Chris. "At Davos, Trump Dismisses Climate Crisis." *Los Angeles Times*, January 22, 2020, A5.

Mercieca, Jennifer R. *Demagogue for President: The Rhetorical Genius of Donald Trump*. College Station: Texas A&M University Press, 2020.

Milbank, Dana. "Donald Trump Is a Bigot and a Racist." *Washington Post*, December 1, 2015.

Miles, Margaret R. "The Body and Human Values in Augustine of Hippo." In *Grace, Politics, and Desire: Essays on Augustine*, edited by Hugo A. Meynell. Calgary: University of Calgary Press, 1990.

Miller, Alice. *The Drama of the Gifted Child: The Search for Self.* Translated by R. Ward. New York: Basic Books, 1981.

Mills, Watson E. *Mercer Dictionary of the Bible*. Macon, GA: Mercer Press, 1994.

Morris, Henry R. *The Long War against God*. New York: Master Books, 2000.

Murphy, John. "Our Mission and Our Moment: George W. Bush and September 11." *Rhetoric and Public Affairs* 6 (2003): 607–632.

Nabokov, Vladimir. "The Art of Literature and Common Sense." In *Lectures on Literature*, edited by Fredson Bowers. New York: Mariner Books, 2002.

Naifeh, Steven, and Gregory White Smith. *Van Gogh: A Life*. New York: Random House, 2012.

Nicolson, Adam. *The Making of Poetry: Coleridge and the Wordsworths, and Their Year of Marvels*. New York: Farrar, Straus and Giroux, 2020.

Nisbet, Robert. *History of the Idea of Progress*. New York: Basic Books, 1980.

Nussbaum, Martha C. *Political Emotions: Why Love Matters for Justice*. Cambridge, MA: Harvard University Press, 2013.

Obama, Barack. "A More Perfect Union." Address. Philadelphia, March 18, 2008.

——. "Inaugural Address." Washington, DC, January 21, 2009.

O'Donnell, John R., and James Rutherford. *Trumped! The Inside Story of the Real Donald Trump—His Cunning Rise and Spectacular Fall*. New York: Simon and Schuster, 1988.

O'Leary, Stephen, and M. McFarland. "The Political Use of Mythic Discourse:

Prophetic Interpretation in Pat Robertson's Presidential Campaign."
Quarterly Journal of Speech 75 (1989): 433–452.

Ouaknin, Marc-Alain. *Mysteries of the Kabbalah.* Translated by Josephine Bacon.
New York: Abbeville Press, 2000.

Parmet, Herbert S. *Eisenhower and the American Crusades.* New York: Macmillan
Co., 1972.

Pearsall, Paul. *Awe: The Delights and Dangers of Our Eleventh Emotion.* Deerfield
Beach, FL: Health Communications, Inc., 2009.

Piff, Paul K., Pia Dietze, Matthew Feinber, Daniel M. Stancato, and Dacher Keltner.
"Awe, the Small Self, and Prosocial Behavior." *Journal of Personality and Social
Psychology* 108 (2015): 883–899.

Pinsky, Mark I. "Meet the New Evangelicals." *Los Angeles Times,* September 16,
2006, B15.

Poulakos, John. "Special Delivery: Rhetoric, Letter Writing, and the Question
of Beauty." In *The Ethos of Rhetoric,* edited by Michael J. Hyde. Columbia:
University of South Carolina Press, 2004.

Quintilian. *Institutes of Oratory.* Translated by H. E. Butler. Cambridge, MA:
Harvard University Press, 1980.

Rafter, Nicole. *Shots in the Mirror: Crime Films and Society.* New York: Oxford
University Press, 2000.

Rees, Martin. *Before the Beginning: Our Universe and Others.* Reading, MA: Perseus
Books, 1997.

Ricoeur, Paul. "Experience and Language in Religious Discourse." In
Phenomenology and Theology, edited by Chrétien et al., 16–33. Paris:
Criterion, 1992.

Riswold, C. D. "A Religious Response Veiled in a Presidential Address: A Theological
Study of Bush's Speech on 20 September 2001." *Political Theology* 5 (2004):
39–46.

Roetzel, Calvin J. *The Letters of Paul: Conversations in Context.* Atlanta: John Knox
Press, 1975.

Roosevelt, Franklin D. "Acceptance of the Democratic Presidential Nomination,"
June 27, 1936.

Rousseau, Theodore. *Selections from His Writing.* New York: Metropolitan Museum of Art, 1979.

Rudd, Melanie, Kathleen D. Vohs, and Jennifer Aaker. "Awe Expands People's Perception of Time, Alters Decision Making, and Enhances Well-Being." *Psychological Science* 23 (2012): 1130–1136.

Scarry, Elaine. *On Beauty and Being Just.* Princeton, NJ: Princeton University Press, 1999.

Schneider, Kirk J. *Awakening to Awe: Personal Stories of Profound Transformation.* New York: Jason Aronson, 2009.

Scholem, Gershom. *Kabbalah.* New York: Meridian, 1974.

Schwartz, Frederick A. O., Jr., and Aziz Z. Huq. *Unchecked and Unbalanced: Presidential Power in a Time of Terror.* New York: New Press, 2007.

Schweitzer, Albert. *Paul and His Interpreters.* New York: Macmillan, 1951.

Seigworth, Gregory J., and Melissa Gregg. *The Affect Theory Reader.* Durham, NC: Duke University Press, 2010.

Shafer, Jack. "Donald Trump Talks Like a Third-Grader." *Politico Magazine*, August 13, 2006.

Shiota, Michelle N., Dacher Keltner, and Amanda Mossman. "The Nature of Awe: Elicitors, Appraisals, and Effects on Self-Concept." *Cognition and Emotion* 21 (2007): 944–963.

Smith, Craig R. *Confessions of a Presidential Speech Writer.* East Lansing: Michigan State University Press, 2014.

———. "Does Trump's Fascist Rhetoric Foreshadow Fascist Action?" *Communication Currents*, June 18, 2019. https://www.natcom.org/communication-currents.

———. "Existential Responsibility and Roman Decorum: A New Praxis." *Western Journal of Communication* 56 (1992): 68–89.

———. "Heidegger's Theory of Authentic Discourse." *Analecta Husserliana*, vol. 15, edited by Calvin Schrag, 209–217. Dordrecht, Holland: D. Reidel Publishing Co., 1983.

———. "Martin Heidegger and the Dialogue with Being." *Communication Studies* 36 (1985): 256–269.

———. "Moving Federal Court Appointments into the Public Sphere." *Controversia:*

The International Journal of Argumentation 4 (2006): 15–50.

——. *The Quest for Charisma: Christianity and Persuasion.* Westport, CT: Praeger Press, 2000.

——. *Rhetoric and Human Consciousness: A History.* 5th ed. Long Grove, IL: Waveland, 2017.

——. *Romanticism, Rhetoric and the Search for the Sublime.* Newcastle upon Tyne, UK: Cambridge Scholars Publishing, 2018.

Smith, Craig R., and Paul H. Arntson. "Identification in Interpersonal Relationships: One Foundation of Creativity." *Southern Communication Journal* 57 (1991): 61–72.

Smith, Craig R., and Michael J. Hyde. "Rethinking 'The Public': The Role of Emotion in Being-with-Others." *Quarterly Journal of Speech* 77 (1991): 446–466.

Smith, Craig R., and Theodore Prosise. "The Supreme Court's Ruling in *Bush v. Gore*: A Rhetoric of Inconsistency." *Rhetoric and Public Affairs* 4 (2001): 605–632.

Smith, Francis Marie, and Thomas A. Hollihan. "'Out of Chaos Breathes Creation': Human Agency, Mental Illness and Conservative Arguments Locating Responsibility for the Tucson Massacre." *Rhetoric and Public Affairs* 17 (2014): 577–584.

Smith, Linda L. *Annie Dillard.* New York: Twayne, 1991.

Smith, Margaret Chase. "Conscience of a Republican." *Congressional Record,* Senate, 81st Cong., 2nd sess. (1 June 1950): 7894–7895.

Spaeth, Ryu. "Donald Trump Has Come Up with His Clinton Nickname." *New Republic,* April 17, 2016.

"Spread of Propaganda by White Supremacists Soars." *Los Angeles Times,* February 13, 2020, A9.

Steward, Katherine. "Eighty-One Percent of White Evangelicals Voted for Trump." *The Nation,* November 17, 2017.

Stewart, John. *Bridges Not Walls.* New York: Random House, 1986.

——. "Foundations of Dialogic Communication." *Quarterly Journal of Speech* 64 (1968): 183–201.

Sullivan, Margaret. *Ghosting the News.* New York: Columbia Global Reports, 2020.

Susskind, Leonard. *The Cosmic Landscape: String Theory and the Illusion of Intelligent Design.* New York: Little, Brown and Co., 2006.

Tachman, Brian. "End Times Pastor Tom Horn: Donald Trump Could Be the Messiah or His Forerunner." *Right Wing Watch*, December 15, 2016.

———. "Pat Robertson: God Is Working on Behalf of Trump." *Right Wing Watch*, February 16, 2016.

Team Fix. "The Fox News GOP Debate Transcript Annotated." *Washington Post*, March 3, 2016.

Terrill, Robert E. "Unity and Duality in Barack Obama's 'A More Perfect Union.'" *Quarterly Journal of Speech* 95 (2009): 363–386.

Thucydides. *History of the Peloponnesian War.* Translated by Rex Warner. New York: Penguin Books, 1954.

Trudeau, Gary. "Doonesbury." *Los Angeles Times*, August 6, 2006, H5.

Truman, Harry S. "Veto Message." In *Documents of American History*, edited by Henry S. Commager, 578–582. Englewood Cliffs, NJ: Prentice-Hall, 1973.

Trump, Donald. "Excerpts from the Acceptance Speech: 'Americanism . . . will be our credo.'" *Los Angeles Times*, July 22, 2016, A3.

Tyler, Poyntz. *Immigration and the United States.* New York: H.W. Wilson Co., 1956.

van Emeren, Frans H., Rob Grootendorst, and Francisca Snoeck Henkemans. *Fundamentals of Argumentation Theory: A Handbook of Historical Backgrounds and Contemporary Developments.* Mahwah, NJ: Lawrence Erlbaum Associates, 1996.

Wallnau, Lance. "Prophecy God Sent Donald Trump to Wage War against Destructive Spirits." *Charisma News*, August 16, 2016.

Wander, Phillip. "The Rhetoric of American Foreign Policy." *Quarterly Journal of Speech* 70 (1984): 344–357.

Washington, George. "First Inaugural Address." In *Inaugural Addresses of the Presidents of the United States.* Washington, DC: Government Printing Office, 1974.

Webster, Daniel. *The Papers of Daniel Webster: Speeches and Formal Writings.* Edited by Charles Wiltse and Alan R Berolzheimer. Vol. 2. Hanover, NH: University Press of New England, 1987.

Weinberg, Steven. *Facing Up: Science and Its Cultural Adversaries.* Cambridge, MA: Harvard University Press, 2001.

Weisman, A. D. *The Existential Core of Psychoanalysis: Reality, Sense and Responsibility.* Boston: Little, Brown and Co., 1965.

West, Mark, and Chris Carey. "(Re)Enacting Frontier Justice: The Bush Administration's Tactical Narration of the Old West Fantasy after September 11." *Quarterly Journal of Speech* 92 (2006): 379–412.

Wood, Sara. "Trump Supporters Just Declared Him the Messiah, Jesus Has Returned." *NewCentury Times,* October 1, 2016.

Zaru, Denna. "Michele Bachman: 'God Raised Up Trump to Be GOP Nominee.'" *CNN Politics,* August 31, 2016.

Zauzner, Julie. "In Space John Glenn Saw the Face of God." *Washington Post,* December 8, 2016.

The Zohar. Translated by Daniel C. Matt. 3 vols. Pritzker Edition. Stanford, CA: Stanford University Press, 2004–2006.

Index